Learning from Picturebooks

Picturebooks, understood as a series of meaningful text–picture relations, are increasingly acknowledged as an autonomous subgenre of children's literature. Because they are highly complex aesthetic products, their use is deeply embedded in specific situations of joint attention between a caregiver and a child. This volume focuses on the question of what children may learn from looking at picturebooks, whether printed in a book format, created in a digital format, or self-produced by educationalists and researchers.

Interest in the relationship between cognitive processes and children's literature is growing rapidly, and in this book, theoretical frameworks such as cognitive linguistics, cognitive narratology, cognitive poetics, and cognitive psychology have been applied to the analysis of children's literature. Chapters gather together empirical research from the fields of literary studies, linguistics, and cognitive psychology for the first time to build a cohesive understanding of how picturebooks assist learning and development.

International contributions explore:

- language acquisition
- the child's cognitive development
- emotional development
- literary acquisition ("literary literacy")
- visual literacy.

Divided into three parts considering symbol-based learning, co-constructed learning, and the learning of language skills, this cross-disciplinary volume will appeal to researchers, students, and professionals engaged in children's literature and literacy studies, as well as those from the fields of cognitive and developmental psychology, linguistics, and education.

Bettina Kümmerling-Meibauer is Professor in the German Department at the University of Tübingen, Germany.

Jörg Meibauer is Chair for German Linguistics at the Johannes Gutenberg University of Mainz, Germany.

Kerstin Nachtigäller is a member of the Emergentist Semantics Group at the Center of Excellence Cognitive Interaction Technology, Bielefeld University, Germany.

Katharina J. Rohlfing is Head of the Emergentist Semantics Group at the Center of Excellence Cognitive Interaction Technology, Bielefeld University, Germany.

Explorations in Developmental Psychology series

Books in this series:

1   Developmental Neuropsychology
    Janna Glozman

2   Indigenous Adolescent Development
    Psychological, social and historical contexts
    Les B. Whitbeck, Kelley J. Sittner Hartshorn, and Melissa L. Walls

3   Learning from Picturebooks
    Research from cognitive psychology, early literacy, and child developmental studies
    Edited by Bettina Kümmerling-Meibauer, Jörg Meibauer, Kerstin Nachtigäller, and Katharina J. Rohlfing

Learning from Picturebooks
Perspectives from child development and literacy studies

Edited by
Bettina Kümmerling-Meibauer,
Jörg Meibauer, Kerstin Nachtigäller,
and Katharina J. Rohlfing

LONDON AND NEW YORK

First published 2015
by Routledge
27 Church Road, Hove, East Sussex BN3 2FA

and by Routledge
711 Third Avenue, New York, NY 10017

Routledge is an imprint of the Taylor & Francis Group, an informa business

© 2015 B. Kümmerling-Meibauer, J. Meibauer, K. Nachtigäller, and K. J. Rohlfing

The right of the editors to be identified as the authors of the editorial matter, and of the authors for their individual chapters, has been asserted in accordance with sections 77 and 78 of the Copyright, Designs and Patents Act 1988.

All rights reserved. No part of this book may be reprinted or reproduced or utilized in any form or by any electronic, mechanical, or other means, now known or hereafter invented, including photocopying and recording, or in any information storage or retrieval system, without permission in writing from the publishers.

Trademark notice: Product or corporate names may be trademarks or registered trademarks, and are used only for identification and explanation without intent to infringe.

British Library Cataloguing in Publication Data
A catalogue record for this book is available from the British Library

Library of Congress Cataloging-in-Publication Data
Learning from picturebooks : perspectives from child development and literacy studies \ edited by Bettina Kümmerling-Meibauer, Jörg Meibauer, Kerstin Nachtigäller and Katharina J. Rohlfing.
   pages cm
   Includes bibliographical references and index.
   ISBN 978-0-415-72079-3 (hardback) – ISBN 978-1-315-86671-0 (ebook) 1. Picture books for children–Educational aspects. I. Kümmerling-Meibauer, Bettina.
   LB1044.9.P49L43 2015
   372.133–dc23   2014032425

ISBN: 978-0-415-72079-3 (hbk)
ISBN: 978-1-315-86671-0 (ebk)

Typeset in Galliard
by Wearset Ltd, Boldon, Tyne and Wear

Contents

List of figures vii
List of tables viii
Notes on contributors ix

Understanding learning from picturebooks: an introduction 1
BETTINA KÜMMERLING-MEIBAUER, JÖRG MEIBAUER, KERSTIN NACHTIGÄLLER, AND KATHARINA J. ROHLFING

PART I
Symbol-based learning in picturebooks 11

1 Picturebooks and early literacy: how do picturebooks support early conceptual and narrative development? 13
BETTINA KÜMMERLING-MEIBAUER AND JÖRG MEIBAUER

2 An examination of factors that affect young children's learning and transfer from picturebooks 33
PATRICA A. GANEA AND CAITLIN F. CANFIELD

3 What the child can learn from simple descriptive picturebooks: an inquiry into *Lastwagen/Trucks* by Paul Stickland 51
JÖRG MEIBAUER

4 The development of color vision and of the ability to appreciate color in picturebooks 71
MEI YING BOON AND STEPHEN J. DAIN

PART II
Co-constructed learning from picturebooks 97

5 Gesturing in joint book reading 99
    KATHARINA J. ROHLFING, ANGELA GRIMMINGER, AND
    KERSTIN NACHTIGÄLLER

6 Growing vocabulary in the context of shared book reading 117
    PAMELA BLEWITT

7 Distributed cognition in early literacy 137
    LESLEY LANCASTER AND ROSIE FLEWITT

8 Affective interaction during classroom picturebook reading 156
    ELENI MOSCHOVAKI AND SARA MEADOWS

PART III
Learning language skills from picturebooks 179

9 Word learning via shared storybook reading 181
    JESSICA S. HORST

10 What good is a picturebook? Developing children's oral
    language and literacy through shared picturebook reading 194
    ELAINE REESE

11 Tense acquisition with picturebooks 209
    LINDA STARK

    Index 228

Figures

1.1	Illustration from *"Cleanliness" starring Johnny Toothbrush* by Virginia Parkinson and Marjorie Wales	26
3.1	A taxonomy of picturebooks	53
3.2	Book cover of *Lastwagen* by Paul Stickland	55
4.1	A 4.3-year-old child observing one test card within a lightbox	83
4.2	Overall preferences as a function of age group (6-month divisions) and color vision test errors (no errors, one major error, two major errors)	85
4.3	Strength of color preferences by age group	86
5.1	Mother and child gesturing to a picturebook	100
5.2	Examples of the pictures used in the books	104
5.3	Pointing to and labeling depicted objects	107
5.4	Pointing while asking questions and eliciting the names of objects from the child	108
5.5	Pointing to relations	109
5.6	With the pointing finger of her left hand, the mother points to a group of similar objects	110
5.7	Pointing to real objects	111
6.1	Fast mapping of a new word, illustrated using the word "airplane"	118
6.2	Slow mapping includes identifying typical functions, activities, parts, and perceptual features of a word's referents	120
6.3	Mean number of information units of all types in 3- and 5-year-olds' definitions of familiar test words	122
6.4	Picturebook featuring the unfamiliar target words "dibble" and "davenport"	125
6.5	Three-year-olds' performance on tests of six target words	129
7.1	Mike's plane	151
8.1	Teacher's affective strategies during book reading	162
8.2	Children's display of affective engagement	165
11.1	Illustration from Harmen van Straaten and Arnica Esterl: *Es war einmal eine Ente*	223

Tables

3.1	A comparison of the German and English texts of *Lastwagen/Trucks*	57
3.2	A comparison of the text lengths of *Lastwagen/Trucks*	61
4.1	Vision as a function of age	79
7.1	Talk between Jake and his mother	145
8.1	Number of children, duration of stories, and presentation style of each story session	160
9.1	Shared storybook reading studies testing noun word learning as a function of repeated readings	186
10.1	Effects of an enhanced dialogic reading training on children's narrative production skills	201
11.1	Communicative parameters of conceptual oral and written language	214
11.2	Overview of the findings of the picturebook analysis	220

Contributors

Pamela Blewitt is Professor of Psychology at Villanova University, in Villanova, Pennsylvania. She holds a Master's degree from Columbia University in special education, and a PhD from the University of Rochester in developmental psychology. She conducts research on the growth of vocabulary in young children and on the cognitive and environmental processes that support vocabulary growth. She is especially concerned with identifying strategies for helping parents and teachers support the language development of young children. She has co-authored a text on lifespan human development for helping professionals, which is widely used in the United States and is in its fourth edition. She also serves on the boards of nonprofit organizations dedicated to advocating for improvements in the accessibility and affordability of high-quality early child care and education.

Mei Ying Boon, BOptom(Hons), PhD, is Lecturer at the School of Optometry and Vision Science, University of New South Wales, Sydney. Her research interests are in the dynamic aspects of the normally maturing and aging visual system as understood using both psychophysical and electrophysiological techniques, in particular color, luminance, and motion perception. She has particular expertise in the nonlinear dynamic analysis of children's visual evoked potentials. Besides aiming at an understanding of the normally developing visual system, her research seeks to understand how vision may be changed during the abnormal development of the visual system (e.g. in amblyopia) and in response to ocular disease (e.g. in low vision) and the measurement and mitigation of any functional impact on quality of life, including ability to participate socially and in activities of daily living.

Caitlin F. Canfield is Postdoctoral Research Training Fellow at New York University School of Medicine. She works on the Bellevue Project for Early Language, Literacy, and Education Success, which is a multidisciplinary research laboratory that attempts to ensure optimal language development and school readiness for young children in low-income families by promoting parent–child interactions. She received her PhD in Developmental Psychology from Boston University, and her research focuses on how infants and young children learn through language and social interaction, and the factors that lead to individual differences in that learning. She has studied infants' early word learning, as well as young children's learning both from others and through picturebooks.

Stephen J. Dain PhD, BSc(Hons) (City University, London), is Research Professor at the University of New South Wales after retiring in 2006 as Professor and Head of the School of Optometry and Vision Science. He is Director of the Optics and Radiometry Laboratory, which is accredited under ISO 17025 for calibrations and measurements in optics, light, and color. His main research interests are in the fields of color vision and occupational aspects of vision. He has over 130 refereed publications. He is a Fellow of the College of Optometrists, the American Academy of Optometry, the Illuminating Engineering Societies of Australia and New Zealand, and the Metrology Society of Australia. He is an honorary life member of both the Colour Society of Australia and the International Colour Vision Society, where he served on the committee for 15 years. He is an Associate Editor of *Color: Research and Application* and a member of the Editorial Board of *Clinical and Experimental Optometry*. He is involved in national and international standards writing on eye protection. He has received awards for his work for Standards Australia and the National Association of Testing Authorities.

Rosie Flewitt is Senior Lecturer in Early Years Education at the Institute of Education, London, and a member of MODE (Multimodal Methodologies for Researching Digital Data and Environments), a National Centre for Research Methods Node, based in the London Knowledge Lab (http://mode.ioe.ac.uk). Her research and teaching focus on the complementary areas of young children's communication, language and literacy development, and inclusive education, with expertise primarily in multimodal and ethnographic approaches to the study of early learning. Throughout her career, she has been developing and refining multimodal methodological, analytic, and theoretical frameworks for the study of how children make and express meaning through combinations of communicative modes (such as spoken and written language, gesture, images, and sounds) as they engage with written, oral, visual, and digital texts both at home and in early education.

Patricia A. Ganea is Developmental Psychologist at the University of Toronto. She received her undergraduate degree from the University of Bucharest (1996), where she studied psychology and philosophy. After completing her doctoral degree in Developmental Psychology at the University of Virginia (2004), she worked as a Postdoctoral Fellow at Northwestern University and as an Assistant Professor in the Psychology Department at Boston University. Her research focuses on the social, linguistic, and representational aspects of young children's learning and it has been funded through grants from the National Science Foundation in the United States and the Social Sciences and Humanities Council in Canada. In 2014, she received the Ontario Early Researcher Award from the Ministry for Research and Innovation.

Angela Grimminger has worked as Laboratory Coordinator of the Emergentist Semantics Group within the Center of Excellence Cognitive Interaction Technology (CITEC) at Bielefeld University, Germany, since 2008. She received her Master's degree in Clinical Linguistics from Bielefeld University in 2011. In her Master's thesis, she investigated maternal gestural behavior towards their language-delayed or typically developed children in a task-oriented dialogue. In her PhD project, funded by the Deutsche Forschungsgemeinschaft (DFG) since 2012, she longitudinally investigates the relationship between gestural and verbal development and the role of familiarity for gestural communicative behavior, and follows her research interests in multimodal input, infants' communicative development, and late-talking children.

Jessica S. Horst is an Associate Professor in Psychology at the University of Sussex, UK. She received her undergraduate degree in Philosophy and Psychology with a minor in German Language and Literature from Boston University in 2001, and her PhD in Psychology from the University of Iowa in 2007. Her doctoral research on how children remember words learned via referent selection earned awards from both the American Psychological Association and the Society for Research in Child Development. She currently directs the WORD Lab, where her team studies not only the cognitive processes involved in word learning via fast mapping, but also incidental word learning from storybooks. Her storybook methods are currently being used by several children's centers across the UK to promote joint storybook reading among young children and their parents.

Bettina Kümmerling-Meibauer is Professor in the German Department at the University of Tübingen. Her research interests focus on international children's literature, picturebook research, children's films, comics, Romantic children's literature, Jewish children's literature, canon studies, and the close connection between literacy studies and children's literature. Her books include *Klassiker der Kinder- und Jugendliteratur* (2 vols., 1999), *Kinderliteratur, Kanonbildung und literarische Wertung* (2003), and *Kinder- und Jugendliteratur. Eine Einführung* (2012). She is an active international editor of research volumes on picturebook theory, including *New Directions in Picturebook Research* (2010), *Emergent Literacy: Children's Books from 0 to 3* (2011), *Manga's Cultural Crossroads* (2013), and *Picturebooks. Representation and Narration* (2014), and co-editor of the international book series Children's Literature, Culture and Cognition (John Benjamins). She was speaker of the international research project Children's Literature and European Avant-Garde, funded by the European Science Foundation. Joint work with Jörg Meibauer focuses on cognitive picturebook theory as well as on lying in children's literature.

Lesley Lancaster is Reader in Multimodal Literacy in the Education and Social Research Institute at Manchester Metropolitan University, and a member of the Centre for Cultural Studies of Children and Childhood. Her current research interests include children's early symbolic learning, writing in early childhood, distributed cognition, and multimodal analysis, with recent publications and conference papers reflecting these interests. She is on the editorial board of the *Journal of Early Childhood Literacy*, was a member of the UK Early Language and Communication Project, and Director of the ESRC-funded project Grammaticisation in Early Mark Making. She teaches in the fields of literacy and applied linguistics at undergraduate and doctoral levels, and in the past she has worked as a member of a literacy advisory team, as a researcher at the National Foundation for Educational Research, and as a teacher.

Sara Meadows is Senior Lecturer and Director of MEd Psychology of Education programme, Graduate School of Education, University of Bristol. She researches and teaches how different factors come together to bring about happier or unhappier development for children. She is interested in developing evidence-based and policy-relevant models of how complex factors such as parental education, teen parenthood, and poverty affect child development. As a psychologist rather than an educationalist, she uses the concepts and the methods of developmental psychology as a way of understanding what children are experiencing at home and at school, and the ways in which they grow up as learners. Her teaching involves partnership between researchers' interest in clarifying causes and teachers' interest in determining the best thing to do, with each side challenging and testing the other in positive ways. Much of her current research is with the Children of the Nineties study (ALSPAC – www.bristol.ac.uk/alspac). She has been looking at the consequences of causal pathways involved in the effects of early childhood education, teenage parenthood, and maternal depression on children's development. She also examined the effects of an innovative new national curriculum on early reading and arithmetic. These studies, and her books, illustrate the complexity of what happens in children's development. Achieving a better understanding is crucial for teachers, parents, and policymakers concerned with children.

Jörg Meibauer holds the chair of German Language and Linguistics at the Johannes Gutenberg University in Mainz and is Affiliated Professor at the University of Stockholm. His research focuses on the grammar of German, word formation, linguistic pragmatics, lexical acquisition, and the linguistics of children's literature. His books include *Rhetorische Fragen* (1986), *Modaler Kontrast und konzeptuelle Verschiebung* (1994), *Pragmatik* (1999), *Einführung in die germanistische Linguistik* (co-authored, 2001), *Schnittstellen der germanistischen Linguistik* (co-authored, 2007), and *Lying at the Semantics–Pragmatics Interface* (2014). Joint work with Bettina Kümmerling-Meibauer focuses on cognitive picturebook theory as well as lying in children's literature.

Eleni Moschovaki is a Chartered Psychologist who works as a School Adviser for Preschool Education in the Regional Directorate of the North Eastern Aegean, Greece. She was awarded her Master's and doctoral degrees from the University of Bristol and holds a degree in Early Childhood Education (University of the Aegean) and Sociology (Panteion University of Athens). She has worked as a kindergarten teacher in Greece and currently organizes and takes part in INSET courses for teachers. Her research interests are kindergarten classroom practice, young children's cognitive and affective engagement during picturebook reading, emergent literacy and assessment, emotional literacy, and conflict resolution in young children. Her publications have appeared in research books and journals.

Kerstin Nachtigäller has worked as Psychologist in a Social Pediatrics Center at the EKO (Evangelisches Krankenhaus Oberhausen) in Germany since 2013. Her main function is the diagnosis of developmental delay and mental disorders in children and adolescents. Since 2008, she has been a member of the Emergentist Semantics Group (Center of Excellence, Cognitive Interaction Technology) at Bielefeld University, where she works on her dissertation, "Long-Term Word Learning in 2-Year-Old Children". Her PhD project, supported by the Volkswagen Foundation, is concerned with word learning from pictures by 2-year-old children. Fast and slow mapping mechanisms of word learning as well as child-directed narrative input are particularly considered as important factors of influence. In 2008 she received her Diploma in Psychology at Bielefeld University.

Elaine Reese is Professor of Psychology at the University of Otago. She received her MA and PhD in Developmental Psychology from Emory University in Atlanta, Georgia, and has worked at the University of Otago since 1993. She conducts longitudinal studies of cognitive and social development, and is an adviser for the Growing Up in New Zealand longitudinal study. She also serves as editor for the *Journal of Cognition and Development*. Her co-edited book *Contemporary Debates in Childhood Education and Development* was published by Routledge in 2012, and her book *Tell Me a Story: Sharing Stories to Enrich Your Child's World* was published by Oxford University Press in 2013.

Katharina J. Rohlfing received her Master's degree in Linguistics, Philosophy, and Media Studies from the University of Paderborn, Germany, in 1997. As a member of the Graduate Program Task-Oriented Communication, she was awarded a PhD degree in Linguistics from Bielefeld University, Germany, in 2002. In 2006, with her interdisciplinary project on the Symbiosis of Language and Action, she became a Dilthey Fellow (VolkswagenStiftung). Since 2008, she has been Head of the Emergentist Semantics Group within the Center of Excellence Cognitive Interaction Technology (CITEC) of Bielefeld University. Her habilitation in 2009 on early semantics attests to her interest in the interface between cognitive development and the early stages of language acquisition. Her contributions to early literacy pursue the questions of how parents shape the book-reading situation and the value of semantically structured input to word learning in young children.

Linda Stark graduated from the Johannes Gutenberg University Mainz with a teaching degree for secondary schools in 2011. Since April 2012, she has been a researcher in the German Department for Linguistics at Bochum University, where she teaches courses for Bachelor and Master students. In her PhD project, she examines the relationship between children's literature, literacy, and language acquisition with regard to the German past tenses.

Understanding learning from picturebooks
An introduction

Bettina Kümmerling-Meibauer, Jörg Meibauer, Kerstin Nachtigäller, and Katharina J. Rohlfing

Picturebooks are a species of children's literature. Typically, their use is embedded in situations of a caregiver's and child's joint attention to them. Therefore, the specific makeup of picturebooks and its embedment within a specific reading situation is an object of research. This collection focuses on the question of what children may learn from looking at picturebooks. It reports on commercial picturebooks as well as on artificial picturebooks made for experimental purposes.

What is a picturebook?

In general, a book is a three-dimensional object that contains information. From a cultural-historical perspective, it is the most important medium for the communication of ideas by means of printed texts. However, with respect to this characterization, two caveats must be entered. One is that there are e-books in which the book content is represented electronically. The second is that there are picturebooks in which there is no text at all ("textless picturebooks"). These may tell a story or simply depict interesting objects ("early-concept books").

Typically, a picturebook is a book that conveys information through either a series of picture–text combinations or a series of pictures only. In contrast to "illustrated books", in which the illustrations play a subordinate role, text and pictures in picturebooks intimately depend on each other. Picturebooks with text–picture combinations, then, are characterized by a mutual interaction of words and pictures. Usually they tell a story – that is, they are narrations. But there are also picturebooks that contain only descriptions ("descriptive picturebooks"). The main target groups that picturebooks are created for are preschool and primary-school children. The first picturebooks are read by 9- to 12-month-olds. However, there are picturebooks for adults as well (Beckett 2012). In this book, we will focus on picturebooks that address children.

Picturebook research focuses on the description and explanation of the peculiar relation between pictures and texts, be it from a theoretical, a historical, a cognitive, a narratological, or a pedagogical perspective, to name only the most prominent areas of research. While some researchers focus on investigating the complex relationships between pictures and texts, others emphasize the close connection between picturebook comprehension and visual literacy (for different approaches, see Kiefer 1985; Nodelman 1988; Nikolajeva and Scott 2001; Colomer et al. 2010; Kümmerling-Meibauer 2011, 2014). The topical issue of how children interpret the meaning of pictures and texts has been discussed in several studies, for instance Arizpe and Styles (2003) and Evans (2009). Some recent studies primarily turn towards the cognitive aspects of picturebooks, undergirding the impact of cognitive studies on the further development of a theory of picturebooks (Kümmerling-Meibauer and Meibauer 2013).

Typical questions asked in these areas include: How do verbal and visual information contribute to the narrative meaning in picturebooks? When were the first picturebooks created, how did they develop over time, and what socio-cultural changes have affected the content, structure, and ideological messages of picturebooks? What cognitive abilities are needed when interpreting the picturebooks' content? How can picture–text combinations or combinations of pictures tell a story? How are picturebooks actually used and how can picturebook reading be taught? In this book, we combine some of these questions in a truly interdisciplinary perspective.

What is learning?

Another seminal question is how children can learn from picturebooks. This demands an answer to the question of what learning is (Jarvis and Watts 2012). Jarvis (2009: 25) proposes a very broad definition of "learning", according to which learning is "the combination of processes throughout a lifetime whereby the whole person [...] experiences social situations, the content of which is then transformed cognitively, emotively or practically [...] and integrated into the individual person's biography resulting in a continually changing [...] person". Most important is the insight that learning is a continuous progress that has to do with arranging and rearranging experiences. While learning is conceived of as something that happens on the basis of social experiences, it is also plausible to assume that innate cognitive abilities support this process. For instance, parts of the visual system – which makes it possible to perceive and interpret pictures – are innate.

Joint attention to a picturebook certainly is a situation in which experiences occur on a number of levels (Suggate and Reese 2012). Learning by picturebooks, so we assume, contributes to the child's development. It is based on a complex interplay of activated cognitive and emotional abilities, in particular those that have to do with the still emerging visual and language systems. In addition, it is embedded within a social interaction.

What constitutes a learning situation?

The typical learning situation we focus on is constituted by a caregiver or caregivers (that is, parents, siblings, friends, grandparents, or other persons), a child or group of children, and the picturebook. Children can also look at picturebooks for themselves. Not much is known about the impact of these different persons on the reading process or how they shape the children's way of interacting with this medium. For instance, can children discover the value of picturebooks by themselves or do they need to be introduced to the way of interacting with the medium? Does sex or gender play an important role in the process of how picturebooks are presented to children? Do fathers read to their daughters in a different way than to their sons? Do we read differently to a group of multicultural and multilingual children in kindergarten? What differentiates the reading situation of a single child and a caregiver from that of a group of children and an adult mediator, as usually occurs in nurseries, kindergartens, and schools?

From a narratological point of view, a further party involved in the process has to be highlighted, namely the author and/or illustrator. Thus, the child will learn eventually to recognize that the caregiver is only the transmitter of information coded in the picture–text combinations, not the creator. Yet this status as a transmitter seems to be important for this special learning situation because, ideally, the caregiver knows the child and has an individual social and emotional relation to her or him.

These aspects already point to the complexity of the reading situation. One way of accessing such a complexity is to study the child's learning process under controlled settings in the laboratory, as several contributions to this collection demonstrate.

What can be learned?

Learning from picturebooks may take place on a number of various levels. Most importantly, it concerns visual learning – that is, the ability to interpret pictorial information in an adequate way (Kress and van Leeuwen 1996; Painter *et al.* 2013). Picturebooks' texts and accompanying narratives concern language acquisition: not only the acquisition of vocabulary (the lexicon), but also the acquisition of grammar and pragmatics. Since picturebooks are literature (and this holds for narrative and descriptive books alike), it is obvious that children will learn about fiction, literary characters, narration, and all aspects that distinguish literary texts from naturally occurring everyday conversation (cf. Nikolajeva 2014 on the significance of children's literature for this specific learning situation). In addition, children learn that the creation of pictures is an art – that is, something intentionally made for aesthetic purposes (Golomb 2011). Picturebooks may also enhance the child's world knowledge, implying factual knowledge or knowledge about individual, cognitive, and other related topics (Siegal 2008; Pritchard 2010; Pinkham *et al.* 2012). Since pictures and texts relate to emotions, children will learn about the reflection of emotions, all the more so as the reading situation itself is emotionally loaded and goes together with emotional attachment (Reese 2013). Moreover, the information provided in picturebooks triggers processes of moral and social learning, for example by telling a story that teaches a moral lesson.

How does learning from picturebooks happen?

Many variables can influence the particular reading situation: whether a book is being read for the first time or the tenth time, whether there is a responsiveness on the part of the caregiver or not, whether the reading happens in a car when heading off on vacation or in the child's bedroom before going to sleep. The child's age and sex/gender are important, as is her or his general curiosity, intelligence, and linguistic competence and performance. In short: there are many various variables that have to be taken into account, and the construction of a general model of "learning from picturebooks" seems by no means easy. We think that the chapters in this book will contribute to further understanding of this process, as they link to important contributions under the umbrella term of "early literacy". Several impressive handbooks represent ongoing research and findings in this field (Neuman and Dickinson 2003–2011; Olson and Torrance 2009; Hall *et al.* 2013; Stone *et al.* 2013; Wolf *et al.* 2013; Larson and Marsh 2014; Nunes and Bryant 2014). "Learning from picturebooks" is surely a topic that will benefit from interdisciplinary work.

The contributions

The topics sketched in previous sections are to the fore of this collection, which addresses the joint relation between book reading, language acquisition, cognitive development, and literacy learning. Because of their unique picture–text relations and their general importance for early literacy, picturebooks play a significant role in a number of research fields, including studies on the relevance of picturebooks for early language acquisition, visual and emotional perception, the investigation of joint reading processes, and the child's developing sense of different cognitive and semantic concepts.

However, as of yet there are hardly any monographs or collections focusing on the impact of empirical studies and studies on cognitive processes on the investigation of picturebooks. Usually, relevant studies in the field of linguistics, literary studies, cognitive psychology, and picturebook research are scattered in diverse journals, collections, and monographs. Scholars often work in their own fields without knowing much about investigations and research undertaken in other disciplines, although the mutual exchange of knowledge and academic discussion would certainly be very stimulating and fruitful.

Hence, one important aim of this collection is to gather together these different findings and recent discussions and to show how they are interrelated with regard to the examination of children's developing linguistic, cognitive, emotional, and aesthetic/literary competencies by means of picturebooks and the social interaction they are embedded in.

The chapters cover different topics that touch upon important issues concerning the investigation of picturebooks with regard to perceptual, cognitive, and linguistic aspects, such as color perception, the impact of gestures and affective presentation on the child's appreciation of picturebooks, the significance of word learning and early mark making (as a precursor for learning to draw and write), the enhancement of knowledge of the world, and the difference between narrative and descriptive picturebooks, as well as their influence on developing narrative skills.

Scholars working in the fields of linguistics, literacy studies, psychology, and picturebook research have written the chapters for this collection. In view of the interdisciplinary character of this collection, each chapter briefly refers to the state of the art, thus contributing to a better understanding and evaluation of the analysis. Moreover, whenever experiments are presented, the contributors will explain their design and introduce the reader to the underlying theoretical framework.

The collection is divided into three parts. The first part focuses on the cognitive processes that guide children's learning when looking at picturebooks. The second concentrates on the joint and shared attention to picturebooks and demonstrates how caregivers and other sources shape and scaffold the process of learning. The third part discusses the advantages of picturebooks for the development of language skills.

In Chapter 1, Bettina Kümmerling-Meibauer and Jörg Meibauer address the question of how picturebooks might foster the conceptual development of children. The authors propose that picturebooks usually are sensitive to children's early cognitive abilities, and that they constitute a specific input for children's cognitive and narrative development. As a plea for a developmental approach to picturebooks, the chapter highlights the importance of early-concept books and concept books that promote the acquisition of conceptual classes. In addition, the authors show that early picturebooks enhance the young child's understanding of simple narrative texts. By focusing on picturebooks that deal with the topic of hygiene, the authors demonstrate the significance of the narrative–descriptive bifurcation that emerges even in picturebooks addressed to children younger than 4 years of age. In a final step, they discuss the issues of genres and literary characters, and how these aspects contribute to the child's increasing comprehension of the picturebooks' narrative functions.

Patricia A. Ganea and Caitlin F. Canfield in Chapter 2 present a research summary that focuses on the question of how children acquire and transfer new knowledge from picturebooks. Investigating the influence of picturebooks on children's learning in the domain of object representation, action knowledge, and biological knowledge, the authors discuss the factors that affect these learning processes and the transfer from picturebooks to the real world. In particular, Ganea and Canfield summarize their findings by showing that some characteristics of picturebooks may facilitate learning, whereas others can be detrimental. Overall, the results of their research contribute to the better understanding of the basic processes involved in young children's interaction with pictorial symbols. The authors highlight the important role picturebooks play in framing young children's knowledge about the real world and conclusively discuss how best to use picturebooks to teach children new information.

In Chapter 3, Jörg Meibauer demonstrates how the model developed in the first chapter can be transferred to a close linguistic and cognitive analysis of a single picturebook. The author has chosen the simple descriptive picturebook *Trucks* (1986) by Paul Stickland and its German version, *Lastwagen*, to demonstrate that this underestimated book type serves important functions in multifarious ways. Besides dealing with objects that are of interest to the child, simple descriptive picturebooks lead children into the comprehension of taxonomic systems. Notably, they rehearse an appropriate vocabulary, including syntactic, morphological, and semantic information. Moreover, they are introduced into textual properties of descriptive texts, for instance anaphoric elements and relative clauses. Finally, Meibauer maintains that simple descriptive picturebooks may be superior to their narrative competitors in that they trigger more of children's own narratives than the narrative ones do.

The contribution of Mei Ying Boon and Stephen J. Dain, Chapter 4, centers on the significance of color in picturebooks. The authors briefly introduce the techniques used in the scientific study of visual development before proceeding with a thorough review of the development of color vision from early infancy up to adolescence. In order to scrutinize existing research on children's visual development, the authors experimentally investigate young children's preferences for grayscale versus full color illustrations in picturebooks. Their testing of 94 preschool children illustrates that this age group already prefers color to grayscale and black-and-white images. In this respect, the authors also discuss the difficulties concerning the most effective methods of investigation, which depend on the age of the target group. Nevertheless, they conclude that colors play an important role in the young child's ability to understand picturebook stories and to construct a coherent interpretation of the text–picture relationship.

In Chapter 5, Katharina J. Rohlfing, Angela Grimminger, and Kerstin Nachtigäller argue that joint book reading constitutes a specific situation which is mainly determined by interaction routines. These routines include verbal as well as nonverbal behavior. The authors maintain that nonverbal behavior is especially important in interaction with very young children, who, instead of communicating solely verbally, make use of their gestural repertoire in their communication and rely on caregivers' gestural input in order to make sense of the picturebook's content. In their longitudinal study, the authors analyze how pointing gestures are a crucial part of interaction routines in book reading and how they are correlated with children's later vocabulary growth. They distinguish diverse strategies, namely pointing with labeling, pointing with asking questions, and specific pointing patterns. In a final step, they discuss how these strategies might be particularly effective in fostering children's vocabulary skills.

How joint reading of picturebooks might help children increase their vocabulary is a main theme of Pamela Blewitt's chapter, Chapter 6. Blewitt emphasizes that children associate new words with referents (fast mapping) and that they elaborate the meanings of familiar words (slow mapping) during shared bookreading. While the first learning strategy increases the breadth of the child's lexicon, the second strategy results in greater depth of vocabulary. Blewitt analyzes different adult reading strategies, considering the question of how they contribute to young children's vocabulary growth. Experimental studies indicate an increasing learning effect in children when readers use strategies such as encouraging children's engagement by asking questions and by responding appropriately to children's verbalizations. Blewitt stresses that these reading routines generally promote children's word learning. In addition, she stresses that it is primarily children from lower socioeconomic groups, who often lag behind other children in vocabulary growth, that benefit from such reading strategies.

Lesley Lancaster and Rosie Flewitt in Chapter 7 take a critical attitude towards the position that literacy learning is a mental activity, characterized by distinct boundaries between mind, body, and events. These authors suggest that early symbolic learning requires a sharing of the cognitive load, distributed between participants, tools, and settings. This network seems to elicit a distribution of cognitive work between these different elements that enables young children to act as creative and independent interpreters and producers of texts, and to work with abstract graphic concepts during early mark-making and reading activities. Therefore, the authors attempt a reintegration of cognition with the social and cultural activity that surrounds young children's earliest participation in reading, writing, and other graphic activities. They explore these contentions through a consideration of studies they have carried out, examining how children under the age of 4 interpret and produce factual texts in a home setting.

Eleni Moschovaki and Sara Meadows' study, Chapter 8, examines the affective dimension of reading books aloud in Greek kindergarten schools with a variety of book genres. They found that the teachers' affective strategies include voice intonation, dramatization, and personal involvement comments, whereas the children's affective engagement is displayed through dramatization, language play, and personal engagement comments. A strong bidirectional relationship emerged between teachers' use of affective strategies and children's display of affective engagement. The sequential analysis yielded reciprocal effects between teachers' comments of personal involvement and children's reactions of personal engagement, between teachers' dramatization and children's dramatization, and between teachers' intonation and children's display of personal engagement. Moreover, text features such as rhyming were found to prompt children's language play. The findings are discussed in relation to research on book-reading styles and young children's developmental outcomes.

In Chapter 9, Jessica S. Horst reviews young children's ability to learn words via shared storybook reading and reflects methodological aspects of using shared storybook reading to experimentally test children's word learning. Horst then evaluates how well children really do learn words via shared storybook reading, focusing on recent research with preschool-aged children. Converging evidence demonstrates that children learn words particularly well when the same stories are read repeatedly. Horst relates this research to similar findings in other areas of psychology. In addition, a section of the chapter elaborates on the respective advantages and disadvantages of commercially available books and self-developed texts. Hence, this chapter informs our understanding of children's novel word learning via shared storybook reading and provides insights into aspects of picturebooks that have to be considered when using them as tools for investigating young children's vocabulary acquisition.

Chapter 10, by Elaine Reese, investigates the various ways children's oral language skills and literacy develop through shared picturebook reading interactions. She focuses on different components of oral language – vocabulary, narrative, phonological awareness – and shows how each of them is supported by picturebook interactions. In this respect, Reese maintains that young children acquire new words and knowledge of story structure from picturebook reading, especially when adults ask questions during the reading. Repeated readings of the same book help children consolidate new words and concepts, primarily when the adults' questions become more difficult with each successive reading. Although young children do not appear to acquire knowledge of the sounds of words or decoding skills through these reading sessions, they can acquire these skills when adults focus specifically on the sounds of words or on print during the interactions. Reese concludes with recommendations for parents and teachers on how to share picturebooks with young children.

Finally, in her corpus analysis in Chapter 10 Linda Stark focuses on the extent to which picturebooks are adapted to the children's developmental stages of tense acquisition in German. She concentrates on the acquisition of the past tense, which is no longer used in many varieties of spoken German but is a standard tense in written German with a specific narrative function. In contrast, the perfect tense is the main tense used in spoken language when referring to the past. This fact raises the question of how children learn the past tense before acquiring written language in its proper sense. The author argues that picturebooks support this acquisition task. In contrast to spoken language, and as a result of their specific and complex text–picture relationships, picturebooks can illustrate the different contexts of use in a lively fashion. In this regard, Stark demonstrates that the use of different tenses in picturebooks reflects the consecutive phases of tense acquisition.

The present collection provides readers with a broad range of new approaches to the investigation of picturebooks and how they contribute to young children's language acquisition, cognitive and emotional development, and emerging literacy skills. Moreover, it attests to the rapidly evolving field of interdisciplinary and international research on a multimodal medium whose complexity increasingly challenges scholars of different disciplines, but also attracts people who (professionally) work with children.

Acknowledgments

We are grateful to the Center for Interdisciplinary Research (ZIF) at the University of Bielefeld, which generously supported the international workshop "Literacy under the Focus of Language and Cognitive Development" (March 22–23, 2012) and thus made this publication possible.

We are also grateful to Björn Technau for checking our English.

The publishers have made every effort to contact authors/copyright holders of works reprinted in *Learning from Picturebooks: Perspectives from Child Development and Literacy Studies*. If we have been unable to trace any copyright holders, then we welcome correspondence from the individuals or companies concerned.

References

Arizpe, Evelyn and Morag Styles. 2003. *Children Reading Pictures: Interpreting Visual Texts*. London: RoutledgeFalmer.
Beckett, Sandra. 2012. *Crossover Picturebooks: A Genre for All Ages*. New York: Routledge.
Colomer, Teresa, Bettina Kümmerling-Meibauer, and Cecilia Silva-Díaz, eds. 2010. *New Directions in Picturebook Research*. New York: Routledge.
Evans, Janet, ed. 2009. *Talking Beyond the Page. Reading and Responding to Picturebooks*. London: Routledge.
Golomb, Claire. 2011. *The Creation of Imaginary Worlds: The Role of Art, Magic and Dreams in Child Development*. London: Jessica Kingsley Publishers.
Hall, Kathy, Teresa Cremin, and Barbara Comber, eds. 2013. *International Handbook of Research on Children's Literacy, Learning and Culture*. Oxford: Blackwell.
Jarvis, Peter 2009. *Learning to Be a Person in Society*. London: Routledge.
Jarvis, Peter and Mary Watts, eds. 2012. *The Routledge International Handbook of Learning*. London: Routledge.
Kiefer, Barbara. 1985. *The Potential of Picturebooks: From Visual Literacy to Aesthetic Understanding*. New York: Merrill Prentice Hall.
Kress, Gunther and Theo van Leeuwen. 1996. *Reading Images: The Grammar of Visual Design*. London: Routledge.
Kümmerling-Meibauer, Bettina, ed. 2011. *Emergent Literacy: Children's books from 0 to 3*. Amsterdam: John Benjamins.
Kümmerling-Meibauer, Bettina, ed. 2014. *Picturebooks: Representation and Narration*. New York: Routledge.
Kümmerling-Meibauer, Bettina and Jörg Meibauer. 2013. "Towards a cognitive theory of picturebooks". *International Research in Children's Literature* 6(2): 143–160.
Larson, Joanne and Jackie Marsh., eds. 2014. *The Sage Handbook of Early Childhood Literacy*. 2nd edition. London: Sage.
Neuman, Susan B. and David K. Dickinson, eds. 2003–2011. *Handbook of Early Literacy Research*. 3 vols. New York: Guilford Press.
Nikolajeva, Maria. 2014. *Reading for Learning. Cognitive approaches to children's literature*. Amsterdam: John Benjamins.
Nikolajeva, Maria and Carole Scott. 2001. *How Picturebooks Work*. New York: Garland.
Nodelman, Perry. 1988. *Words about Pictures: The Narrative Art of Children's Picture Books*. Athens, GA: University of Georgia Press.
Nunes, Terezinha and Peter Bryant, eds. 2014. *Handbook of Children's Literacy*. Dordrecht: Kluwer.
Olson, David R. and Nancy Torrance, eds. 2009. *The Cambridge Handbook of Literacy*. New York: Cambridge University Press.
Painter, Clare, J. R. Martin, and Len Unsworth. 2013. *Reading Visual Narratives: Image Analysis of Children's Picture Books*. Sheffield: Equinox.

Pinkham, Ashley M., Tanya Kaefer, and Susan B. Neuman, eds. 2012. *Knowledge Development in Early Childhood: Sources of Learning and Classroom Implications.* New York: Guilford Press.
Pritchard, Duncan. 2010. *What Is This Thing Called Knowledge?* 2nd edition. London: Routledge.
Reese, Elaine. 2013. *Tell Me a Story: Sharing Stories to Enrich Your Child's World.* New York: Oxford University Press.
Siegal, Michael. 2008. *Marvelous Minds: The Discovery of What Children Know.* Oxford: Oxford University Press.
Stone, C. Addison, Elaine Silliman, Barbara J. Ehren, and Geraldine P. Wallach, eds. 2013. *Handbook of Language and Literacy Development and Disorders.* 2nd edition. New York: Guilford Press.
Suggate, Sebastian and Elaine Reese, eds. 2012. *Contemporary Debates in Childhood Education and Development.* London: Routledge.
Wolf, Shelby A., Karen Coats, Patricia Enciso, and Christine A. Jenkins, eds. 2013. *Handbook of Research on Children's and Young Adult Literature.* New York: Routledge.

Part I
Symbol-based learning in picturebooks

1 Picturebooks and early literacy
How do picturebooks support early conceptual and narrative development?

Bettina Kümmerling-Meibauer and Jörg Meibauer

Introduction

This contribution builds upon two strands of our joint research. The first is to explore the interaction between language acquisition and the acquisition of children's literature (Meibauer 2011; Kümmerling-Meibauer and Meibauer 2013). The second is to explore the nature of picturebooks with respect to children's cognitive development of which language development is a part (e.g. Kümmerling-Meibauer and Meibauer 2005, 2011c). Our basic assumptions can be put into the following hypotheses guiding our research (Kümmerling-Meibauer and Meibauer 2013).

Assumption 1

Children's literature is a specific input in the process of language acquisition. A theory of language acquisition has to reflect on how this specific input supports the acquisition process.

We will show that picturebooks reflect children's early development. In particular, picturebooks support children's conceptual development by showing them pictures that reflect relevant categories, and by engaging them in conversations about concepts and categories.

Assumption 2

Children's literature is important for the acquisition of literature in general. A theory of literature acquisition has to consider how the use of children's literature supports literature acquisition.

Since there is no narrative without descriptive content, we will show that early descriptive picturebooks lay the ground for narrative picturebooks. Moreover, the early acquisition of narratives is seen as the basis for later literature acquisition.

Assumption 3

A crucial property of children's literature is to be accommodated to the cognitive and linguistic abilities of children in different developmental stages. A theory of children's literature has to explain this property.

We will show that there is an adaptation to the child's cognitive and linguistic abilities. However, for lack of space we cannot deeply go into the realm of poetic, aesthetic, and emotional aspects of early literature. We leave that for another occasion.

Against the background of these assumptions, the outline of our contribution is as follows. In the next section, we will deal with what we call "picturebook spurt", a neologism coined on the basis of the term "vocabulary spurt", which is used in research on lexical acquisition. The third section focuses on the descriptive–narrative distinction that plays a crucial role when it comes to the young child's acquisition of narrative abilities. The fourth section addresses the significance of knowledge acquisition and how children learn from testimony, based on picturebooks that impart knowledge about hygiene. The fifth section delves into the impact of literary characters and genres upon children's conceptual development. Finally, we will draw some conclusions from our investigations and address future research topics.

Picturebook spurt: from conceptual classes to early narratives

In Kümmerling-Meibauer and Meibauer (2005, 2011a), we developed the category of "early-concept books" and elaborated on noun- and verb-related early concepts. The notion of early-concept book refers to those picturebooks that show single objects from the child's surroundings, such as a ball, a doll, an apple, or a chair. Prominent examples have been created by Dutch illustrator Dick Bruna, but also by renowned artists such as Tana Hoban, Emmanuel Sougez, Edward Steichen, and Andy Warhol.[1] These picturebooks target children between 12 and 18 months of age and usually do not contain any text; sometimes a single word denotes the depicted object. Since they are the first picturebooks very young children typically encounter, at least in Western countries, they introduce the child not only to the "rules of book behaviour" (Lewis 2001: 135) – that is, sitting still, turning the pages, looking and pointing at the pictures – but also to basic skills of perception, such as (1) the differentiation between figure and ground; (2) the recognition of lines, points, and colors as inseparable parts of the depicted item; (3) the understanding that two-dimensional images stand for three-dimensional objects; and (4) the knowledge of learned visual schemata (Nodelman 1988; Nikolajeva 2003; Kümmerling-Meibauer and Meibauer 2005: 332f.). Besides acquainting children with crucial visual codes that induct them into visual literacy, these picturebooks also support the young child's lexical acquisition. It is not merely a coincidence that the depicted objects are labeled through nouns. Nouns play an important role in the early lexicon, since approximately 44 percent of the first 50 words learned by children are nouns (Bloom 2000). However, understanding the meaning of words is quite a demanding task because children have to learn the prototypical features that constitute a concept (Murphy 2002). A concept comprises the verbal knowledge that enables the child to refer to a given entity. Thus, if a child has acquired the concept DOLL, she or he is able to refer to dolls. In this regard, a picture of a doll might support the child's acquisition of concepts (for a more detailed analysis, see Kümmerling-Meibauer and Meibauer 2011a).

Hence, we propose the notion "early-concept book" for this book type because its basic function is fostering the acquisition of early concepts. Early concepts belong to the young child's early lexicon and are usually acquired between 12 and 18 months of age. These early concepts do not only encompass nouns, but also verbs, such as *to have*, *to make*, *to play*, and *to eat*. Although plenty of early-concept books focus on nouns, there are also early-concept books that display actions which are expressed by verbs. Helen Oxenbury's *Playing* (1981) and Judith Drews' *Antons ganze Welt* (Anton's Whole World, 2010) are two examples of early-concept books that focus on verbal concepts. Consequently, early-concept books have important properties from the point of view of cognitive and conceptual development.

Nouns and verbs surely play an important role in the early lexicon, but children between 12 and 18 months of age already know other word categories as well: for example, adjectives (*hot*, *high*), personal-social words (*yes*, *hello*, *thanks*), relational words (*there*, *again*), pronouns (*you*, *my*) and onomatopoetic words (*bow-wow*) (Barrett 1995; Clark 1993; Dromi 1987; Kauschke 2000; Kauschke and Hofmeister 2002; Meibauer and Rothweiler 1999). These word categories, as well as abstract concepts such as LOVE, are not easy to depict, and yet there are attempts to visualize them, as for instance in Annette Langen's *Noch mal! Meine ersten Lieblingswörter* (Once Again! My First Favorite Words, 2012), in which children are introduced to personal-social words (*bye-bye*, *hello*) and relational words (*more*, *there*), among others. Nevertheless, since the 1970s early-concept books focusing on adjectives, onomatopoetic words and antonyms have come to the fore. In Tana Hoban's *Push/Pull – Empty/Full* (1973), the properties are arranged in accordance with the contrast principle of antonyms (big–little; dark–light) and illustrated by objects that prototypically present the respective properties, such as a stone for "heaviness" or a feather for "lightness". Onomatopoetic words expressed by noises turn up in the French book *Le livre des bruits* (The Book of Noises, 2004) by Soledad Bravi, while antonyms are frequently used in Didier Cornille's *Mini maxi. Le livre des contraires* (The Book of Contrasts, 2009). Interestingly, in order to depict these parts of speech the presence of objects is essential. Activities, properties, and noises are usually depicted with respect to objects, since it is hard, if not impossible, to depict them purely as concepts.

While many of these words still belong to the child's early lexicon, these books present a transition from the early-concept book to another book type that might be called "concept book". In contrast to early-concept books displaying common objects from different conceptual domains, concept books go a step further in that they depict objects that belong to a single conceptual domain, such as toys, animals, vehicles, food, or clothes. Typical examples of this book type are Helmut Spanner's *Mein Spielzeug* (My Toys, 1989) and Chez Picthall's *Baby Sees Farm Animals* (2008). Picturebooks that display abstract concepts, for example colors, shapes, numbers, and letters, can also be assigned to this book category. Prominent examples are Tana Hoban's *Red, Blue, Yellow Shoe* (1986), Keith Haring's *Ten* (1998), and Dick Bruna's *B Is for Bear* (1967). These concept books usually do not have any text at all, but sometimes include single words on the same page or alternate pages that denote the objects or the objects' characteristics (color, shape, number). Although these picturebooks depict objects that refer to nominal concepts as well, the words expressing these concepts mostly do not occur in the child's early lexicon but are acquired later, when children are about 18 to 24 months old, or perhaps even older. This age span is characterized by a vocabulary spurt. While most children have a repertoire of 50 words by the age of 18 months, the lexicon seems to "explode" after that stage, and children acquire new words on a daily basis, thus enlarging their lexicon and knowledge about concepts at an astonishing pace.

However, the vocabulary spurt goes hand in hand with a picturebook spurt. The expanding market of picturebooks for young children is responsible for an increasing range of topics, themes, genres, and styles. This development leads to the creation of book types that serve different purposes at the same time. They might be used for a pointing and naming game, for searching for hidden things, for stimulating a question–answer dialogue, for categorizing, for the comprehension of speech acts and deixis, and even for a basic understanding of poetic practices, such as rhyme, rhythm, and emphasis. Nevertheless, these picturebooks still have discernible key concepts.

First of all, concept books mainly serve to support the young child's acquisition of categorization. Categorization enables the child to build up a network of interrelated concepts. Furthermore, acquisition of conceptual domains not only expands the child's lexicon but might also be regarded as a first step towards an understanding of coherence, in this special case by a coordination of objects belonging to the same conceptual domain (Rakison and Oakes 2003). Therefore, this book type is an extension of the early-concept book focusing on nominal concepts. Some concept books have commonalities with picture dictionaries, in that they show several (five to seven) objects on a page with labels printed below or besides them.

Paul Stickland's *A Child's Book of Things* (1990) depicts simple scenes, such as eating breakfast in the kitchen, gardening, or bathing, and combines them with single items from these scenes represented on the opposite page. Stickland's picturebook engages the child in two activities: first, to name and to describe the things and actions shown in the scene; and second, to search for the single items displayed on the opposite page. The child is thus prepared to focus on a complex image that connects objects belonging to one or two conceptual domain(s). This procedure marks a transition to the more sophisticated "descriptive frames", which still belong to the category of conceptual domains.

Picturebooks focusing on "scripts" are distinguished by intricate pictures showing crowds of people and objects that are all in the same location or setting, such as a farmyard, a building yard, or a train station. In addition, these picturebooks contain texts that describe the illustrations by stressing the main events in the image. Hence, this book type supports the ability to categorize – that is, the mapping of conceptual domains to a "frame" – and also introduces linguistic features that prepare the child for an understanding of a narrative (Jones 1996). These features concern coordination, subjunction, and anaphor. This book type is connected with the aforementioned concept books and picturebooks focusing on frames: each double spread can be looked at on its own, since its text is never related to the preceding or subsequent pages. Nevertheless, the overarching frame links the images together and builds up a sequence of images. Thus, two reading strategies are interconnected: while the sequence of images entices the viewer into examining the book from the beginning to the end, the accompanying text usually refrains from this strategy, stimulating the viewer to concentrate on the respective double spread.

The communicative situation is quite different in the case of those picturebooks that focus on "narrative scripts", such as birthday celebrations, shopping tours, train rides, or doctors' visits. This book type also stresses the importance of conceptual domains, but the text–picture relationship is more complex. Joint reading of picturebooks with a narrative script reveals that this book type combines different conceptual levels, i.e. categorization, coherence, and cohesion, that touch upon both the visual and the linguistic level. The essential cohesive elements are page-turners and recurrent visual elements, such as figures or objects that turn up on every double spread, thus encouraging the viewer to page forward and to search for the perseverative visual cues (Gressnich 2012). Recurring linguistic elements are deictic references, anaphor, and subjunction, complemented by direct speech and *wh*-questions which urge the viewer to turn the pages.

Furthermore, the understanding of narrative scripts already requires a basic understanding of theory of mind – usually acquired in a basic form between 24 and 36 months of age – since conceptual/cognitive frames, such as birthday celebrations or shopping tours, constitute a factual context in combination with an intention (Legerstee 2005). Intentionality can only be understood by children when they are already able to ascribe certain purposes to the actions performed by figures in picturebooks. This ability is essential for the understanding of narratives. While descriptive texts refer only to the events and things depicted in the images (adopting deictical references and the pointing gesture used by joint reading of early-concept books), narrative texts go a step further. They emphasize intentions that propel a storyline that is mainly determined by the respective conceptual/cognitive frame (Wellman 1992).

The book types just presented have two properties in common: their focus is (1) on objects, and (2) on what can be done with these objects. The latter demands the incorporation of characters. This essential trait reveals that they belong to the general category "nonfiction book", since they introduce the young child to real objects and their surrounding settings. Nevertheless, they play a crucial role in the child's conceptual and cognitive development, because they prepare for the encounter with more complex nonfiction books on the one hand, and with fictional picturebook stories on the other hand. The underlying problem is the crucial question of how children manage the transition from nonfiction picturebooks focusing on concepts and conceptual domains to narratives, usually displayed in fictional stories.

Exploring the descriptive–narrative distinction

The descriptive–narrative bifurcation obviously starts between the second and third year of age, when children are confronted with picturebooks with simple stories that we would like to term "early narratives" (Meibauer 2014). As studies in developmental psychology and language acquisition have shown, children at 30 months of age and older develop basic narrative strategies and become more or less able to connect sentences in order to build up simple narrative forms (Boueke *et al.* 1995; Kauschke 2000). Descriptive and narrative texts have two properties in common: coherence (a coherent sequence of descriptive passages and events) and cohesion (linear linkage of sentences by means of anaphor, deixis, and so forth). The following aspects distinguish a description from a narrative: a narrative is defined by a climax – that is, a discontinuity turning up in the course of the narrative/story – and by affective markers – that is, the tendency to affect the reader's empathy and emotional involvement. (Note that we use the notion "narrative" as an equivalent to the term "story"; in studies undertaken by scholars such as Bamberg (1997), Boueke *et al.* (1995), Dannerer (2012), and Quasthoff (1976), the term "narrative" (*Erzählung*) is restricted to descriptive (oral) texts, while "story" (*Geschichte*) refers to narratives with a climax and affective markers.)

Besides concept books and books displaying descriptive and narrative frames, children aged between 2 and 3 will gradually also become acquainted with picturebooks that display an early narrative. We have chosen two picturebooks in order to analyze their narrative strategies and to demonstrate their contribution to the young child's conceptual development. In addition, by comparing a nonfiction descriptive picturebook with a picturebook that narrates a fictional story, the nonfiction book–narrative bifurcation will be emphasized.

The first book, *Trucks* by Paul Stickland (1986), belongs to the category of (simple) descriptive picturebooks (see Meibauer, this volume, Chapter 3, for a detailed analysis). It shows different types of trucks and their functions. What distinguishes this picturebook from concept books is the depiction of characters who drive, load, repair, or refuel the trucks, and the addition of one or two sentences assigned to each picture. On each double spread, either one or two trucks are depicted against a negative space, and just a few items, such as trees, a gas pump, scaffolding, serve as indicators for different settings. The trucks are always shown from slightly below, thus adopting a young child's point of view. Although the text is rather descriptive, distinguishing various truck types and describing their specific functions by focusing on different actions, the sentences achieve coherence by deixis, anaphor, and temporal adverbs. An example occurs when a consecutive action is explained in the text. A long-distance lorry and a tow truck are shown on opposite pages, and the text informs the reader about a temporal sequence: the lorry has broken down and the tow truck has arrived to tow the damaged vehicle to a garage. The connection between the sentences is given by anaphor and deictic references. However, this picturebook does not have a climax, nor does it affect the child emotionally. This is due to the fact that the text does not display a continuous character with which the young child might feel empathy; in addition, the short sentences on each double spread describe rather than narrate the event shown in the illustration, because affective markers are totally missing.

While the texts in Stickland's book are restricted to a double spread and generate a description of two subsequent events, the picturebook *Heute spiele ich* (Today I am Playing, 1995) by Angela Wiesner varies between different book types: some pages look like an early-concept book focusing on nominal concepts, others resemble an early-concept book focusing on verbal concepts. The book as a whole, however, can be characterized as a concept book focusing on the conceptual domain "toys". Some pages just show single objects, such as a ball, a pull toy, and a picturebook, whereas other pages depict a young child doing something with objects, such as sitting on a rocking horse or playing with a bucket in the sand pitch. Although the subordinated sentences are more or less descriptive, they challenge the reader by their alternation between two grammatical structures, namely first-person and third-person sentences (see Gressnich and Meibauer 2010). The connection between these sentences is mainly built up by the reference to the young child as the owner of the depicted objects. She either stresses that the playthings belong to her ("my red ball has white dots") or she is doing something with the playthings ("In the sand pitch I need a spade and sand molds"). The enumeration of playthings and actions done with them culminates on the last double spread, where the child is in a swing facing her teddy bear who sits on a wooden duck. Accordingly, the accompanying text changes from *I* to *we*: "And we like best playing together in the garden." When one examines the whole picture sequence, the single illustrations and the text seem interchangeable, because they merely consist of enumerations. However, they lead to a sort of climax in the last sentence.

A unique property of early narratives that attempt to tell a continuous story from the first to the last page is their detachment of concept books and conceptual domains as dominant features. A case in point is *Max blöja* (Max's Napkin, 1994) by Babro Lindgren and Eva Eriksson. The book consists of a picture sequence displaying the protagonist Max, his dog, and his mother. The setting, Max's bedroom, remains the same throughout the story. The book first introduces the protagonist; the dog is introduced on the fifth page, while Max's mother does not appear until page 9, so that the young child is steadily accustomed to the main characters. The text is adjusted to the child's linguistic and narrative capacities, comprising short sentences that consist of three to seven words (in the German translation). Invitations, such as *Look, Max*, direct speech, and the sentences on the right page, such as *Max wants to wee on the floor*, function as page-turners, making the reader curious about what will happen next. Deictic notions like *there*, the repetitive reference to the protagonists as *Max, the dog* or *Mama* (note the disclaimer of anaphors), the simple syntactic structure, and the repetition of utterances support the young child's developing sense of a story. The cartoon-like drawings, the dog wrapped in the napkin, and Max's attempt to behave like a dog create a humorous effect, while the first appearance of Max's mother prepares the reader for an imminent change. Her angry facial expression and her scolding of Max and the dog present the climax of the story, which smoothly merges into the story's conclusion: Max's mother fetches a new napkin, while Max is cleaning the floor with a scrubber. The normal course of events depicted in this picturebook is interrupted by the sudden appearance of Max's mother, thus dividing the narrative into two parts, before and after the climax. Furthermore, the reader is emotionally involved by empathizing with the protagonist Max. Affective markers are inserted into the text and the pictures. Although the text is rather short and the sentences have a simple syntactic structure, the repeated imperative *look* on the first page and the onomatopoetic word *fie* on the ninth page invite the reader to bond with the protagonist.

On the picture level, affection is caused by the changing facial expressions of the figures, ranging from happiness to abashment and anger, supported by related gestures. In sum, then, although this picturebook has a short text and relies on a set of simple visual schemata and cues (same setting, three figures, gradual introduction of the figures), it possesses the basic features of a narrative nevertheless – that is, climax and affective markers. Since the story refers to an event that touches upon the experiences of young children, it might support the young child's progression from descriptive (nonfiction) picturebooks to narrative (fictional) picturebooks, an interface hardly investigated as of yet.

At the beginning of this section, we referred to the descriptive–narrative bifurcation as a seminal aspect of early literacy. Quite surprisingly, the first picturebooks with texts that very young children come across are distinguished by their descriptive approach. The texts are usually short and mostly describe objects and their functions, and sometimes even events that are connected with the objects. Therefore, this book type lays the ground for nonfiction books for children. Although nonfiction books play an increasingly important role in the international book market, they have hardly been investigated in the realm of children's literature research. Both picturebook research and children's literature studies focus on fictional picturebooks and children's books, thus neglecting a huge book corpus that evidently attracts many children, especially those children who are more interested in factual information about diverse topics than in fictional stories that demand their ability to connect with the fictional characters and settings. Studies in narratology have shown that even narrative stories include descriptive passages and that the distinction between descriptive and narrative sections is not always easy to draw (Fludernik 2009). In contrast to descriptive texts, narrative texts are characterized by affective markers on the one hand, and the building of a climax on the other hand. Considering this, one might argue that the descriptive–narrative bifurcation that seemingly emerges in picturebooks targeted at children at the threshold from the second to the third year of age fosters the child's appreciation of the different narrative strategies of picturebooks. In this respect, one might even suspect that the descriptive–narrative bifurcation smoothly passes into a descriptive–narrative continuum, as will be shown in the next section.

Knowledge and testimony: the case of hygiene

Learning from picturebooks has to do with transmitting knowledge. Knowledge, as studied in epistemology, is a multifaceted and complex notion. Pritchard (2010) draws a basic distinction between propositional knowledge and ability knowledge. The former relates to knowledge that is represented in the form of propositional contents (which can be true or false, which can be believed or known), the latter to knowledge related to certain actions (e.g. to swimming) that cannot easily be "translated" into a propositional format. With respect to propositional knowledge, one may distinguish, say, geographical knowledge, linguistic knowledge, mathematical, aesthetic, ethical, and scientific knowledge. It is obvious that all these types of knowledge and many more are conveyed in picturebooks.

This said, it has to be recalled that it is not only knowledge that matters in learning from picturebooks. There are many others things to be learned from picturebooks, for example emotions, moral evaluation, appreciation of art. All of these are domains that cannot be represented in terms of propositional knowledge. Not much is known about the acquisition of these domains via picturebooks.

As Harris (2012) demonstrates, children mostly do not learn from their own experience; instead, from early on, they tend to trust testimony. Testimony is handed over to them by members of their family, such as their parents, grandparents, and siblings. At least in Western cultures, testimony is also spread through picturebooks.

In the joint reading situation, the child is exposed to at least two testifiers: the adult reader and the author. This is an important aspect of a reading situation: the adult, who can be trusted with respect to many nonreading situations, acts as a mediator of knowledge fixed by an author. We do not know anything about the child's concept of the AUTHOR. However, we assume that even young children already conclude that adult readers take the things they say from a certain source, namely the book. And apart from in the case of self-made books, most adult readers will not impose the impression on the child that they themselves are the authors of the book. (Note that authorship seems to be blurred in laboratories where children are confronted with artificial children's books.)

In the following, we will focus on one particular knowledge domain, namely hygiene knowledge.[2] In particular, we will show that descriptive and narrative strategies are often mixed, so that there is a descriptive–narrative continuum that fosters knowledge acquisition. Siegal (2008) reports on experimental findings with respect to children's knowledge about biology, food, and hygiene. He draws on the seminal work of Carey (1985), who assumes that "young children cling to appearances rather than underlying realities that involve true causal mechanisms" (Siegel 2008: 79). For instance:

> in their biological understanding, they think that irritants such as pepper as well as germs transmit appearances that correspond to colds, that traits such as eye color are the result of environmental influence rather than biological inheritance, and that a dead corpse retains certain biological attributes of life.
> (ibid.: 79)

Thus, viewed from an adult (scientific) perspective, children possess false knowledge. Roughly, Carey (2008) distinguishes two developmental phases. In the first phase, until the age of 6, children learn facts about the biological world, for example "that animals are alive and that babies come from inside their mothers and look like their parents" (Siegal 2008: 79). In the second phase, children are said "to begin to construct a coherent framework theory of biology through a process of 'conceptual' change" (ibid.). To be more precise, this change is a "nonconservative conceptual change" in that it "requires a strong restructuring in which previous causal concepts that are 'incommensurable' with the culturally received view are abandoned" (ibid.: 96).

Takashi and Wilkerson (2011) present an impressive study of Japanese books dealing with toilet training. While these books, for instance Mari Mori's *Chii dekita yo!* (I Can Wee, 2006), differ in their approaches to toilet training, they nevertheless are engaged in fostering children's thinking about bodily functions, thus preparing them for a more adult-like conception of contagion and purification. In a nutshell, we would like to argue that books like these prepare children for the "nonconservative conceptual change". Toilet-training books take up the child's interest in their own excrements, as well as their interest in others' excrements. These books build on Japanese cultural and literary traditions, yet try to integrate them into modern scientific thinking. It is said that it is useful to observe one's own feces because it reflects bodily habits and may be indicative of diseases.[3] Most astonishingly, there appears to be a prototypical or archetypical picture of a "poop":

> This archetypical portrayal roughly depicts the shape formed when a soft semi-solid is extruded from a tube or nozzle in a series of ever narrowing concentric circles, a pyramid or pointed swirl similar to that made when soft ice cream is extruded into an ice-cream cone.
> (Takashi and Wilkinson 2011: 182)

Toilet-training board books for very young children also appear in European and North American countries. Their main purpose is to support toddlers and kindergarten children in learning to control their bodily functions and to introduce them to correct toilet behavior. Depending on the respective target groups, the picturebooks provide hygiene knowledge on diverse levels of complexity. While Leslie Patricelli's *Potty* (2010) aims at introducing toddlers to the usage of the potty, Alida Allison's *Toddler's Potty Book* (2003) additionally conveys knowledge about accompanying hygiene measures, such as the washing of one's hands.

Often, and following older literary traditions, toilet-training advice is embedded into humorous narratives, for instance, narratives with farting literary characters, such as Shinta Cho's *The Gas We Pass: A Story of Farts* (1994) and Taro Gomi's bestseller *Everyone Poops* (1998). A comparatively rare example of a German picturebook dealing with excrements is the eminently successful picturebook *Vom kleinen Maulwurf, der wissen wollte, wer ihm auf den Kopf gemacht hat* (The Story of the Little Mole Who Went in Search of Whodunit, 1989) by Werner Holzwarth and Wolf Erlbruch, which has also been quite successful in its English and Japanese translations.

The story starts with the little mole looking out of his hole and an unknown animal leaving its business on the mole's head. Annoyed by this lapse, the mole sets out to find the culprit, checking the excreta of diverse animals, such as a bird's, a horse's, a cow's, and a rabbit's. Finally, with the help of some flies the mole is able to find the responsible animal, a dog, and takes his revenge by leaving his business on the dog's head.

Although the humorous effects are to the fore, the picturebook additionally imparts knowledge about the diverse forms and shapes of the animal's defecations. The underlying message, besides the information that every animal has its own shape of excrements, consists in the testimony that making dirt is a natural process, regardless of whether it concerns animals or people. Of all animals, it is the flies, as the excrement experts, who are able to set the mole on the right track.

Although this picturebook tells a fictional story with anthropomorphized animals, its text and images also convey knowledge about the different excrements of animals and how the shape and consistency of dirt are closely connected to the animals' size and feeding habits. Moreover, descriptive and narrative elements converge in the text. The overarching plot is structured by the typical narrative story design with a beginning, an ending, and a climax, and is complemented by a series of repetitive actions that are divided into a question–answer sequence. The characterization of the animals and their excrements has a descriptive character and is amended by the illustrations.

The descriptive–narrative continuum that determines the majority of picturebooks for young children also emerges in nonfiction books about dental care. A classical representative for this topic is the successful Norwegian book *Karius and Bactus* (1949) by Thorbjørn Egner, which has been translated into several languages and is still available on the book market. This book has served as a model for other picturebooks focusing on dental hygiene. What distinguishes Egner's book is the combination of a fictional story with factual information about dental hygiene. To achieve this goal, Egner uses the strategy of personalizing the germs that are responsible for forms of dental damage, such as caries and plaque. In this respect, the author relies on a specific strategy, namely the tendency of children (and even adults) to conceptualize complex items, such as germs and microbes, as creatures with humanlike features. Therefore, the germs in Egner's book are miniature people who have proper names and wear clothes. Nevertheless, the author succeeds in conveying the necessary knowledge about dental hygiene by means of a somewhat hybrid mixture of fictional and factual elements. A number of picturebooks dealing with dental care followed in Egner's footsteps, showing anthropomorphized germs that populate people's mouths and attack their teeth. Sometimes, articles of dental hygiene like a toothbrush play a crucial role, as in Virginia Parkinson's *"Cleanliness"* (1943). We will come back to this picturebook in the next section when we focus on literary characters.

These dramatic stories merge into descriptive passages providing factual information about dental hygiene that is suitable for children. In contrast, there also exist picturebooks dealing with dental care that matter-of-factly focus on a young child's (first) visit to the dentist. In *Wir besuchen den Zahnarzt* (We Visit the Dentist, 2010) by Christiane Wittenburg with illustrations by Ulla Bartl, a group of five kindergarten children go to the dentist, where they are introduced to what usually happens during a dental surgery and where they are finally advanced to dental care themselves. The children's different emotional reactions, expressed by their facial expressions and assertions, serve as narrative markers that invite the child reader to empathize with the protagonists. Nevertheless, factual information is embedded into the story, thus underscoring the descriptive–narrative continuum of this nonfiction picturebook.

A note on literary characters and genres

In their review of experimental findings, Ganea and Canfield (this volume, Chapter 2) make clear (1) "that picturebooks with realistic pictures provide better support for generalizing information from the pictures to the real world"; and (2) "although features such as the illustrations and type of language do not prevent learning in young children, they may impart incorrect knowledge when they portray the world in an unrealistic manner". The latter remark is directed against, for example, anthropomorphized picturebooks. In particular:

> The children who had heard anthropomorphic language were more likely to say that animals in the real world can have human-like characteristics than were children who were exposed to realistic books. Thus, just as realistic pictures allow infants to generalize labels to novel objects, realistic picturebooks enable preschool children to accurately incorporate the factual information they are exposed to in the books into their conceptions of the real world.
>
> (Ganea and Canfield, this volume)

We think, however, that this generalization might turn out to be far too strong. On the contrary, we suggest that anthropomorphized literary characters may be helpful for conveying reliable knowledge to children. Siegal (2008) stresses that adults as well as children like to draw pictures of germs in which they show anthropomorphic traits. He concludes: "Portraying germs in the form of tiny menacing human-like organisms can be used as a strategy toward improving children's knowledge of health and well-being" (ibid.: 86).

In the picturebook *"Cleanliness"* (1943) by Virginia Parkinson, we find several anthropomorphic characters, i.e. Mr. Do and Mr. Don't, Johnny Toothbrush, and the pelican-doctor Doc Stork. Bob, a little boy, neglects Johnny Toothbrush, and so the latter reasons:

> "Oh dear," he cried so bitterly,
> "How can I change his ways,
> How can I teach him, Cleanliness
> Comes first before he plays!"
> "I guess I'll have to find a way
> So Bob will not forget.
> I'll ask advice of Doctor Stork…
> He's never failed me yet!
> This worry makes me very ill,
> So Doctor Stork will say
> That the quickest way to get me well
> Is to use me every day!"

Doc Stork, when visited by Bob and Johnny, explains to Bob that he should not neglect his friend Johnny because if he did, Johnny would be very sad. Obviously, the idea behind this plot is to use the authority of these anthropomorphic characters to teach cleanliness (in this case, to use the toothbrush regularly; see Figure 1.1). So, these characters may be helpful in transmitting knowledge concerning hygiene. Anthropomorphic characters feature in more nonfiction books than one would expect. For example, some nonfiction picturebooks use matchstick-men characters that have the function of guides and commentators, as in *Grammar Can Be Fun* (1940) by Munro Leaf.[4] Other nonfiction books, in turn, personalize abstract items, such as colors, numbers, and machines. One idea behind this strategy might be an attempt to arouse the child's interest in abstract and oftentimes complex issues. Another prospect certainly consists in facilitating the child's cognitive and emotional attunement with topics that are not easily understandable, such as grammar, mechanical constructions, and physical laws.

As for "realistic pictures", Ganea and Canfield mention that further differentiation is needed. However, we would emphasize that this claim also touches upon the analysis of "unrealistic pictures". For instance, from the perspective of an adult reader, *Fox* (2000) by Margaret Wild and Ron Brooks certainly is a challenging picturebook. Basically, it is a love triangle between a half-blind dog, a broken-winged magpie, and a fox, in which the fox seduces the magpie into leaving the half-blind dog by way of deception. The accompanying pictures give

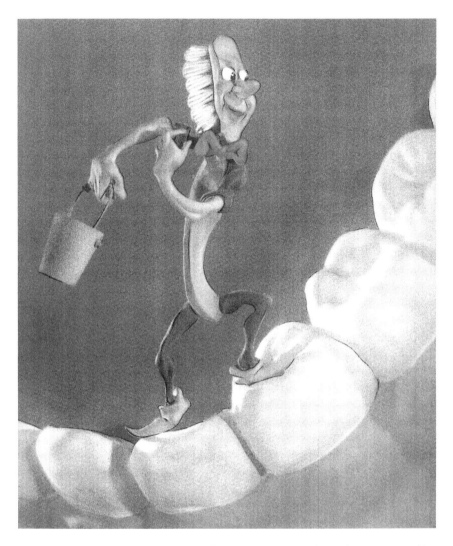

Figure 1.1 Illustration from *"Cleanliness" starring Johnny Toothbrush* by Virginia Parkinson and Marjorie Wales. New York: J. L. Schilling, 1943.

the impression of emotional arousal and despair. In order to reconstruct a possible interpretation of this particular text–picture relation from the point of view of a child reader, Kümmerling-Meibauer and Meibauer (forthcoming, b) analyze the fox as a specific literary character, discuss the notions of deception and seduction (with a view to the child's emerging mind-reading abilities), ask how empathy with literary characters contributes to the child's moral theme comprehension, and include emotional aspects of the pictures (especially those triggered by the colors). The comprehensive analysis shows that *Fox* can be read on multiple levels, so that it qualifies for the status of a genuine crossover picturebook.[5] The point we want to make is simple: unrealistic pictures and animal characters that show human traits may be helpful in a child's acquisition of moral knowledge. So, there is ample room for more subtle experiments on acquiring knowledge from (real) picturebooks. The investigation of the cognitive challenges of personalization and anthropomorphism in picturebooks, whether it concerns fictional stories or nonfiction books, is still in its fledgling stages, but our short overview has hopefully demonstrated that this matter is closely connected with children's cognitive development and knowledge acquisition.

Furthermore, the analysis of literary characters in picturebooks cannot be undertaken without considering the concept of GENRE. Since children evidently come into contact with diverse literary genres, such as fairy tales, nursery rhymes, songs, animal stories, and realistic stories, from very early on, they often learn intuitively the significant features that distinguish these genres. While some genres are relatively easy to recognize, for instance by formulaic expressions ("Once upon a time"), the occurance of animal protagonists, rhymes, and other genres, demand thorough attention to their essential features. We do not know much about children's genre acquisition and genre. The genre concept, however, definitely steers children's anticipations and beliefs concerning the content, structure, characterization of figures, and language of specific stories and books. For lack of effectual research in this domain, we cannot delve into this fascinating material. Nevertheless, we would like to stress the significance of genre knowledge as a crucial component of a developmental scenario that illustrates children's cognitive development via picturebooks.

Conclusions

It goes without saying that our attempts at categorizing different book types and relating them to different developmental stages are only a first step. However, it appears that we can draw some conclusions from our previous analyses.

First, it is realistic to assume that 1-year-olds are not confronted with books focusing on *wh*-questions, and that 4-year-olds are not interested in early-concept books that only show apples or balls. So, the assignment of picturebook types to developmental stages is an empirical task. For instance, we assume that noun-related early-concept books are connected to the developmental stage of the early lexicon (12–18 months, mean length of utterance (MLU): 1), characterized by the naming insight and connected with the pointing and naming game. In addition, we assume that picturebooks presenting a first-person perspective are related to the developmental stage at which the child grasps the concept of a sentence, including some morphosyntax, and forms a theory of mind (thoughts are related to different agents, and indexicals are related to these agents). These processes appear to happen sometime between the ages of

21 and 36 months, with an MLU of between 2 and 4, but more precise knowledge is still needed.

Second, we find picturebooks like the so-called wimmelbook that are related to more than just one developmental stage (Rémi 2011). A wimmelbook is a wordless picturebook which presents a panorama that is rich in characters and detail. The situations shown in these "pluriscenic" settings are familiar to young children. While the different panoramas form separate, independent units, some wimmelbooks, such as those created by Rotraut Susanne Berner (e.g. 2003), connect them to form a continuous narrative (Rémi 2011). This book type activates the reader on different levels, inviting her or him to different modes of reception. What catches the eye is the tight connection to earlier picturebook types. Wimmelbooks display objects and actions carried out with those objects. They arrange the objects so that they can be assigned to conceptual domains, and produce a combination of descriptive and narrative frames. The characteristics of the aforementioned book types, i.e. sequentiality, multidimensionality, categorization, and descriptive–narrative divide, can also be applied to wimmelbooks, although they do not have any text. The wimmelbook, so it seems, thus demands a lot of fine-tuning by adults, who may nevertheless invite children to read them on their own. Wimmelbooks prompt the viewer to diverse approaches, like playing a searching game, attentively looking at the details shown in the panorama, re-narrating the depicted events, and building up connections between different characters and actions. For these reasons, books of this type appeal to different age groups, from very young children up to 5-year-olds.

Third, reconsider what we have called the descriptive–narrative bifurcation. By and large, picturebooks for the very young are nonfiction books, since they focus on things and events. Yet they are only a stepping stone to the acquisition of narrative picturebooks. While these narrative picturebooks still contain descriptive elements, they need more coherence and cohesion, and they need complications and affective markings (cf. Boueke *et al.* 1995; Becker 2011; Quasthoff 1987). Remarkably, this does not render the nonfiction books superfluous; on the contrary, the nonfiction books gain in complexity, and there are even children (maybe boys) who are consistent in preferring nonfiction books. The development of this nonfiction/descriptive–narrative bifurcation is still mysterious territory.

Fourth, we endorse the view that even the first picturebooks enhance an understanding of elements that are important for the acquisition of literary literacy (see Kümmerling-Meibauer and Meibauer 2005, 2011a). These elements are, for instance, sequentiality, contrast, the forming of mental images, and talking about things and events as well as them to shared experiences. In later developmental stages, the child will develop the concepts of STORY or GENRE – that is, concepts that are fostered by picturebook input, yet are achievements of the child at the same time. Thus, the child will detect that there are similarities between picturebooks and her or his own creative stories.

Fifth, while we have highlighted the relation between language development and picturebook spurt (drawing a parallel to the vocabulary spurt), there are several accompanying developmental processes that have an impact on early literacy: the development of playing, including pretend play; and sensorimotor developments leading to different activities, such as opening and closing flaps, looking at hidden things through a peephole, touching cloth, fake fur and other materials representing animals' skin, and making noises. Rhyme has to do with the development of phonological awareness and is very important, of course. The development of painting abilities might be supported by coloring books.

Finally, picturebooks have a crucial impact on the child's knowledge acquisition and her or his approach towards testimony. As regards picturebooks, children acquire knowledge on different levels, ranging from knowledge about their immediate surroundings, usually displayed in early-concept books and concept books, to learning about different knowledge domains, such as vehicles and hygiene, not to mention more complex spheres such as moral knowledge. In addition, the important function of literary characters as mediating agents should not be underestimated in this respect. As narrative and emotional markers, they foster children's empathy and might even support their knowledge acquisition.

This overview is far from complete but has, we hope, evinced the outstanding impact that picturebooks have on the young child's cognitive and narrative development. It goes without saying that such an enterprise can only be satisfactorily accomplished by an interdisciplinary approach, embracing cognitive psychology, linguistics, picturebook research, and education.

Notes

1 For examples, see Kümmerling-Meibauer and Linsmann (2009).
2 Another interesting topic is geographical knowledge, for instance the ability to understand maps. Astonishingly, maps assume a significant role in picturebooks focusing on travels, itineraries, and historical events. See Kümmerling-Meibauer and Meibauer (forthcoming, a).
3 Summarizing the content of the first book in the *The Book of Poop Series* by Murakami Yachiyo, Takashi and Wilkerson (2011: 183) write: "Among the lessons incorporated in this volume we can find the following: bodily functions are not cause for embarrassment; different textures of excrement can be identified and named; your excrement reflects what and how you eat; one should examine one's stools, and make daily observations; don't forget to flush the toilet and wash your hands."
4 See Kümmerling-Meibauer and Meibauer (2014) for a detailed analysis of matchstick men as literary characters in picturebooks.
5 Typical examples of crossover picturebooks are Pop Art picturebooks that were prominent in the 1970s and targeted at children and adults alike (Kümmerling-Meibauer and Meibauer 2011b).

References

Primary sources

Allison, Alida. 2003. *Toddler's Potty Book*. Los Angeles: Price Stern Sloan.
Berner, Rotraut Susanne. 2003. *Winter-Wimmelbuch*. Hildesheim, Germany: Gerstenberg.
Bravi, Soledad. 2004. *Le livre de bruits*. Paris: l'école des loisirs.
Bruna, Dick. 1967. *B Is for Bear*. London: Methuen.
Cho, Shinta. 1994. *The Gas We Pass: A Story of Farts*. La Jolla, CA: Kane/Miller.
Cornille, Didier. 2009. *Le livre des contraires*. Paris: hélium.
Drews, Judith. 2010. *Antons ganze Welt*. Weinheim: Beltz.
Egner, Thorbjørn. 1986. *Karius and Bactus*, translated by Mike Sewig. San Francisco: Meadowbrook Press (original Norwegian edition 1949).
Gomi, Taro. 2001. *Everyone Poops*. La Jolla, CA: Kane/Miller (orginal Japanese edition 1977).
Haring, Keith. 1998. *Ten*. New York: Hyperion Books for Children.
Hoban, Tana. 1973. *Push/Pull – Empty/Full*. New York: Macmillan.
Hoban, Tana. 1986. *Red, Blue, Yellow Shoe*. New York: Macmillan.
Holzwarth, Werner and Wolfgang Erlbruch. 1989. *Vom kleinen Maulwurf, der wissen wollte, wer ihm auf den Kopf gemacht hat*. Wuppertal: Peter Hammer Verlag.
Langen, Annette and Sabine Kraushaar. 2012. *Noch mal! Meine ersten Lieblingswörter*. Münster: Coppenrath.
Leaf, Munro. 1940. *Grammar Can Be Fun*. London: Ward Lock.
Lindgren, Babro and Eva Eriksson. 1994. *Max blöja*. Stockholm: Rabén & Sjögren.
Mori, Mari and Ichiko Fuyuno. 2006. *Chii dekita yo!* Tokyo: Shogakukan.
Oxenbury, Helen. 1981. *Playing*. London: Walker Books.
Parkinson, Virginia and Marjorie Wales. 1943. *"Cleanliness" starring Johnny Toothbrush*. New York: J. L. Schilling.
Patricellli, Leslie. 2010. *Potty*. Somerville, MA: Candlewick Press.
Picthall, Chez. 2008. *Baby Sees Farm Animals*. London: Picthall & Gunzi.
Spanner, Helmut. 1989. *Meine Spielzeug*. Ravensburg, Germany: Ravensburger Buchverlag.
Stickland, Paul. 1986. *Trucks*. York: Methuen Books.
Stickland, Paul. 1990. *A Child's Book of Things*. Yeovil, UK: Matthew Price.
Wiesner, Angela. 1995. *Heute spiele ich*. Ravensburg, Germany: Ravensburger Buchverlag.
Wild, Margaret and Ron Brooks. 2000. *Fox*. Syndey: Allen & Unwin.
Wittenburg, Christiane and Ulla Bartl. 2010. *Wir besuchen den Zahnarzt*. Hamburg: Carlsen.

Secondary sources

Bamberg, Michael, ed. 1997. *Narrative Development: Six Approaches*. Mahwah, NJ: Lawrence Erlbaum.
Barrett, Martyn. 1995. "Early lexical development". In *The Handbook of Child Language*, edited by Paul Fletcher and Brian MacWhinney. 362–292. Oxford: Blackwell.
Becker, Tabea. 2011. *Kinder lernen erzählen. Zur Entwicklung der narrativen Fähigkeiten von Kindern unter Berücksichtigung der Erzählform*. Baltmannsweiler, Germany: Schneider Hohengehren.
Bloom, Harold. 2000. *How Children Learn the Meaning of Words*. Cambridge, MA: MIT Press.

Boueke, Dietrich *et al.* 1995. *Wie Kinder erzählen. Untersuchungen zur Erzähltheorie und zur Entwicklung narrative Fähigkeiten.* Munich: Fink.

Carey, Susan. 1985. *Conceptual Change in Childhood.* Cambridge, MA: MIT Press.

Clark, Eve. 1993. *The Lexicon in Acquisition.* Cambridge: Cambridge University Press.

Dannerer, Monika. 2012. *Narrative Fähigkeiten und Individualität: Mündlicher und schriftlicher Erzählerwerb im Längsschnitt von der 5. bis zur 12. Schulstufe.* Tübingen: Stauffenburg.

Dromi, Esther. 1987. *Early Lexical Development.* Cambridge: Cambridge University Press.

Fludernik, Monika. 2009. *Introduction to Narratology.* London: Routledge.

Gressnich, Eva. 2012. "Verbal and visual pageturners in picturebooks". *International Research in Children's Literature* 5(2): 167–183.

Gressnich, Eva and Jörg Meibauer. 2010. "First-person narratives in picturebooks: An inquiry into the acquisition of picturebook competence". In *New Directions in Picturebook Research*, edited by Teresa Colomer, Bettina Kümmerling-Meibauer, and María Cecilia Silva-Díaz. 191–203. New York: Routledge.

Harris, Paul L. 2012. *Trusting What You're Told: How Children Learn from Others.* Cambridge, MA.: The Belknap Press of Harvard University Press.

Jones, Rhian. 1996. *Emerging Patterns of Literacy: A Multidisciplinary Perspective.* London: Routledge.

Kauschke, Christina. 2000. *Der Erwerb des frühkindlichen Lexikons.* Tübingen: Narr.

Kauschke, Christina and Christoph Hofmeister. 2002. "Early lexical development in German: A study on vocabulary growth and vocabulary composition during the second and third year of life". *Journal of Child Language* 29: 735–757.

Kümmerling-Meibauer, Bettina and Maria Linsmann, eds. 2009. *Literatur im Laufstall. Bilderbücher für die ganz Kleinen.* Troisdorf, Germany: Bilderbuchmuseum Burg Wissem.

Kümmerling-Meibauer, Bettina and Jörg Meibauer. 2005. "First pictures, early concepts: Early concept books". *The Lion and the Unicorn* 29: 324–347.

Kümmerling-Meibauer, Bettina and Jörg Meibauer. 2011a. "Early-concept books: Acquiring nominal and verbal concepts". In *Emergent Literacy. Children's books from 0 to 3*, edited by Bettina Kümmerling-Meibauer. 91–114. Amsterdam: John Benjamins.

Kümmerling-Meibauer, Bettina and Jörg Meibauer. 2011b. "On the strangeness of pop art picturebooks: Pictures, texts, paratexts". *New Review of Children's Literature and Librarianship* 17: 103–121. [Reprinted in: *Picturebooks. Beyond the Borders of Art, Narrative and Culture*, edited by Evelyn Arizpe, Maureen Farrell, and Julie McAdam. 23–41. New York: Routledge, 2013.]

Kümmerling-Meibauer, Bettina and Jörg Meibauer. 2011c. Lügenerwerb und Geschichten vom Lügen. *LiLi. Zeitschrift für Literaturwissenschaft und Linguistik* 162: 118–138.

Kümmerling-Meibauer, Bettina and Jörg Meibauer. 2013. "Towards a cognitive theory of picturebooks". *International Research in Children's Literature* 6(2): 143–160.

Kümmerling-Meibauer, Bettina and Jörg Meibauer. 2014. "Understanding the matchstick man: Aesthetic and narrative properties of a hybrid picturebook character". In *Picturebooks: Representation and Narration*, edited by Bettina Kümmerling-Meibauer. 139–161. New York: Routledge.

Kümmerling-Meibauer, Bettina and Jörg Meibauer. forthcoming, a. "Maps in picturebooks: Cognitive status and narrative functions". *Nordic Journal of Children's Literature Aesthetics/Barnelitterært forskningstidsskrift* (BLFT) 5.

Kümmerling-Meibauer, Bettina and Jörg Meibauer. forthcoming, b. "*Beware of the fox!* Emotion and deception in *Fox* by Margaret Wild and Ron Brooks". In *Challenging and Controversial Picturebooks: Creative and Critical Responses to Visual Texts*, edited by Janet Evans. London: Routledge.

Legerstee, Maria. 2005. *Infants' Sense of People: Precursors to a Theory of Mind*. Cambridge: Cambridge University Press.

Lewis, David. 2001. *Reading Contemporary Picturebooks: Picturing Text*. London: RoutledgeFalmer.

Meibauer, Jörg. 2011. "Spracherwerb und Kinderliteratur". *LiLi. Zeitschrift für Literaturwissenschaft und Linguistik* 162: 11–28.

Meibauer, Jörg. 2014. "Einfachheit, Anpassung und *Early Literacy*". *LiLi. Zeitschrift für Literaturwissenschaft und Linguistik* 174: 9–23.

Meibauer, Jörg and Monika Rothweiler, eds. 1999. *Das Lexikon im Spracherwerb*. Tübingen: Francke.

Murphy, Gregory L. 2002. *The Big Book of Concepts*. Cambridge, MA: MIT Press.

Nikolajeva, Maria. 2003. "Verbal and visual literacy: The role of picturebooks in the reading experience of young children". In *Handbook of Early Childhood Literacy*, edited by Nigel Hall, Judith Larson, and Jackie Marsh. 235–248. London: Sage.

Nodelman, Perry. 1988. *Words about Pictures: The Narrative Art of Children's Picture Books*. Athens, GA: University of Georgia Press.

Pritchard, Duncan. 2010. *What Is This Thing Called Knowledge?* 2nd edition. New York: Routledge.

Quasthoff, Uta M. 1987. "Sprachliche Formen des alltäglichen Erzählens. Struktur und Entwicklung". In *Mündliches Erzählen im Alltag, fingiertes mündliches Erzählen in der Literatur*, edited by Willi Erzgräber and Paul Goetsch. 54–85. Tübingen: Narr.

Rakison, David H. and Lisa M. Oakwa, eds. 2003. *Early Category and Concept Development: Making Sense of the Blooming, Buzzing Confusion*. New York: Oxford University Press.

Rémi, Cornelia. 2011. "The cognitive challenge of the wimmelbook". In *Emergent Literacy: Children's books from 0 to 3*, edited by Bettina Kümmerling-Meibauer. 115–140. Amsterdam: John Benjamins.

Siegal, Michael. 2008. *Marvelous Minds: The Discovery of What Children Know*. Oxford: Oxford University Press.

Takahashi, Kyoko and Douglas Wilkerson. 2011. "Linking behavioural training and scientific thinking: Toilet training picturebooks in Japan". In *Emergent Literacy: Children's books from 0 to 3*, edited by Bettina Kümmerling-Meibauer. 175–192. Amsterdam: John Benjamins.

Wellman, Henry M. 1992. *The Child's Theory of Mind*. Cambridge, MA: MIT Press.

2 An examination of factors that affect young children's learning and transfer from picturebooks

Patricia A. Ganea and Caitlin F. Canfield

Introduction

Children are surrounded by symbols from early in life, and within a few years they must master a variety of educational symbols, including letters, numbers, mathematical symbols, maps, and in some cases musical notation and computer icons. Extensive research points to the importance of beginning to acquire this knowledge in preschool and early elementary school. For example, children who learn letters and their relations to sounds at a young age perform substantially better in later reading, not only in early elementary school but also through high school and perhaps beyond (Foulin 2005; Hulme *et al.* 2012; Levin *et al.* 2006; Stevenson and Newman 1986).

Symbol-mediated experience vastly expands children's horizons by enabling them to learn from a variety of sources and, most importantly, to acquire information beyond the here and now. A common assumption among parents and educators is that symbolic artifacts can be used to *maximize* learning. Pictures, videos, maps, and other symbolic objects are routinely used at home and in preschools to expose young children to new information. Given the widespread practice of using symbolic artifacts to teach children new information, it is important to consider what factors may influence the processes involved in early learning of symbol-mediated information.

One factor that constrains children's learning from symbolic artifacts is their understanding of the symbol-referent relation (DeLoache and Burns 1994). Symbols have a dual nature: they are both objects in and of themselves and at the same time representations of something else (DeLoache 1995, 2002). To acquire information from symbols, children first need to appreciate their representational nature, the fact that they refer to something else. For example, for children to learn and extrapolate new information from a picturebook, they first need to appreciate that information about the objects and events in the book is relevant to the real world. Similarly, to acquire information from video, children first need to understand that video images can represent real events. A good deal of developmental research has shown that understanding the nature of symbol-referent relations can be a difficult task for young children (Callaghan 2000; DeLoache 2002; Harris *et al.* 1997; Liben and Downs 1989; Tomasello *et al.* 1999; Troseth and DeLoache 1998). For example, children around the age of 2 have difficulty using objects symbolically if those objects have other conventional uses, because it is difficult for them to represent both the object's symbolic use and its conventional use (Tomasello *et al.* 1999). It has also been shown that highly salient and interesting objects can be more difficult for children to understand and use as representations of something else (DeLoache 1995, 2002). The more children's attention is focused on the object itself, the less likely they are to appreciate the symbolic relation between the object and its referent.

The dual representation requirements for pictures are reduced because pictures are generally less salient as objects in themselves. This should make it easier for children to use them as sources of information about the world compared to other symbolic objects (i.e. scale models) (DeLoache 2002). Nevertheless, although pictures may be less salient as objects in themselves, they have many physical characteristics (different types of images, sizes, colors, textures) that can influence the extent to which children use them symbolically. Thus, a second factor that can play a significant role in children's learning from symbols involves the physical characteristics of the symbol. Picturebooks form a unique symbolic medium, in that the things they represent can vary from real-world objects, to imaginary entities, and even to other symbols, such as letters and numbers. This added layer of representational complexity should make considerations about the characteristics of the symbolic medium even more important. For example, encouraging children to play with books that have tabs to pull out letters might not help them learn the abstract symbolic content depicted in the book, such as letters or numbers. Symbols that are too interesting in themselves as objects may not function as good teaching tools with young children.

In this chapter, we present research examining young children's learning from their interactions with picturebooks. In particular, we will summarize research showing that some characteristics of picturebooks may facilitate learning better than others. We will begin with a summary of research examining children's understanding of the symbolic nature of pictures.

Learning from picturebooks

American toddlers and young preschoolers spend hours engaged in joint picturebook reading with parents and others (Rideout *et al.* 2003). There is substantial evidence supporting the general benefits of picturebook reading (DeBarsyshe 1993; Sénéchal and Cornell 1993; Sénéchal and LeFevre 2001; Teale and Sulzby 1986; Whitehurst *et al.* 1994; Whitehurst and Lonigan 1998). For example, children who spend more time in picturebook interactions as preschoolers and young toddlers know more about reading when they go to school. Shared book reading contributes to children's knowledge about print, from their initial insight into the difference between words versus pictures (Bialystok 1995; Sulzby 1985) to actually learning to read (Adams 1990; Mason 1980). Furthermore, book-reading interventions with educationally at-risk children have also shown that picturebook reading can lead to an increase in children's concept of print and expressive vocabulary (Whitehurst *et al.* 1994), as well as in their participation in the picturebook interaction (Crain-Thoreson and Dale 1999; McNeill and Fowler 1999).

Another important question that has recently been systematically examined has to do with *content* information young children take away from these interactions. What do children actually learn about the real world from picturebooks? If they were to hear about a novel kind of animal – a zebra, for example – from a picturebook, would they recognize the real animal when seeing one for the first time? More importantly, would they apply to the real animal what they had learned from the book?

Parents and educators assume that very young children extend what they learn from picturebooks to the real world, but this assumption deserves to be systematically examined. In the research reported here, we present a review of young children's learning and generalization of information from picturebooks to real entities. Pictures are symbols that commonly represent entities that can be encountered in the "real world", and recent studies have shown that children as young as 18 months of age understand that a label given to a picture refers to a real object, rather than to only the picture itself (Ganea *et al.* 2009; Preissler and Carey 2004). This means that if a child hears the word "ball" during shared book reading in relation to the book, the child understands that the word refers to both the real object and the depiction of the object in the book. This indicates that the child has achieved an understanding of the referential nature of pictures; she or he realizes that the picture, as a symbol, is related to a real-world referent, and is not solely an artifact in itself (DeLoache *et al.* 1999). This also indicates that the child understands that words refer to conceptual categories that include more than the singular referent with which they are associated at the time of labeling (Gelman and Waxman 2009). In the case of hearing a word in relation to a picture, the child realizes that the word can also refer to a three-dimensional instantiation of the depicted object.

Although children's understanding of the referential relation between a picture and its referent seems to be in place early in their second year of life, their ability to extrapolate information from symbolic depictions to their real counterparts can be disrupted (Ganea *et al.* 2009). Below, we examine what features of picturebooks affect how likely young children are to apply information from the picturebook to the real world. Dimensions on which the pictures in children's books vary include (1) their level of realism; (2) the nature of their relation to their referent (i.e. whether real or fantasy entities are depicted); and (3) the presence of "manipulative" elements (features such as flaps and levers that children can manipulate to interact physically with the book).

We will focus on two general kinds of information that children presumably are exposed to in picturebooks. One involves general information about the world, such as names for objects, properties of objects, and conceptual information. The second involves more abstract information, such as information about letters and numbers. The general goal of the research reviewed here was to identify features of picturebooks that improve or impede the extent and accuracy of young children's learning and generalization from them.

Pictorial realism

The pictures in children's books can vary enormously in how realistic they are, ranging from highly realistic color photographs to simplified and schematic drawings to highly distorted and less realistic cartoons. In a study looking at young children's learning from picturebooks we examined whether young children would *learn* equally well from these different types of pictures. What we were mostly interested in was the extent to which pictorial realism would affect how well children *generalize* information to the real world.

To answer these questions, we taught 15- and 18-month-old children a novel name for a novel object in a naturalistic picturebook interaction. We then assessed how well they extended the label to the real object, as well as how well they generalized the label to a novel exemplar of the object (Ganea *et al*. 2008). Three kinds of books varying in pictorial realism were used in the study. Each book was made up of either highly realistic color photographs, realistic color drawings, or colored cartoons of the objects. The same six familiar objects were depicted once in each book, and the same two novel objects were depicted four times. During a naturalistic picturebook reading interaction, the experimenter drew the child's attention to each picture and talked about each depicted object. She briefly described and labeled one of the novel objects with a novel name ("Look, this is a blicket. See, a blicket. It's shiny and goes round and round. Yeah, that's a blicket."). She also described the other novel object, but she never named it ("Look at this! Wow, this is white and has two strings. Yeah, look at this!").

Three tests were administered. The first sought to determine whether the children actually learned the label. For this test, we showed them the pictures of the two novel objects and asked them to "show the blicket". Both the 18- and the 15-month-olds overwhelmingly chose correctly, indicating they had learned the novel label from the brief picturebook interaction. Thus, the children remembered the novel object that was labeled during the picturebook interaction. This indicates that children as young as 15 months can learn new information from picturebooks. There was no difference in performance as a function of the three types of pictures.

Our primary interest concerned the next test, in which we showed children the two novel objects in real life. We wanted to find out whether they would extend the label they had learned from the picturebook to the real object. The 18-month-olds extended the label to the real object in all three picture conditions. For the 15-month-olds, only the children who had interacted with the realistic books (ones with photographs or drawings) extended the label to the real referent. The 15-month-olds in the cartoon condition failed to extend what they had learned from the book to the real object.

Further, we wanted to see whether the children would generalize the label to a new instance of the object differing by a single feature from the object that they had seen depicted. When shown novel exemplars from the same category of objects (same kind of object but differently colored), the 18-month-olds who had seen the photographs or realistic drawings generalized the label to the new exemplar, but those who had seen cartoons did not. The 15-month-olds generally failed to generalize the label they had learned from the picturebooks to the novel exemplar of the target object, regardless of which kind of pictures they learned the name from.

This study establishes that picturebook interactions can be an effective means of teaching new information to very young children. Both the 15- and 18-month-olds in this study readily learned a novel name for an unfamiliar object from a very brief picturebook interaction. This research supports the basic assumption made by parents and educators alike that very young children do learn from picturebook interactions (van Kleeck 2003). It is important to note that in this study the objects were depicted alone on the page and that the background was blank. Books for young children come in a variety of arrangements and it would be important to examine whether children learn equally well from other types of early books that show objects grouped together on a page or against more detailed backgrounds, or showing objects from the same or a different category. Kümmerling-Meibauer and Meibauer (2011) provide an insightful analysis of the structure of books for children between 0 and 3 years of age that could be used as a guideline in experimentally testing what types of early books facilitate conceptual development in young children during shared picturebook reading.

The research discussed also reveals the importance of physical similarity between symbol and referent for young children's exploitation of the relation between them. Generalization of the novel name from the picture to the referent occurred more reliably from more realistic photographs and drawings than from less realistic cartoons. The importance of using more iconic pictures to teach children new information has also been illustrated in other studies with toddlers. Simcock and DeLoache (2006) found that 18- to 30-month-old toddlers can better imitate a sequence of actions with novel objects if it is portrayed in books with realistic photographs than if it is portrayed in books with line drawings. Thus, the pictorial realism effect does not seem to be limited to learning a particular type of content, but rather the nature of pictures can have a general influence on children's ability to take away information from the pages of a book. In terms of practical implications, this research tells us that if we want children to apply the information they learn from picturebooks to the real world, we need to consider the nature of the pictures in the book. The results presented here indicate that picturebooks with realistic pictures provide better support for generalizing information from the pictures to the real world.

Recent studies with younger infants show that even at 13 months of age, infants have the ability to transfer information across symbolic media. Keates *et al.* (2014) presented 13-, 15-, and 18-month-olds with picturebooks that showed and described an adult interacting with a target object that displayed a non-obvious property (i.e. the object lit up when touched). The adult was also shown interacting with a nontarget object, one that did not have a nonobvious property. When presented with the real referents and new exemplars of real referents (the same objects in a different color), children in all age groups transferred the nonobvious property to the target object – that is, they attempted the specific action that was depicted in the book to trigger the non-visible property of the object. This study indicates that young children not only can learn properties of objects from a pictorial representation of the object, but also can generalize that information to the general category of real objects.

The above studies indicate that children's referential understanding of pictures emerges early in life and that, despite some limitations in transfer from pictures to the real world, children understand that a basic function of pictures is to refer to something other than themselves. An important issue to consider is whether children's ability to generalize information they encounter in picturebooks to real objects is dependent on exposure to symbolic media early on in life. Experience with representational media can vary widely across cultures and it is important to examine whether children growing in different cultural settings would display a similar pattern of learning and generalization from picturebooks. Recent findings from a study conducted with children from a rural village in Tanzania who had no prior exposure to pictures indicates that lack of exposure and interaction with symbolic media may lead to significant delays in learning and generalization from picturebooks (Walker *et al.* 2013; see also Callaghan *et al.* 2012). In this study, children who had no prior pictorial experience were not able to generalize a label for a novel object from a photograph to the real world until nearly a year after this skill develops in children with rich picture-symbol exposure.

Fantasy pictures and language

A common feature of pictorial depictions in children's books is their fantastical nature. Infants and young children are exposed to a variety of pictures that depict reality in a distorted, fantastical way. For example, animals in children's books are commonly depicted wearing clothes and are portrayed and described as engaging in human-like activities (e.g. pigs building houses, bunnies going to school, dogs driving cars). Even inanimate entities, such as trains, cars, and lamps, are anthropomorphized: they are often depicted with faces and emotions, and are endowed with the ability to talk, laugh, and think. To what extent do picturebooks illustrating and describing nonhuman creatures and physical artifacts as intentional beings affect what children take away from pictures and apply to the real world? In other words, do young children assume that what is depicted in fantasy picturebooks applies to reality?

Previous research has shown that pictures can have a strong effect on children's beliefs about reality. Research with older children has shown that 6-year-olds believe in illogical transformations depicted in pictures even when they contradict events that they themselves had observed in the real world (O'Connor *et al.* 1981). We expect this effect to be even stronger for younger children who have limited knowledge about the nature of the relation between pictures and the referents they depict. Is children's ability to learn and transfer new information from picturebooks to the real world affected by the fantastical nature of pictures in books and by the type of language used to describe actual events in the world?

Ganea *et al.* (2011) varied the type of language used in picturebooks to teach preschool children about color camouflage in animals. In this study, children were read a story about color camouflage in frogs; half of the children were read picturebooks with realistic pictures and language, while the other half were read books with realistic pictures and intentional language. In this latter condition, the language used to describe the animals was anthropomorphized (the animals had names and they were described in intentional terms). After hearing the story, children were able to apply the concept of color camouflage when asked about photographs of a novel animal (butterflies), regardless of the type of book they saw. For example, when asked to indicate which of two depicted animals would be more likely to fall prey to a predatory bird, 3- and 4-year-old children correctly selected the animal whose color did not match the background. By 4 years of age, they were also able to provide appropriate factual explanations and transfer their new knowledge to live animals (Ganea *et al.* 2011). The 4-year-olds justified their choice by explicitly referring to information encountered in the book about color camouflage. For example, when asked to choose a safe place for a live animal to live in, they considered whether the color of the animal matched the test displays.

Although this study seems to indicate that the type of illustrations and language used in picturebooks makes little difference in children's learning, this is not entirely the case. Anthropomorphized picturebooks elicit a different, but equally important, limitation in children's learning. When tested on fantastical elements of books in addition to factual information, 4- and 5-year-olds (but not 3-year-olds) are more likely to also transfer fantastical, anthropomorphic characteristics to real animals when they have been exposed to anthropomorphic stories than when they have been exposed to realistic stories (Ganea *et al.* 2014). Thus, although features such as the illustrations and type of language do not prevent learning in young children, when they portray the world in an unrealistic manner they may play into children's natural anthropomorphic tendencies and, in doing so, may impart incorrect knowledge.

Ganea and colleagues (2014) looked at what picturebook elements most influence children's learning of facts about novel animals. They tested children from three age groups: 3-, 4-, and 5-year-olds. In the first study, an experimenter read three picture storybooks that contained realistic illustrations and either realistic or anthropomorphic language to each child. Each book imparted factual information about a different novel animal. After each book was read, the experimenter left the room to "find the next book", and a second experimenter showed the child a photograph of the animal and asked them questions about the animal in the photograph. The second experimenter emphasized that she was asking about the real animal, saying, "Look! I have a picture of a real cavy! Can you help me answer some questions about this real cavy? Do cavies eat grass?" and continuing on with additional questions. The questions included factual questions from the books, factual questions that were not in the books, and anthropomorphic questions. Children in both conditions were asked the same questions.

The results of this study, Study 1, indicated that, as in previous studies, children did learn from the picturebooks, regardless of whether they heard realistic or anthropomorphic language. Although children performed at chance levels in answering the factual questions that were not found in the books, children in all three age groups were significantly above chance in correctly answering the factual questions from the books. Thus, children in both book conditions learned new facts from the books. However, both 4- and 5-year-olds were more likely to answer anthropomorphic questions incorrectly, attributing human-like characteristics to the animals, if they heard the anthropomorphic stories. Three-year-olds attributed anthropomorphic characteristics to animals regardless of story type.

To determine whether illustrations, in addition to language, play a role in children's learning, Study 2 used the same procedure as Study 1, but with half the children hearing picturebooks with realistic language and anthropomorphic illustrations, and the other half of the children hearing books with both anthropomorphic language and illustrations. The results of this study expanded on those found in Study 1, indicating that illustrations also play a role in children's learning: children had difficulty transferring the new facts from the story to the real world if the picturebook they read contained *both* anthropomorphic illustrations and anthropomorphic language.

Taken together, these studies show that the types of books young children are exposed to affect their conception of reality. The children who had heard anthropomorphic language were more likely to say that animals in the real world can have human-like characteristics than were children who were exposed to the realistic books. Thus, just as realistic pictures allow infants to generalize labels to novel objects, realistic picturebooks enable preschool children to accurately incorporate the factual information they are exposed to in the books into their conceptions of the real world.

Fantastical illustrations and language may also affect children's ability to transfer more complex information to the real world. In another study, after hearing a story about a child who used a tool to obtain a toy that was out of reach, 4-year-old children were able to apply that solution when faced with a similar problem and provided with the necessary equipment (Richert *et al.* 2009). However, children were more likely to do so when the story from which they learned the solution was realistic. This is true when problem solutions are demonstrated in a simple framework, as well as when they are embedded in a more complex story context, as would be typical of commercial children's books (Richert and Smith 2011).

Further, Walker *et al.* (2014) have demonstrated that children learn and transfer causal information better when the information is presented in a story context "close" to the real world – that is, one more similar to reality – than in a context that is more dissimilar to the real world. For instance, children were more likely to link a cause and effect (e.g. sneezing from smelling a certain flower) for an experimenter's behavior if they first heard about the causal relation in a story about a boy who participated in realistic activities (e.g. having a picnic) than after hearing about a boy who had a more fantastical experience (e.g. conversing with a tree).

Collectively, these studies indicate that young children are capable of learning new information about the world from picturebooks, but that this learning works best when children are exposed to realistic stories and images. Children may disregard content information when it is portrayed in a format that they cannot directly relate to their own experience – that is, in a "far" fantastical context.

Manipulative books

Several books that are currently popular for young children fall in the category of "manipulative" books. These are books that invite children to physically interact with them, through elements such as flaps to lift, dials to turn, textures to feel, tabs to pull, and so on. Also included in this category are "pop-up" books incorporating pseudo-three-dimensional elements. Although such elements may make a book interesting and engaging to young children, they may not be advantageous for learning. The extraneous manipulative elements may actually distract children from the relevant content material. Instead of focusing on learning new information from the book, children may focus only on lifting the flaps and pulling the tabs. To the extent that the manipulative elements engage children, they may also distract children, and thus might undermine the teaching purpose of these books.

To examine the effect of manipulative features on how well children learn from books, Chiong and DeLoache (2012) taught 30- to 36-month-olds alphabet letters using one of three alphabet books. One commercial book, *My ABC Book* (Izawa 1971; plain book), was chosen because of its simplicity, and the other book, *First Concepts ABC* (Graham and Pinnington 2002; manipulative book), was chosen because of its complexity. Specifically, the plain book showed letters that were consistent in size, color, and position. Each letter was paired with one picture (i.e. A for apple). In contrast, the manipulative book incorporated manipulative features such as flaps to lift, shiny materials to touch, and tabs to pull, and it contained a great deal of variation in displaying other elements on the page. For instance, it had letters that varied in size, color, and position, and each letter was paired with as many as three different pictures (i.e. T for twin, tire, and truck). The third book was a two-dimensional copy of the manipulative book, obtained by scanning the manipulative book. Thus, this book contained most of the visual elements of the manipulative book, minus its manipulative features.

Children were first tested on their prior letter knowledge. Then, in a naturalistic picturebook interaction, the experimenter taught children four novel letters. Children were then given a letter identification task in which all four target letters were shown and they were asked, "Can you show me the letter ____?"

The results showed that children who interacted with the plain book and the 2D book version performed significantly above chance level on the letter identification task, whereas the children in the manipulative book condition did not. Also, the children who interacted with the plain book recognized significantly more letters than the children who interacted with the manipulative book. These results suggest that young children learn better from books that present information in a simple format. The results further suggest that manipulative elements can distract young children from the relevant material and thereby hinder their learning.

A similar negative effect of manipulative features on children's learning has been found for the learning of facts and labels about real animals from picturebooks. Preschool-aged children were better able to recall facts about real animals from picturebooks that did not contain manipulative features (Tare *et al.* 2010). These findings suggest that manipulative elements in books draw the child's attention *away* from the information to be learned. The elements in the manipulative book that were used in these studies did not directly involve the letter (e.g. the flap to lift or shiny texture to feel was next to or around the letter) or the fact to be learned. Would manipulative elements designed to draw children's attention to the to-be-learned information enhance learning?

For example, teachers in Montessori preschools use sandpaper letters to teach the alphabet, having children trace the letters with a finger. In this case, the manipulative element (e.g. the sandpaper) is incorporated into the letter itself. Here, the manipulative feature is intended to draw the child's attention to the letter, thus possibly facilitating learning (Lillard 2005).

To test this possibility, Chiong and DeLoache (2012) conducted a second study in which 30- to 36-month-olds interacted with an alphabet book containing either sandpaper letters or regular printed letters. The alphabet books were very simple; each contained large alphabet letters accompanied by one picture. Half the children in each book condition were asked to point to the target letters, and the other half were asked to trace the target letters with their finger. Following the book reading, the children were given a letter identification task. Children in the sandpaper book condition performed significantly above chance levels on this task. However, the results showed no significant difference in performance between the children who interacted with the plain versus the sandpaper book, or between the children who traced versus pointed to the letters. Thus, the sandpaper book did not seem to hinder children's learning. Furthermore, although the children who traced with the sandpaper book did not learn significantly more letters than the children in the other groups, they were the only group to perform above chance on the letter identification task. This suggests that a manipulative element that draws children's attention to the relevant, to-be-learned information might actually facilitate learning.

The above findings suggest that manipulative features that highlight the information to be learned through symbolic media can have a positive impact on children's learning. Recent touch-screen technology provides the opportunity for researchers and educators to consider a wide variety of interactive features (sounds, movements, contingent events) by which to present educational material to young children. It is important that we investigate what types of features offer the best support for children's learning. A recent study using electronic books shows that books in which the animations and interactive elements served to highlight target words increased children's understanding of those words after repeated exposure, even when no adult aided in the children's book interactions (Smeets and Bus 2014).

Together, these studies have important implications for the design of children's books for educational purposes. Books for young children should be interesting and engaging, but should not incorporate features that distract children from the information provided.

Parent interaction style

Another topic that deserves more attention is how different types of books affect the manner in which parents read books with their children. Children's learning from books is influenced by the type of interaction they have with their parents in picturebook reading interactions (Blewitt, this volume, Chapter 6; Rohlfing *et al.*, this volume, Chapter 5; Sénéchal *et al.* 1995). How does the presence of manipulative features affect parent–child picturebook interactions?

Chiong (2008) asked mothers of 30- to 36-month-olds to read three different alphabet books with their child. Of the three books, one was chosen for its simplicity, and the other two for their manipulative features. Two of the books, plain and manipulative, were the same as the ones described earlier (Chiong and Deloache 2012). The third book (embedded) displayed highly complex letters embedded within pictures. For example, the "O" was the body of an ostrich, and the "H" was part of a house where the sides of the house were the sides of the letter. The mothers were asked to read all three books as they naturally would at home, in a counterbalanced order.

The analyses involved measures of vocalizations and the manner in which both the mothers and the children interacted with the different aspects of the books (letter, picture, manipulative elements, etc.). The type of book influenced how mothers read the books to their children. For instance, when mothers interacted with the plain book, they were more likely to point to the letters and pictures, and they also labeled the letters more than when they interacted with the manipulative or the embedded books. Thus, mothers tended to focus more on the relevant information with the plain book than with the other two books. The analyses involving children's behaviors showed a similar pattern of results, in that they vocalized most often about the letters and pictures with the plain book. Children interacted the most with the manipulative book, as they either pointed to its extraneous elements or lifted the flaps in the book. Thus, again, the type of book can alter the aspects of the book that the child is focusing on.

This study suggests that books that contain extraneous features can change the nature of shared book reading and may lead both young children and their parents away from the main information of the book. As was shown in the study described here, parents tend to draw less attention to the relevant information in the book and the children tend to focus on interacting physically with the book. This combination can lead to a diminished focus on learning.

Improving preschoolers' learning from picturebooks

Although children's learning from picturebooks during the preschool years seems tenuous, they do, nevertheless, absorb a great deal of information through book reading. This is true both in controlled settings, in which researchers have created or selected picturebooks that include simple stories and involve specific features, as in many of the studies discussed above, and in typical parent–child reading interactions with commercially available picturebooks that may contain more complex storylines and use various physical and story elements that may make learning more difficult. How do children overcome their limitations? How are they able to apply concepts learned in a distracting and fantastical framework to their own real-world experiences? It turns out that there are several ways we can address the limitations stated above and aid children's learning, and that many of these things are naturally involved in many picturebook interactions.

Parental input

Children's learning and transfer of information from picturebooks can be aided by parental input during book-reading episodes, especially when parents provide information outside of the text. For instance, children learn better from picturebooks when they are asked questions during reading interactions (Blewitt *et al.* 2009; Blewitt, this volume, Chapter 6), and when a parent or other reader points to relevant pictures and adds brief explanations (Brett *et al.* 1996; Sénéchal *et al.* 1995). One specific way in which parental talk can enable children to understand that story elements relate to a "kind" or richly structured category is through the use of generics.

Generic noun phrases refer to kinds in an abstract sense, drawing attention to characteristics of a whole category rather than the individuals that are part of that category (e.g. "Birds fly"). By 4 years of age, children grasp the nature of generic noun phrases and are able to make generalizations about categories from these statements (Hollander *et al.* 2002). Thus, when parents use generics during picturebook interactions, children can interpret these statements as conveying general knowledge about the world. This may enable transfer of knowledge in young children, because it indicates that the generic information is true not just of the picturebook character but of all animals, people, or artifacts in that category. Both mothers and children are more likely to use generics and refer to categories when talking about symbolic representations of objects, such as pictures, than when interacting with objects themselves (Gelman *et al.* 2005). This may be especially true of the representations found in picturebooks. In one study of maternal speech during picturebook reading, 92 percent of mothers produced at least one generic noun phrase (Pappas and Gelman 1998). Interestingly, while mothers' nongeneric phrases tended to closely match the pictures they looked at – for instance, using a singular noun when only one animal was present on the page – their generic phrases seemed independent of the page, and were almost always plural in form. Gelman and others have suggested that these "errors" actually indicate that such generic noun phrases refer to an abstract whole category, and not to a specific instance or to an instance present in the current environment (ibid.).

Context

In addition to the types of input that parents provide, the types of picturebook interactions that children experience can enhance their learning. Preschool children often hear picturebooks read in a variety of contexts: preschool teachers may read books to an entire class, children may participate in story-reading groups at their local libraries, and they may have one-on-one interactions with parents and others in which a picturebook is read with no other distractions. Such one-on-one interactions seem to aid learning and transfer of knowledge. Children are better able to apply to the real world knowledge and problem solutions embedded in fantastical stories when they hear the stories one-on-one (Richert and Smith 2011).

The context in which information is learned and later on retrieved can affect young children's successful acquisition of knowledge in other ways as well. Children tend to perform best when the context in which they have to use the knowledge in question is similar to the context in which they learned the information. Context is especially important in very young children (Rovee-Collier and Dufault 1991), and contextual cues – created by both limiting and varying the learning context – may enable young preschoolers to generalize what they have learned to new situations or category members (Goldenberg and Sandhofer 2013). This context can include the physical environment, as children do better when tested in the room where they had read the picturebook, but also the similarity between the pictorial depictions and their real-world counterparts. For instance, toddlers are more likely to generalize and transfer information from highly iconic images (photographs) that share more features with the real-world referents than from less iconic images (cartoons) (Ganea *et al.* 2008).

Finally, one of the best ways to improve children's learning from picturebooks is through repetition. In younger toddlers, repetition enhances imitation of novel actions (Simcock and DeLoache 2008) and word learning (Horst, this volume, Chapter 9; Schafer 2005). Hearing the same story multiple times even aids learning in 3-year-olds. Cornell and colleagues (1988) found that both testing and rereading help children at this age remember story events, and they argue that both of these effects stem from additional learning, rather than the prevention of forgetting. Repetition of the same story also enhances preschool children's recall and retention of new words. Even when children hear and see a new word–object association the same number of times in different reading contexts (i.e. reading three different books that feature the same word–object pairing), they do not perform as well as they do after repetition (i.e. hearing the same story three times) when tested on those new words (Horst *et al.* 2011; Horst, this volume, Chapter 9). Thus, it seems that, of all contextual aids, repeated presentation may serve to enable children's learning and transfer of information best.

Throughout the preschool years, children can learn a variety of information from picturebooks. They can learn basic facts and concepts, as well as more complex ideas, such as causal information and theories. What is more, at this age children can take this information and apply it to the real world – both to the specific animals and events they have learned about, and to novel instances that they have never encountered before. Although this learning is evident even when stories do not accurately depict the world, it is stronger when the child is learning from realistic contexts, and can get thrown off track by too much distraction, either within the story, as when the book portrays a world too far from reality, or in the physical structure of the book itself, as is the case with manipulative features. However, the good news is that we can facilitate and enhance children's learning, and even help them to learn in contexts in which it is usually more difficult.

Conclusions

The goal of this chapter has been to argue that in order to use picturebooks effectively to teach children, we need to consider what children know of the nature of the symbols, and what kinds of symbols to use and how. As research illustrates, children sometimes fail to acquire information from the picturebooks to which they get exposed. For example, children interacting with a book that has many manipulative features may not be focusing on the information to be learned but rather on how the book can be used as a toy.

Picturebooks can be useful in teaching young children, but we carefully need to consider how their physical characteristics may influence what children take away from them. As illustrated by the research reviewed here, by the end of their second year children can already acquire new information about the world from picturebooks. They can learn novel words, novel properties for objects, and novel actions. They can also learn abstract information, such as information about letters. However, certain kinds of picturebooks better facilitate their learning and generalization from books. We have shown, for instance, that children learn and generalize better from books that have more realistic pictures, such as photographs and realistic drawings, than from less realistic books containing cartoons. We have also shown that children learn letters better from books that are simple than from books that have a lot of exciting physical features. Finally, we have shown that children transfer information from a story context to the real world when the story context resembles the real world to a large extent.

We – parents and educators – need to facilitate children's learning of symbol-mediated information by making the symbol–referent relation explicit through increased resemblance between the picturebook and the real world, and by encouraging children to focus on the symbolic content.

References

Primary sources

Graham, Neville and Andrea Pinnington. 2002. *First Concepts ABC*. New York: St. Martin's Press.

Izawa, Tadasu. 1971. *My ABC Book*. Tokyo: Zokeisha Publications.

Secondary sources

Adams, Marilyn Jager. 1990. *Beginning to Read: Thinking and Learning about Print*. Cambridge, MA: MIT Press.

Bialystok, Ellen. 1995. "Making concepts of print symbolic: Understanding how writing represents language". *First Language* 15: 317–338.

Blewitt, Pamela, Keiran M. Rump, Stephanie E. Shealy, and Samantha A. Cook. 2009. "Shared book reading: When and how questions affect young children's word learning". *Journal of Educational Psychology* 101(2): 294–304.

Brett, Arlene, Liz Rothlein, and Michael Hurley. 1996. "Vocabulary acquisition from listening to stories and explanations of target words". *Elementary School Journal* 96(4): 415–422.

Callaghan, Tara C. 2000. "Factors affecting children's graphic symbol use in the third year: Language, similarity, and iconicity". *Cognitive Development* 15(2): 185–214.

Callaghan, Tara C., Philippe Rochat, and John Corbit. 2012. "Young children's knowledge of the representational function of pictorial symbols: Development across the preschool years in three cultures". *Journal of Cognition and Development* 13(3): 320–353.

Chiong, Cynthia. 2008. "The effect of different types of books on the nature of mother–child book-reading interactions". *Dissertation Abstracts International: Section B: The Sciences and Engineering* 68: 6997.

Chiong, Cynthia and Judy S. DeLoache. 2012. "Learning the ABCs: What kinds of picture books facilitate young children's learning?" *Journal of Early Childhood Literacy* 13(2): 225–241.

Cornell, Edward H., Monique Sénéchal, and Lorri S. Broda. 1988. "Recall of picture books by 3-year-old children: Testing and repetition effects in joint reading activities". *Journal of Educational Psychology* 80(4): 537–542.

Crain-Thoreson, Catherine and Philip S. Dale. 1999. "Enhancing linguistic performance: Parents and teachers as book reading partners for children with language delays". *Topics in Early Childhood Special Education* 19(1): 28–39.

DeBaryshe, Barbara D. 1993. "Joint picture-book reading correlates of early oral language skills". *Journal of Child Language* 20(2): 455–461.

DeLoache, Judy S.. 1995. "Early symbol understanding and use". *Psychology of Learning and Motivation* 33: 65–114.

DeLoache, Judy S. 2002. "The symbol-mindedness of young children". In *Child Psychology in Retrospect and Prospect: The Minnesota Symposia on Child Psychology*, edited by Willard W. Hartup and Richard A. Weinberg. 73–101. Mahwah, NJ: Lawrence Erlbaum.

DeLoache, Judy S. and Nancy M. Burns. 1994. "Early understanding of the representational function of pictures". *Cognition* 52(2): 83–110.

DeLoache, Judy S., Olga A. Peralta de Mendoza, and Kathy N. Anderson. 1999. "Multiple factors in early symbol use: Instructions, similarity, and age in understanding a symbol–referent relation". *Cognitive Development* 14(2): 299–312.

Foulin, Jean Noel. 2005. "Why is letter-name knowledge such a good predictor of learning to read?" *Reading and Writing* 18(2): 129–155.

Ganea, Patricia A., Megan Bloom-Pickard, and Judy S. DeLoache. 2008. "Transfer between picture books and the real world by very young children". *Journal of Cognition and Development* 9(1): 46–66.

Ganea, Patricia A., Melissa L. Allen, Lucas Butler, Susan Carey, and Judy S. DeLoache. 2009. "Toddlers' referential understanding of pictures". *Journal of Experimental Psychology* 104(3): 283–295.

Ganea, Patricia A., Lili Ma, and Judy S. DeLoache. 2011. "Young children's learning and transfer of biological information from picture books to real animals". *Child Development* 82(5): 1421–1433.

Ganea, Patricia A., Caitlin F. Canfield, Kadria Simons-Ghafan, and Tommy Chou. 2014. "Do cavies talk? The effect of anthropomorphic picture books on children's knowledge about animals". *Frontiers in Psychology* 5.

Gelman, Susan A. and Sandra R. Waxman. 2009. "Response to Sloutsky: Taking development seriously: Theories cannot emerge from associations alone". *Trends in Cognitive Sciences* 13(8): 332–333.

Gelman, Susan A., Robert J. Chesnick, and Sandra R. Waxman. 2005. "Mother–child conversations about pictures and objects: Referring to categories and individuals". *Child Development* 76(6): 1129–1143.

Goldenberg, Elizabeth R. and Catherine M. Sandhofer. 2013. "Same, varied, or both? Contextual support aids young children in generalizing category labels". *Journal of Experimental Child Psychology* 115(1): 150–162.

Harris, Paul L., Robert D. Kavanaugh, and Laura Dowson. 1997. "The depiction of imaginary transformation: Early comprehension of a symbolic function". *Cognitive Development* 12(1): 1–19.

Hollander, Michelle A., Susan A. Gelman, and Jon Star. 2002. "Children's interpretation of generic noun phrases". *Developmental Psychology* 38(6): 883–894.

Horst, Jessica S., Kelly L. Parsons, and Natasha M. Bryan. 2011. "Get the story straight: Contextual repetition promotes word learning from storybooks". *Frontiers in Psychology* 2: 1–11.

Hulme, Charles, Claudine Bowyer-Crane, Julia M. Carroll, Fiona J. Duff, and Margaret J. Snowling. 2012. "The causal role of phoneme awareness and letter-sound knowledge in learning to read combining intervention studies with mediation analysis". *Psychological Science* 23(6): 572–577.

Keates, Jeany, Susan A. Graham, and Patricia A. Ganea. 2014. "Infants transfer nonobvious properties from pictures to real-world objects". *Journal of Experimental Child Psychology* 125: 35–47.

Kümmerling-Meibauer, Bettina and Jörg Meibauer. 2011. "Early-concept books: Acquiring nominal and verbal concepts". In *Emergent Literacy: Children's Books from 0 to 3*, edited by Bettina Kümmerling-Meibauer. 91–114. Amsterdam: John Benjamins.

Levin, Iris, Sivan Shatil-Carmon, and Ornit Asif-Rave. 2006. "Learning of letter names and sounds and their contribution to word recognition". *Journal of Experimental Child Psychology* 93(2): 139–165.

Liben, Lynn S. and Roger M. Downs. 1989. "Understanding maps as symbols: The development of map concepts in young children". *Advances in Child Development and Behavior* 22: 145–201.

Lillard, Angeline Stoll. 2005. *Montessori: The Science behind the Genius*. New York: Oxford University Press.

Mason, Jana M. 1980. "When do children begin to read? An exploration of four year old children's letter and word reading competencies". *Reading Research Quarterly* 15: 203–227.

McNeill, Joyce H. and Susan A. Fowler. 1999. "Let's talk: Encouraging mother–child conversations during story reading". *Journal of Early Intervention* 22(1): 51–69.

O'Connor, Joseph, Harry Beilin, and Gary Kose. 1981. "Children's belief in photographic fidelity". *Developmental Psychology* 17(6): 859–865.

Pappas, Athina and Susan A. Gelman. 1998. "Generic noun phrases in mother–child conversations". *Journal of Child Language* 25(1): 19–33.

Preissler, Melissa A. and Susan Carey. 2004. "Do both pictures and words function as symbols for 18- and 24-month-old children?" *Journal of Cognition and Development* 5(2): 185–212.

Richert, Rebekah A. and Erin I. Smith. 2011. "Preschoolers' quarantining of fantasy stories". *Child Development* 82(4): 1106–1119.

Richert, Rebekah A., Alison B. Shawber, Ruth E. Hoffman, and Marjorie Taylor. 2009. "Learning from fantasy and real characters in preschool and kindergarten". *Journal of Cognition and Development* 10(1–2): 41–66.

Rideout, Victora J., Elizabeth A. Vandewater, and Ellen A. Wartella. 2003. "Zero to six: Electronic media in the lives of infants, toddlers, and preschooler". *The Henry J. Kaiser Family Foundation*. www.kff.org/entmedia/3378.cfm (accessed May 25, 2004).

Rovee-Collier, Carolyn and Debra Dufault. 1991. "Multiple contexts and memory retrieval at three months". *Developmental Psychobiology* 24(1): 39–49.

Schafer, Graham. 2005. "Infants can learn decontextualized words before their first birthday". *Child Development* 76(1): 87–96.

Sénéchal, Monique and Edward H. Cornell. 1993. "Vocabulary acquisition through shared reading experiences". *Reading Research Quarterly* 28: 360–375.

Sénéchal, Monique and Jo-Anne LeFevre. 2001. "Storybook reading and parent teaching: Links to language and literacy development". In *The Role of Family Literacy Environments in Promoting Young Children's Emerging Literacy Skills: New Directions for Child and Adolescent Development*, edited by Pia Rebello Britto and Jeanne Brooks-Gunn. 39–52. San Francisco: Jossey-Bass.

Sénéchal, Monique, Edward H. Cornell, and Lorri S. Broda. 1995. "Age-related differences in the organization of parent–infant interactions during picture-book reading". *Early Childhood Research Quarterly* 10(3): 317–337.

Simcock, Gabrielle and Judy DeLoache. 2006. "Get the picture? The effects of iconicity on toddlers' reenactment from picture books". *Developmental Psychology* 42(6): 1352.

Simcock, Gabrielle and Judy DeLoache. 2008. "The effect of repetition on infants' imitation from picture books varying in iconicity". *Infancy* 13(6): 687–697.

Smeets, Daisy J. H. and Adriana G. Bus. 2013. "The interactive animated e-book as a word learning device for kindergartners". *Applied Psycholinguistics*: 1–22. doi:10.1017/S0142716413000556

Stevenson, Harold W. and Richard S. Newman. 1986. "Long-term prediction of achievement and attitudes in mathematics and reading". *Child Development* 57: 646–659.

Sulzby, Elizabeth. 1985. "Children's emergent reading of favorite storybooks: A developmental study". *Reading Research Quarterly* 20: 458–481.

Tare, Medha, Cynthia Chiong, Patricia Ganea, and Judy DeLoache. 2010. "Less is more: How manipulative features affect children's learning from picture books". *Journal of Applied Developmental Psychology* 31(5): 395–400.

Teale, William and Elizabeth Sulzby. 1986. *Emergent Literacy: Writing and Reading*. Norwood, NJ: Ablex.

Tomasello, Michael, Tricia Striano, and Philippe Rochat. 1999. "Do young children use objects as symbols?" *British Journal of Developmental Psychology* 17(4): 563–584.

Troseth, Georgette L. and Judy S. DeLoache. 1998. "The medium can obscure the message: Young children's understanding of video". *Child Development* 69(4): 950–965.

van Kleeck, Anne. 2003. "Research on book sharing: Another critical look". In *On Reading Books to Children: Parents and Teachers*, edited by Anne van Kleeck, Steven A. Stahl, and Eurydice B. Bauer. 271–319. Mahwah, NJ: Lawrence Erlbaum.

Walker, Caren M., Alison Gopnik and Patricia A. Ganea. 2014. *Learning to learn from stories: Children's developing sensitivity to the causal structure of fictional worlds. Child Development*. DOI: 10.1111/cdev.12287.

Walker, Caren M., Lisa B. Walker, and Patricia A. Ganea. 2013. "The role of symbol-based experience in early learning and transfer from pictures: Evidence from Tanzania". *Developmental Psychology* 49(7): 1315–1324.

Whitehurst, Grover J. and Christopher J. Lonigan. 1998. "Child development and emergent literacy". *Child Development* 69(3): 848–872.

Whitehurst, Grover J., David S. Arnold, Jeffery N. Epstein, Andrea L. Angell, Meagan Smith, and Janet E. Fischel. 1994. "A picture book reading intervention in day care and home for children from low-income families". *Developmental Psychology* 30(5): 679–689.

3 What the child can learn from simple descriptive picturebooks

An inquiry into *Lastwagen/Trucks* by Paul Stickland

Jörg Meibauer

Introduction

Simple descriptive books for children between the ages of 2 and 3 are definitely not the focus of picturebook research, let alone the focus of literary studies. For instance, there is no article on descriptive books in the recent *Oxford Handbook of Children's Literature* (Mickenberg and Vallone 2011). This is in sharp contrast to the huge interest these books may arouse in children. It is also in contrast to the important historical contribution that descriptive books have made to children's literature in general. Arguably, *Orbis sensualium Pictus* (The Visible World, 1658) by Johannes Amos Comenius is one of the first works of children's literature (Fassbind-Eigenheer and Fassbind-Eigenheer 2002). Why do most adult scholars – with the notable exception of researchers engaged in the children's literature–education interface – neglect the study of these books? The reasons are obvious. From their point of view, these books do not contain an interesting story, the pictures merely represent everyday objects, and the apparent joy they may trigger is a superficial and somewhat trivial phenomenon not worth pursuing. But these attitudes are only prejudices. At least from the point of view of a cognitive theory of picturebooks, this view seems completely misguided (see Kümmerling-Meibauer and Meibauer 2013).

In their excellent review of *Nonfiction Literature for Children*, Kiefer and Wilson (2011) point out that there is a lack of sophisticated research into nonfiction literature: not only do we find much conceptual confusion, but there is also a lack of serious analysis of single nonfiction texts. I would like to add that embedding into theories of literary development is nearly nonexistent, because nonfiction literature is typically separated from fiction literature and thus excluded from in-depth research.

In Kümmerling-Meibauer and Meibauer (2005, 2011), we argue that early-concept books – that is, wordless books for the very young that show only pictures of everyday objects – are very important when it comes to the understanding of early literacy. And the same is true with respect to simple descriptive books like the one I am about to analyze in more detail. The main distinction between early-concept books and simple descriptive books, then, is that only the latter contain text.[1]

What is, then, a "simple descriptive picturebook"? I will assume that a prototypical picturebook is a series of picture–text combinations. The attribute "simple" means that there are not many items in the pictures and not many sentences on the pages; simple picturebooks are thus opposed to complex picturebooks containing more pictorial and textual information. But keep in mind the gist of this contribution: simple picturebooks are not as simple as they might appear. This will become clearer when we go on.

The attribute "descriptive" means that there is no story told. The term is thus opposed to "narrative". Narrative picturebooks for the very young are also neglected in picturebook research (see Kümmerling-Meibauer and Meibauer, this volume, Chapter 1). Yet they attract more interest, because they are developmentally connected to narrative texts for older children. There are several other notions referring to descriptive books that are used in the literature: (1) nonfiction literature (Kiefer and Wilson 2011); (2) information(al) books; and (3) expository books. I prefer to speak of descriptive picturebooks, because "nonfiction literature" is a negative term. "Information" is also part of fictional/narrative literature, of course, as is an "expository" style. It goes without saying that description may be part of narration, and vice versa. Hence, there may be degrees of hybridity in the descriptive–narrative continuum (Kiefer and Wilson 2011: 291). Speaking of descriptive books still has the advantage of settling them within a comprehensive theory of description ("descriptology"; see Klotz 2013).

These distinctions leave us with the taxonomy shown in Figure 3.1.

Examples of these book types are:

- early concept-book: Dick Bruna: *Erste Bilder* (1973) (see Kümmerling-Meibauer and Meibauer 2005);
- simple descriptive picturebook: Paul Stickland: *Trucks* (1986) (see the present chapter);
- complex descriptive picturebook: David Macaulay: *Cathedral: The Story of Its Construction* (1973);
- wimmelbook: Ali Mitgutsch: *Rundherum in meiner Stadt* (1988) (see Rémi 2011);
- simple narrative picturebook with text: Barbro Lindgren and Eva Eriksson: *Max blöja* (1994);
- complex narrative picturebook without text: David Wiesner: *Flotsam* (2006);
- complex narrative picturebook with text: Anthony Browne: *Voices in the Park* (1998).

It goes without saying that this taxonomy is by no means exhaustive and that there are many intermediate or overlapping categories. For example, there are wimmelbooks that display text. Textless wimmelbooks, in contrast, are "narrative" insofar as the pictures can tell simple stories. In sum, the taxonomy shows that the distinction "descriptive–narrative" matters, as well as the distinctions "simple–complex" and "plus text–minus text".

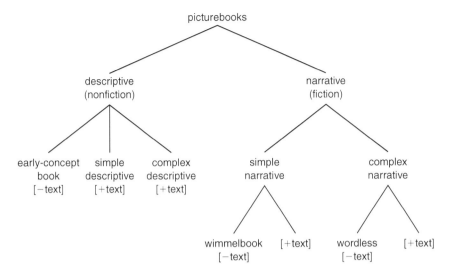

Figure 3.1 A taxonomy of picturebooks.

This contribution starts from the assumption that simple descriptive picturebooks serve important functions on a number of levels. First of all, they deal with objects that are of interest to the child. This seems to be a trivial statement; however, when it comes to general knowledge about the world, it must be explained why trucks are more interesting than, say, toothbrushes. Second, they introduce a taxonomic system, since they bring the depicted objects into a certain order. Taxonomies are very important from a cognitive point of view, since categorization – that is, subsuming an exemplar under a certain category – is essential for understanding our surroundings. Third, they teach appropriate vocabulary including morphosyntactic and semantic information. Building up a complex dictionary, including learned or technical lexemes, is important for language acquisition and for learning in general. Fourth, they introduce the child to textual properties of descriptive texts, for example anaphoric elements.[2] It is clear that anaphoric processes, including coherence and cohesion, are also important for narrative texts. Moreover, simple descriptive picturebooks may be superior to their narrative competitors in that they trigger more of children's own narratives than the narrative ones do. Thus, Torr and Clugston (1999: 25) find in their experiments that

> the discourse surrounding the informational book was greater in quantity, contained more cognitively demanding questions, more conditional clauses and more interactions involving reasoning and technical terminology. These findings suggest that the informational picturebook has distinctive features that encourage and support children in their construction of new knowledge and patterns of reasoning.

(See also Moschovaki and Meadows 2005; Duke *et al.* 2012; Pinkham 2012.) Indeed, this could be an interesting reason why some children seem to prefer descriptive books over narrative books.

Learning the meaning of a complex word like *Langholzlaster* ("lumber truck") is a big challenge for a 2-year-old. Yet there are several developmental processes that make this possible. From early on, children are interested in the meaning and concepts of words (Smiley and Huttenlocher 1995; Bloom 2000; Gelman 2006; Rohlfing 2013). They are ready to analyze complex words and their components, and engage in the coining of new words in order to fill lexical gaps (Clark 1993; Meibauer 1995; Rainer 2010; Schipke and Kauschke 2011). Moreover, they use contextual (pragmatic) information to make progress (Clark and Amaral 2010). Numerous studies have shown that the reading situation is one important way in which children learn about language.

Simple as they may be, simple descriptive picturebooks participate in at least two "big" issues that have been recently put onto the agenda of research into children's cognition and culture. The first is children's knowledge acquisition; the second is how children learn from testimony. *The Discovery of What Children Know*, the subtitle of Siegal's book *Marvelous Minds* (2008), is indeed a major task of children's epistemology. There is research on what children know about astronomy, geography, biology, food, hygiene, life and death, numbers, and arithmetic. Yet there are many more fields that are the subject of children's knowledge acquisition. Certainly, knowledge about trucks does not qualify as a scientific domain; however, it is important for everyday life, as I will point out in more detail. Second, there is research on the question of how children learn from testimony. It is clear that children do not discover the whole world on their own. From early on, they rely on what they are told by others (Harris 2012). I think that the input from children's literature is one such source of testimony. When trucks are described in a picturebook for 2-year-olds, children assume that the information given is reliable.

This chapter deals with just one simple descriptive picturebook, *Trucks/Lastwagen* by Paul Stickland. The aim of the chapter is to point out how this picturebook may be related to the questions addressed in the introduction. As a linguist, I will highlight linguistic aspects of this picturebook. My point is that descriptive picturebooks have much to do with linguistics because information about the world is given qua linguistic structure. The outline of the chapter is as follows. In the next section, I describe the pictures in *Trucks*, drawing on the recent theory by Painter *et al.* (2013). In the third section, I will go into the textual makeup, contrasting the English version with the German version. In the fourth section, I will simulate the developmental perspective of a child in order to illuminate what a simple descriptive picturebook may mean to them. In the final section, I will address further research questions.

The pictures

The book contains pictures of 11 trucks and the people working with these trucks. The trucks are depicted in bright watercolors. Primary colors such as red, yellow, green, and blue are used. Usually there is an empty (white) background. Some pictures show additional background elements, such as trees or a building to be erected. The trucks are posited on a line symbolizing the ground on which they are standing or being driven. They are depicted from the perspective of a child so that they appear huge (see Figure 3.2). The depiction of the tires is very salient and not completely realistic. They are too big in comparison to the truck as a whole. The trucks are in different positions; they are depicted from the front or from behind, always simulating three-dimensionality.

As far as I can tell, we do not know much about depiction styles in descriptive picturebooks for young children.[3] It seems to me that we can describe the depiction style of *Trucks* as (1) realistic and (2) generic. As far as (1) is concerned, it is worth pointing out that the trucks are shown as they naturally occur. In particular, they do not have faces or other properties that real trucks

Figure 3.2 Book cover of *Lastwagen* by Paul Stickland, published by Ars Edition (Munich), n.d.

do not have. This remark is not trivial. Think of the many depictions of trains, cars, etc. addressed to children in which these things are anthropomorphized, such as *Thomas the Tank Engine* (1946) by the Reverend Wilbert Awdry, or *The Story of the Little Red Engine* (1945) by Diana Ross and Leslie Wood. As regards (2), I would like to borrow from the distinction between minimalist, generic, and naturalistic depiction styles made by Painter *et al.* (2013: 34–35). While these depiction styles are related to the depictions of literary characters and are hence subsumed under the heading of "pathos", a transfer to the depiction of things is tempting. The minimalist depiction style goes together with "appreciative" pathos; this style is used, for example, in Dick Bruna's work (see his *Miffy* (*Nintje*) series, 1955 et seq.). The generic depiction style is related to "emphatic" pathos; indeed, the trucks are generic – they can be perceived as prototypical exemplars of their kind – yet they trigger the empathy and emotional attention of the child viewer. For the generic depiction style, it seems important that there is a balance between giving too much and too little detail. (The worldwide success of *Trucks* might indicate that the balance is successful.)

Beside pathos, Painter *et al.* (2013: 35–36) deal with ambience as well. Ambience, they point out, "will be regarded as a visual meaning system for creating an emotional mood or atmosphere, principally through the use of color". The effects of color are to be seen in the parameters of vibrancy, warmth, and familiarity. Let us apply these parameters to *Trucks*. The "muted" choice within the parameter of vibrancy certainly creates a gentle feeling, as Painter *et al.* (2013: 37) put it. As for the parameter of warmth, we find warm (red, orange, yellow hues) as well as cool colors (blue, green, aqua hues). Finally, familiarity

> is realised by the amount of colour differentiation in the image. The basic principle here is that the more different colours are present in the image, the greater the sense of the familiar, since we usually experience the world day to day in all its variety of colour.
>
> (ibid.: 38)

In this sense, the colorful pictures of *Trucks* are adapted to the child's everyday experience.

The text

Trucks, first published in 1986, has been translated into several languages. It belongs to a set of similar books focusing on other vehicles (fire engines, excavators, tractors, cars, boats, planes, and trains). In Table 3.1, J1 and J2 refer to the jacket pages. The book contains 14 pages, some of them without any text (i.e. only with a picture).

In order to give a more detailed picture of the intricacies of a simple text presented to children between 2 and 3 years of age, I will point out some of its linguistic properties, dealing with phonology, morphology, syntax, semantics, and

Learning from descriptive picturebooks 57

Table 3.1 A comparison of the German and English texts of *Lastwagen/Trucks*

Page	German text	English text
J1	Lastwagen	Trucks
J2	–	–
1 Title	Paul Stickland Lastwagen *ars edition*	Trucks Paul Stickland Methuen Children's Books
2	Der grüne Pritschenwagen bringt Rohre zu einer Baustelle.	Two flatbed trucks. The green one is delivering pipes to a building site.
3	Der gelbe kommt gerade zurück. Er kann wieder beladen werden.	The yellow one is on its way back to reload.
4	Der Baustofflaster hat einen Spezialkran, mit dem man Ziegelsteine auf- und abladen kann.	A builder's truck has a special crane for loading and unloading bricks.
5	–	–
6	Dieser Fernlaster hat einen Motorschaden.	This lorry has broken down.
7	Der Abschleppwagen ist gekommen. Er wird den Laster in die Werkstatt bringen.	The breakdown truck has arrived to tow it to a garage.
8	Aus diesem Tankwagen werden die unterirdischen Benzinlager einer Tankstelle gefüllt.	The tanker fills the garage's underground tanks as the red lorry gets petrol from the pump.
9	Unterdessen bekommt der rote Lastwagen Dieselöl aus der Zapfsäule.	
11	Solche Fernlastwagen transportieren die Güter in Containern.	Container lorries drive huge distances, taking goods direct from ship to warehouse.
12	Sie können mit einem Kran leicht auf einen Eisenbahnwaggon oder ein Schiff umgeladen werden.	
13	Ein Langholzlaster fährt Baumstämme aus dem Wald zum Stapelplatz des Sägewerks.	The trees have been cut down, and are being taken by special lorry from the forest to the timber yard.
14	–	–
J4	In diesem Bilderbuch finden Kinder ab 2 bis 3 Jahren die verschiedensten Lastwagen.	All kinds of trucks for the very young.

pragmatics in turn.[4] I assume that the text will be read to the child by an adult or older sibling. Note that the English and the German texts are not in a one-to-one correspondence. Thus, I present word-by-word translations in the examples that follow.

Phonology

Interestingly, the text starts with a contrast focus. The two color words *grün* ("green") and *gelb* ("yellow") stand in a semantic opposition. When the text is read to a child, the reader should pose a strong accent on the first syllables of each contrasted word. (Quite possibly, this is a source of error when reading the text for the first time.)

1   Der GRÜne Pritschenwagen bringt Rohre zu einer Baustelle. Der GELbe kommt gerade zurück.
    "The green flatbed truck is delivering pipes to a building site. The yellow one is on its way back."

In addition, in the second sentence, *Pritschenwagen* ("flatbed truck") is left out (by way of ellipsis) and has to be reconstructed. Thus, *der grüne Pritschenwagen* ("the green flatbed truck") and *der gelbe Pritschenwagen* ("the yellow flatbed truck") are contrasted with each other.

Morphology

A look at the verbal constructions reveals several tenses and different constructions. Besides the simple present we find:

2 [3]   a. kommt ... zurück   (particle verb)
           "comes ... back$_{PART}$"
        b. kann ... beladen werden   (present tense modal passive)
           "can ... reload AUX"
        c. auf- und abladen kann   (modal construction)
           "up- and download can"
  [7]   d. ist ... gekommen   (perfect tense)
           "has ... come"
        e. wird ... bringen   (future tense)
           "will ... bring"
  [8]   f. werden ... gefüllt   (present tense passive)
           "are ... filled"
  [12] g. können ... umgeladen werden   (present tense modal passive)
           'can ... reload AUX'

What is astonishing, however, and central to the topic of this chapter, is the rich set of complex nominal compounds:

3   Pritsche+n+wagen, Bau+stelle, Bau+stoff+laster, Spezial+kran, Ziegel+stein, Fern+last+er, Motor+schaden, Ab+schlepp+wagen, Werk+statt, Tank+wagen, Benzin+lager, Tank+stelle, **Last+wagen**, Diesel+öl, Zapf+säule, Fern+last+wagen, Eisen+bahn+waggon, Lang+holz+laster, Baum+stamm, Stapel+platz, Säge+werk

Hence, 21 out of 99 words are complex nouns. While *Last+wagen* ("truck") is a nominal compound, *Last+er* (meaning also "truck") is an *-er* derivation with a nominal base. Thus, this pair may give insight into patterns of word formation. Moreover, the elements *Laster* and *Wagen* are morphological heads of some complex words. So, we find *Fern+laster* as well as *Tank+wagen*.

Syntax

There is only one complex sentence, namely [4]. The embedded sentence is a relative clause.

4   Der Baustofflaster hat [einen Spezialkran$_h$], [mit dem$_h$] man Ziegelsteine auf- und abladen kann.
    "The builder's truck has a special crane by which one can load and unload bricks."

We find several anaphors creating textual coherence:

5   a.   [Der gelbe$_i$] kommt gerade zurück. Er$_i$ kann wieder beladen werden.
         "The yellow one is just coming back. It can be reloaded again."
    b.   [Der Abschleppwagen$_j$] ist gekommen. Er$_j$ wird den Laster in die Werkstatt bringen.
         "The breakdown truck has arrived. It will bring the truck into the garage."
    c.   Solche Fernlastwagen transportieren die Güter in [Containern$_k$]. Sie$_k$ können mit einem Kran leicht auf einen Eisenbahnwaggon oder ein Schiff umgeladen werden.
         "Such long-distance trucks transport goods in containers. They can easily be reloaded with a crane onto a railway wagon or a ship."

Moreover, we find ellipsis, as in the case of *der gelbe* [Lastwagen] in [3], and the elliptical coordination *auf- und abladen*, which has to be interpreted as *aufladen und abladen*.

Semantics

We find definite and indefinite articles as well as demonstrative pronouns:

6   a.   der Baustofflaster
         the build+stuff+truck
         "the builder's truck"

b. ein Langholzlaster
a long+wood+truck
"lumber truck" (see *special lorry* in the English original text)
c. dieser Fernlaster; an diesem Tankwagen
this distant+truck; at this tank+truck
"this long-distance truck; at this tanker"
d. solche Fernlastwagen
"such long-distance trucks"

The general topic of the book is of course the presentation and naming of different kinds of trucks. These names constitute a lexical field. As an archlexeme, we find *Lastwagen*. Note, however, that this term is first mentioned on page 9.

7   Lexical field of nouns denoting types of trucks:
Pritschenwagen, Baustoffflaster, Fernlaster, Abschleppwagen, Tankwagen, *Lastwagen*, Fernlastwagen, Langholzlaster

Note that in the English original, we find *container lorry*, while in the German version we find *Fernlaster* ("long-distance truck"). In addition, the original simply speaks of "special lorry", whereas the German version uses the more specific *Langholzlaster* (lit. long+wood+truck, "lumber truck").

Recall that *Wagen* and *Laster* are both morphological heads, for example in *Tank+wagen* and *Fern+laster*. In addition, they are semantic heads: thus, a "Tankwagen" is a type of "Wagen" and a "Fernlaster" is a type of "Laster." *Wagen* and *Laster* are related by hyponymy, *Wagen* being the hyperonym, *Laster* the hyponym. Thus, every "Laster" is a "Wagen" but not every "Wagen" is a "Laster".

Pragmatics

In picturebooks, the pictures provide a context for the text. Therefore, indexical elements point to the things or events that are depicted. For example, the expressions *der grüne Pritschenwagen, dieser Fernlaster*, and *solche Fernlastwagen* refer to the pictures in which such kinds of trucks are shown.

The speech acts used in this text are assertives. However, it is not simply asserted that the green flatbed truck is delivering pipes to a building site; it is explained. The presupposition is that the child does not already know these facts; therefore, an expert is explaining these facts to the child. This is of course typical of descriptive books.

We do not know whether a child listener correctly attributes this information to a certain speaker. For instance, if Ken's father is reading the text to his son, is it possible that Ken believes that his father has so much knowledge about trucks? Or does Ken form the concept of an anonymous expert author and knows that his father is only the transmitter of the words the author-speaker has laid down in the past? As far as I know, we do not really know of to whom testimony is attributed from the child's perspective.

The overarching theme (also called "question under discussion" or "quaestio") is of course information about trucks. There is no introduction to this theme, there is no complication, there is no solution, and there is no ending. Narrative elements are simply not there.

Yet there is some tension in the description that has to do with the movements and specific tasks of the trucks. For example, in [2] and [3] the child has to understand that the two flatbed trucks share a common task. Similarly, in [6] and [7] the function of the breakdown truck is to help the lorry; hence, the two trucks cooperate. Furthermore, in [8] and [9] it is shown (but only in the German version) that the tanker delivers the gas that is needed by another truck, so again we find a cooperative relation between the trucks.

In sum, *Trucks* is helpful in constructing knowledge concerning trucks. Learning about trucks has to do with acquiring basic knowledge such as that (1) trucks have functions; (2) trucks transport goods, e.g. bricks, gasoline, wood; (c) trucks have drivers and the drivers do something with the trucks – for example, they load them; and (4) trucks are named after the goods or after their functions. Possibly this knowledge is integrated into a truck frame that will be expanded in the course of further development.

Comparison of the German and English texts

We cannot go deeply into quantitative aspects of the length of texts and sentences. It must suffice here to notice that length is not trivial with respect to acquisitional tasks. A well-known methodological tool for the comparison of children at different ages is to compare the mean length of their utterances – that is, to find out their MLU value. So, if the MLU of the textual input is measured, one finds a higher MLU in the English text than in the German text (Table 3.2). We cannot go into the question of whether English sentences are longer than German sentences in general. However, if it is assumed that children in the acquisitional process aim at being able to produce longer sentences, then it can be concluded that the English text is somewhat more demanding and, maybe, more effective.[5]

Suppose little Ken is bilingual; as a matter of fact, he has the English as well as the German version at hand. Then he might find out that both texts give different information. For instance, take the last sentence in the two books:

Table 3.2 A comparison of the text lengths of *Lastwagen/Trucks*

	German	English
Words	99	99
Sentences	12	9
Mean length	8.2	11.0

8   a. The trees have been cut down, and are being taken by special lorry from the forest to the timber yard.
     b. Ein Langholzlaster fährt Baumstämme aus dem Wald zum Stapelplatz des Sägewerks.

While in the first conjunct of [8a] it is explicitly expressed that trees have been cut down, this information remains implicit (it is presupposed) in [8b]. In contrast, while the truck is vaguely described as a "special lorry" in [8a], it gets a more explicit term in [8b], *Langholzlaster*, which can be paraphrased as "truck that transports long timber".

Let us now consider the text–picture relation, which is at the heart of picturebooks. In early-concept books, we have the prototypical case of a one-to-one correspondence between pictures and verbal information. For instance, there is a picture of a ball on the right-hand side of a double spread, and the word *ball* is printed on the left-hand side (Kümmerling-Meibauer and Meibauer 2011). In simple descriptive picturebooks, however, we find (1) cases where the textual information surmounts pictorial information, and (2) cases where pictorial information surmounts textual information.

For instance, in the German version of [12] it is said that containers can easily be reloaded onto a railway carriage or ship by means of a crane, but the corresponding picture is left to Ken's imagination; it is not depicted. On the other hand, most pictures contain more information than the text. This is trivially so when the picture stands for itself and is not accompanied by any text. But even in normal text–picture configurations, there are aspects (that Ken is potentially interested in) which are not verbally expressed in the accompanying text. For instance, in [8] the 15 logo-like yellow stars on a red circle (similar to the Caltex sign) are quite salient for Ken, but there is no further information about them.

Hence, what we find in a simple descriptive picturebook like *Trucks* is a careful balancing of textual and pictorial information, thus supporting the child's interest in adding lacking information, be it from the perspective of the text or the perspective of the picture. Interestingly, the books under consideration slightly differ in the information they offer to readers.

A developmental scenario

Before embarking on the following developmental scenario, let me start with a cautionary note.[6] What I am striving for – and what is much needed – is an integrative picture that is able to bring together findings from both naturalistic and experimental studies. The format of a developmental scenario is an appropriate method for this purpose as it fleshes out the situation of a fictive model recipient. In this way, it is possible to hint at research questions that often are not even asked in purely experimental work.[7]

Let us assume that Ken's father, Ben, bought *Trucks* from the local bookseller.[8] He read on the back flap (and believed) that this book is suited "for the very young". His son Ken is very young indeed: it was his second birthday four weeks ago. Moreover, Ben thinks that Ken could be interested in learning more about trucks. He has observed Ken's attention whenever a truck enters the little street where the family lives.[9]

Ken, being 25 months of age, certainly does not know much about types of trucks and their different functions, but he knows something about language and concepts, of course. Let us assume that Ken already knows about 200 words (supposing that he knew 50 words at 1;8 and then acquired 5 new words each week). In this still small lexicon, there are many nouns, comparatively few verbs, and some adjectives (see Kauschke and Hofmeister 2002). It is clear that Ken has to learn more vocabulary.

Verbs are very important to him, since verbs organize sentence structure via their argument structure. Ben supposes that Ken still does not know the verbs *to deliver*, *to load*, *to arrive*, *to fill*, *to drive*, and *to cut*, for instance. But Ben is not sure. Maybe Ken has overheard one or more of these words on occasion, so that they may be part of his passive lexicon.

To be sure, it is unreasonable to assume that he possesses several words denoting types of trucks, so here is Ken's chance to enhance his truck lexicon.

Ben is right in assuming that Ken is interested in trucks. When Ken was still a baby, he became interested in moving objects. While some objects were self-moving, other objects moved when they were caused to move, for instance balls. Trucks belong to the class of self-moving objects; however, Ken suspects that the driver is an actor that causes trucks to move. Moreover, trucks are movable objects that make noises. A ball, in contrast, is an object that does not make noises. So what is the reason behind these noises? Animals, for example, are moving objects that appear to produce noises by themselves. The noises produced by trucks seem to stem from the motor. The motor is something that makes noises and has the force to propel the truck. Finally, trucks are very large objects, at least in comparison to little Ken. And he knows already that trucks are somewhat dangerous. This is something his parents told him on several occasions.

Ken, being 25 months old, has just started to coin new words. His lexicon is still small, so compounding is a strategy for enlarging it when the situation requires. Typically, these new words are nominal compounds (cf. Clark 1993; Meibauer 1995).[10] When Ken is reading *Trucks* together with his father, Ben, and his mother, Betty, he detects and feels assured that there are many complex nouns referring to the objects he is interested in. These nouns are fast-mapped – that is, they are stored in his memory. Moreover, since these nouns are related (they denote subcategories of trucks), they are semantically connected in his lexicon.

Since the text is read to him repeatedly, Ken learns how the words are pronounced. This helps him with the segmentation of the words. Moreover, Ken experiences that his mother Betty pronounces some words in a slightly different manner than his father does. Nevertheless, he detects that these words are the same, be they spoken by Ben or by Betty.

During the third year, there is an increase in the mean length of utterance. At 3;0, most children have an MLU value of 3 – that is, their utterances contain three words on average. Ken will be no exception, but most of his utterances still consist of only two words. Confronted with *Trucks*, he hears very long and complex sentences that surmount his own abilities. For instance, he will be able to produce embedded sentences at 3;0, but *Trucks* already contains an embedded sentence, namely [4] in the German version and [8] in the English version. Typical embedded sentences in German have SOV (subject–object–verb), while typical root sentences have SVO. In the two-word stage, German children posit the infinite verb at the second (last) position. So, they have to learn to move the verb when using root sentences (this happens around 2;6) and to leave the verb in its position in embedded sentences (cf. Gretsch 2013; Kauschke 2012). Moreover, they have to master the verbal inflection.

It goes without saying that knowledge of grammar and texts is still restricted at 25 months of age. As a matter of fact, Ken will learn a huge number of things about grammar and usage during his third year of life. For instance, he learns to avoid ellipsis of subjects and function words; and he uses different sentence types, including embedded sentences. Moreover, he learns to use obligatory articles and to get the agreement between subject and verb right. Case, number, tense, and further morphological and syntactic properties of sentences are still difficult for Ken; however, even in this respect he will make some progress within his third year of life. In all these dimensions, he receives input by reading a simple descriptive book like *Trucks* together with one of his parents.

As we have seen before, his knowledge of texts, especially of the main textual properties of cohesion and coherence, is still restricted. So, there is an interesting aspect here: on the one hand, the text is quite demanding for Ken, since it contains complex words and sentence structures; on the other hand, it is an easy read, since there are no complex characters and narrative plots. To learn something about trucks and about grammar and lexicon is sufficient for 25-month-old Ken. Maybe when he is confronted with fictional characters like trains that can speak (e.g. *Thomas the Tank Engine*), he will not be happy about this jump from reality to fiction.

Perhaps Ken is primarily interested in the pictures, not in the accompanying text. The pictures depict trucks and selected parts of their surroundings in a special way. There are no detailed backgrounds. The trucks appear as huge objects seen from the perspective of a small girl or boy. The main relation shown in the pictures is the one between the truck and a person who has some function with respect to the trucks. The pictures are not very detailed; they are more realistic than naturalistic. Yet there is some special information given in the pictures that add realism and lead to further thinking about them. For instance, there are traffic lights, license plates, and even reflections of the forest on the chromes parts of the special lorry that transports wood. What is also salient to Ken is the position of the tires, which gives an indication of the direction in which the truck will turn when moving. All these things invite further pointing and asking.

Trucks has no introduction, no climax, no complications, no ending – in short, all elements of a narrative are lacking. This does not mean, however, that this simple text has no connection to narration at all. Indeed, some of the textual elements can be found in narratives, too. First, you find contrasts on a number of levels: contrasts between pictures, contrasts between lexical items denoting trucks, and contrasts between sentences such as in [2], [3] or [8]:

9   Two flatbed trucks. The green one is delivering pipes to a building site. The yellow one is on its way back to reload.
10 The tanker fills the garage's underground tanks as the red lorry gets petrol from the pump.

Second, since the picture–text sequences are ordered, there is a moment of sequentiality. For instance, the huge red truck transporting wood is at the end of the book.

Certainly Ken's ability to tell a story must still develop. And we know from numerous inquiries into children's narrative skills that there is a long road ahead. Empirical research shows that these skills develop gradually, from 3;0 years onwards until adolescence (cf. Bamberg 1987, 2005; Boueke *et al.* 1995; Becker and Quasthoff 2005; Dannerer 2012). What is remarkable, however, is the fact that all narratives, the child's own narratives as well as the narratives of professional authors, contain descriptive parts. Indeed, it is a key feature of every narrative that it contains descriptive elements. Hence, Ken's interest in trucks might constitute a building block for his later interest in descriptive passages as part of a narrative.

Furthermore, it could be that descriptive books have a greater impact on the child's own narratives than fictional books. Of course, Ben will have a major role here. Ken and Ben may develop stories in which they drive huge trucks across the deserts, for example. Trucks transporting dangerous materials are potential characters in these stories. In contrast, a story overloaded with fictional characters may not function as a trigger for the child's own narratives in a similar way. Perhaps descriptive books offer material that children can manipulate and rearrange according to their needs at a certain point of their development.

Outlook

The fictive developmental scenario embeds *Trucks* into the world of a little boy and reveals how this book may function in this world, and how a child can "learn" from this book. "Learning" is a multifaceted notion that can be spelled out in a number of ways. A very general definition of "learning" has been proposed by Jarvis (2009: 25):[11]

> The combination of processes throughout a lifetime whereby the whole person – body (genetic, physical and biological) and mind (knowledge, skills, attitudes, values, emotions, meaning, beliefs and senses) – experiences

social situations, the content of which is then transformed cognitively, emotively or practically (or through any combination) and integrated into the individual person's biography resulting in a continually changing (or more experienced) person.

If we take this definition seriously, it is obvious that "learning from picturebooks", including one particular person's learning from one particular picturebook, is a complex process.

Ganea and Canfield (this volume, Chapter 2) report experimental findings according to which young children prefer realistic picturebooks, and have an early preference for "realistic color photographs". Yet it has to be emphasized that learning from picturebooks happens also, and very importantly, from narrative books (fantasy, tales, etc.). It is not restricted to so-called information or reality, since there is also learning with respect to emotions, aesthetic values, and fiction. In addition, an early preference for "realistic color photographs" does not prevent children from appreciating, for instance, Dick Bruna's abstract drawings. So, there is much room for more naturalistic experimental research – that is, research focusing on individual development and authentic picturebooks.

Kiefer and Wilson (2011: 291) approve of the taxonomy by Lounsberry (1996: 29), according to which nonfiction books can be subcategorized as follows:

- lives (diaries, memoirs, autobiographies, biographies);
- events (histories, journalism);
- places (travel writing, nature writing, science writing);
- ideas (essays, including religious and philosophical work).

Specifically, they state that "Lounsbury's explanation works just as well for studying children's nonfiction as it does for adult nonfiction". I do not agree. Simple descriptive picturebooks certainly are nonfiction; however, trucks, animals, things of everyday life do not fit into the above categories. Yet they regularly show up in children's literature for the very young. Books like *Trucks* are more demanding than early-concept books as described by Kümmerling-Meibauer and Meibauer (2011), yet they display simple descriptive texts that contrast with the complex genres listed in Lounsbury's classification.

Recently, Bernstein (2013) suggested to view children's literature in the context of material culture and play. In contrast, I would propose that children's literature should be appreciated as an important subject of a cognitive theory of language and literature acquisition. However, Bernstein is right in that she focuses on relations between children's literature and play. It seems to me that little Ken compares the pictures of *Trucks* with his own toy trucks and that he can even transfer knowledge he acquires from the text to his play with his trucks. On being confronted with hybrid toy trucks (e.g. books in the form of toy trucks) which are available in his local bookstore, he will notice a category mistake.

Much more may be asked about simple descriptive picturebooks. Are they a separate genre and, if so, are there subgenres? To what extent are children able to distinguish between narrative and descriptive picturebooks? What can children of both sexes learn from descriptive picturebooks? Are they able to transfer knowledge from picturebooks to reality (cf. Ganea *et al.* 2011)? Are simple descriptive picturebooks better for learning than narrative picturebooks? Is there competition between them or do they complement each other? I cannot go into these questions in any detail. I think that there is ample room for experimental research into descriptive picturebooks (see Torr and Clugston 1999; Moschovaki and Meadows 2005). My main goal here was to show that simple descriptive picturebooks like *Trucks* should by no means be underrated.

Notes

1 There are early-concept books that contain, for instance, the word *apple* in addition to the picture of an apple. *Apple*, however, is not a text. I assume that a minimal text consists of at least two sentences or utterances. Cf. the very wide notion of text adopted by Lancaster and Flewitt (this volume, Chapter 7), who assume that even bedrooms and photographs are texts.
2 For instance, *it* is an anaphor referring back to *the lorry* in the following text:

   This lorry has broken down. The breakdown truck has arrived to tow it to a garage.

3 However, see Painter *et al.* (2013). The styles mentioned by Ganea and Canfield (this volume, Chapter 2), i.e. "highly realistic color photographs", "simplified and schematic drawings", "highly distorted and less realistic cartoons", do not exhaust the variety of styles to be found in picturebook art, let alone the problem of how to define these styles. It is unclear to me why children should prefer the former across the board since these styles deliver distinct kinds of information and are connected to distinct aesthetic values.
4 It goes without saying that it is not possible to relate all of these descriptive findings to recent language acquisition research in a sensible way. For a comprehensive survey on first language acquisition, see Clark (2003).
5 See Clark and Kurumada (2013) for a recent analysis of brevity in language acquisition.
6 There are many methodological approaches to early literacy, ranging from naturalistic, parent-observer studies to experimental, eliciting studies in laboratory settings. Typically, the latter are quite restricted in scope, mainly because of statistical requirements. First of all, in order to isolate and control variables, they often use self-made picturebooks. Second, they elicit children's knowledge in more or less artificial laboratory settings. Third, they typically are cross-sectional studies – that is, they cannot cover the longitudinal development of an individual. Fourth, the participants chosen are not representative of the respective society. In contrast, parent-observer studies display a richness of data on different observational levels. However, their drawback is the lack of control of variables. Moreover, generalizations with respect to cohorts of children are not possible. Yet these studies often present data that are not easily captured in laboratory settings. Impressive parent-observer studies include those by Lowe (2007), who studies the literary development of her two children Rebecca and Ralph, and Rainer (2010), who studies the acquisition of word formation by his daughter Carmen.
7 Cf. the observational-descriptive method applied by Lancaster and Flewitt (this volume, Chapter 7), which is intended to give an idea of what "distributed cognition" is about.

8 There is some evidence that in reading situations, fathers behave differently from mothers. Moreover, mothers and fathers, respectively, react differently depending on the sex of their children. See Elias (2009) for a comprehensive study of fathers' reading behavior.
9 Compare Jake's fascination with farming, farming machinery (tractors), and farm animals, as well as Mike's interest in planes, as described by Lancaster and Flewitt (this volume, Chapter 7).
10 Hiebert and Bravo (2010) point out that early morphological knowledge, like early phonological knowledge, may promote later success in reading abilities. With respect to morphological input, *Trucks* may play a small part in this process.
11 See also the articles in Jarvis and Watts (2012).

References

Primary sources

Browne, Anthony. 1998. *Voices in the Park*. London: Transworld Publishers.
Bruna, Dick. 1973. *Erste Bilder*. Ravensburg, Germany: Otto Maier.
Lindgren, Barbro and Eva Eriksson. 1994. *Max blöja*. Stockholm: Rabén & Sjögren.
Macaulay, David. 1973. *Cathedral: The Story of Its Construction*. Boston: Houghton Mifflin.
Mitgutsch, Ali. 1988. *Rundherum in meiner Stadt*. Ravensburg, Germany: Otto Maier Verlag.
Stickland, Paul. 1986. *Trucks*. Text by Mathew Price. London: Methuen Children's Books.
Stickland, Paul. n.d. *Lastwagen*. Translated by Friedrich Langreuter. Munich: Ars Edition.
Wiesner, David. 2006. *Flotsam*. Boston: Houghton Mifflin.

Secondary sources

Bamberg, Michael. 1987. *The Acquisition of Narratives: Learning to Use Language*. Berlin: Mouton de Gruyter.
Bamberg, Michael, ed. 2005. *Narrative: State of the Art*. Amsterdam: John Benjamins.
Becker, Tabea and Uta Quasthoff, eds. 2005. *Narrative Interaction*. Amsterdam: John Benjamins.
Bernstein, Robin. 2013. "Toys are good for us: Why we should embrace the historical integration of children's literature, material culture, and play". *Children's Literature Association Quarterly* 38(4): 458–463.
Bloom, Paul. 2000. *How Children Learn the Meanings of Words*. Cambridge, MA: MIT Press.
Boueke, Dietrich *et al.* 1995. *Wie Kinder erzählen. Untersuchungen zur Erzähltheorie und zur Entwicklung narrativer Fähigkeiten*. Munich: Fink.
Clark, Eve V. 1993. *The Lexicon in Acquisition*. Cambridge: Cambridge University Press.
Clark, Eve V. 2003. *First Language Acquisition*. Cambridge: Cambridge University Press.
Clark, Eve V. and Patricia Matos Amaral. 2010. "Children build on pragmatic information in language acquisition". *Linguistics Compass* 4(7): 445–457.
Clark, Eve V. and Chigusa Kurumada. 2013. "'Be brief': From necessity to choice". In *Brevity*, edited by Laurence Goldstein. 233–248. Oxford: Oxford University Press.

Dannerer, Monika. 2012. *Narrative Fähigkeiten und Individualität. Mündlicher und schriftlicher Erzählerwerb im Längsschnitt von der 5. bis zur 12. Schulstufe*. Tübingen: Stauffenburg.

Duke, Nell K., Anne-Lise Halvorsen, and Jennifer A. Knight. 2012. "Building knowledge through informational text". In *Knowledge Development in Early Childhood: Sources of Learning and Classroom Implications*, edited by Ashley Pinkham, Tanya Kaefer, and Susan B. Neuman. 205–219. New York: Guilford Press.

Elias, Sabine. 2009. *Väter lesen vor. Soziokulturelle und bindungstheoretische Aspekte der frühen familialen Lesozialisation*. Weinheim: Juventa.

Fassbind-Eigenheer, Ruth and Bernhard Fassbind-Eigenheer. 2002. *Was sagt der Text? Was zeigt das Bild? Vom Orbis Pictus zum Photobilderbuch. Text und Bild in der historischen Entwicklung des Sachbilderbuches*. Zürich: Schweizerisches Jugendbuchinstitut.

Ganea, Patricia A., Lili Ma, and Judy S. DeLoache. 2011. "Young children's learning and transfer of biological information from picture books to real animals". *Child Development* 82(5): 1421–1433.

Gelman, Susan A. 2006. "Early conceptual development". In *Blackwell Handbook of Early Childhood Development*, edited by Kathleen McCartney and Deborah Phillips. 149–167. Malden, MA: Blackwell.

Gretsch, Petra. 2013. "Satztyp und Spracherwerb". In *Satztypen des Deutschen*, edited by Jörg Meibauer, Markus Steinbach, and Hans Altmann. 815–845. Berlin: De Gruyter.

Harris, Paul L. 2012. *Trusting What You're Told: How Children Learn from Others*. Cambridge, MA: The Belknap Press of Harvard University Press.

Hiebert, Elfrieda H. and Marco Bravo. 2010. "Morphological knowledge and learning to read in English". In *The Routledge International Handbook of English, Language and Literacy Teaching*, edited by Dominic Wyse, Richard Andrews, and James Hoffman. 87–95. New York: Routledge.

Jarvis, Peter. 2009. *Learning to be a Person in Society*. London: Routledge.

Jarvis, Peter and Mary Watts, eds. 2012. *The Routledge International Handbook of Learning*. London: Routledge.

Kauschke, Christina. 2012. *Kindlicher Spracherwerb im Deutschen. Verläufe, Forschungsmethoden, Erklärungsansätze*. Berlin: De Gruyter.

Kauschke, Christina and Christoph Hofmeister. 2002. "Early lexical development in German: A study on vocabulary growth and vocabulary composition during the second and third year of life". *Journal of Child Language* 29: 735–757.

Kiefer, Barbara and Melissa I. Wilson. 2011. "Nonfiction literature for children: Old assumptions and new directions". In *Handbook of Research on Children's and Young Adult Literature*, edited by Shelby A. Wolf, Karen Coats, Patricia Enciso, and Christine A. Jenkins. 290–299. New York: Routledge.

Klotz, Peter. 2013. *Beschreiben. Grundzüge einer Deskriptologie*. Berlin: Schmidt.

Kümmerling-Meibauer, Bettina and Jörg Meibauer. 2005. "First pictures, early concepts: Early-concept books". *The Lion and the Unicorn* 29: 324–347.

Kümmerling-Meibauer, Bettina and Jörg Meibauer. 2011. "Early-concept books: Acquiring nominal and verbal concepts". In *Emerging Literacy. Children's books from 0 to 3*, edited by Bettina Kümmerling-Meibauer. 91–114. Amsterdam: John Benjamins.

Kümmerling-Meibauer, Bettina and Jörg Meibauer. 2013. "Towards a cognitive theory of picturebooks". *International Review of Children's Literature* 6(2): 143–160.

Lounsbury, Barbara. 1996. "Anthology introduction". In *Writing Creative Nonfiction: The Literature of Reality*, edited by Gay Talese and Barbara Lounsberry. 29–31. New York: HarperCollins.

Lowe, Virginia. 2007. *Stories, Pictures and Reality: Two Children Tell*. London: Routledge.

Meibauer, Jörg. 1995. "Neugebildete -er-Derivate im Spracherwerb. Ergebnisse einer Langzeitstudie". *Sprache und Kognition* 14: 138–160.

Mickenberg, Julia L. and Lynne Vallone, eds. 2011. *The Oxford Handbook of Children's Literature*. New York: Oxford University Press.

Moschovaki, Eleni and Sara Meadows. 2005. "Young children's spontaneous participation during classroom book reading: Differences according to various types of books". *Early Childhood Research and Practice* 7(1): 1–21.

Painter, Clare, J. R. Martin, and Len Unsworth. 2013. *Reading Visual Narratives: Image Analysis of Children's Picture Books*. Sheffield: Equinox.

Pinkham, Ashley M. 2012. "Learning by the book: The importance of picture books for young children's knowledge acquisition". In *Knowledge Development in Early Childhood: Sources of Learning and Classroom Implications*, edited by Ashley M. Pinkham, Tanya Kaefer, and Susan B. Neuman. 90–108. New York: Guilford Press.

Rainer, Franz. 2010. *Carmens Erwerb der deutschen Wortbildung*. Vienna: Verlag der Österreichischen Akademie der Wissenschaften.

Rémi, Cornelia. 2011. "The cognitive challenge of the wimmelbook". In *Emergent Literacy: Children's books from 0 to 3*, edited by Bettina Kümmerling-Meibauer. 115–140. Amsterdam: John Benjamins.

Rohlfing, Katharina J. 2013. *Frühkindliche Semantik*. Tübingen: Narr.

Schipke, Christine S. and Christina Kauschke. 2011. "Early word formation in German language acquisition". *First Language* 31(1): 67–82.

Siegal, Michael. 2008. *Marvelous Minds: The Discovery of What Children Know*. Oxford: Oxford University Press.

Smiley, Patricia and Janellen Huttenlocher. 1995. "Conceptual development and the child's early words for events, objects, and persons". In *Beyond Names for Things: Young Childrens's Acquisition of Verbs*, edited by Michael Tomasello and William E. Merriman. 21–61. Hillsdale, NJ: Lawrence Erlbaum.

Torr, Jane and Lynn Clugston. 1999. "A comparison between informational and narrative picture books as a context for reasoning between caregivers and 4-year-old children". *Early Child Development and Care* 159(1): 25–41.

4 The development of color vision and of the ability to appreciate color in picturebooks

Mei Ying Boon and Stephen J. Dain

Introduction

Picturebooks may be described as sequences of picture–text relations. The pictures are an integral part of the picturebook. Neither the text nor the pictures should stand alone. The exploration of this specific relationship is a fundamental task of picturebook theory (Nodelman 1988; Lewis 2001; Nikolajeva and Scott 2001). There are also textless picturebooks, for instance early-concept books or relatively complex picture narratives. In these cases, the meaning of the single pictures or of the story connected to the sequence of pictures has to be interpreted by the viewer.

Quite often, pictures are seen as mere illustrations, and the idea that children have to learn to interpret pictures, just as they have to learn to understand the meaning of texts, is not always appreciated by picturebook theorists. This contribution focuses on one particular property of pictures, namely color.

What one finds are considerations of the functions of pictures, often from the perspective of pedagogic or literacy enhancement. Thus, it has been pointed out that pictures may engage children with "reading" (or even "literature") without being able to be read in the literal sense (Kiefer 1995; Jones 1996; Nikolajeva 2003). There is a division of labor in that the child looks at the pictures while a caregiver reads the text. There are, of course, numerous actions such as pointing or gesturing that accompany this situation of common attention, thus supporting the child's learning about the specific picture–text relations.

Pictures may trigger enjoyment in the viewer, a process that is not easy to understand and has hardly been investigated from a cognitive point of view. Enjoyment is thought to be essential in the learning process, as it motivates and engages children to read and to continue to want to read (Apseloff 1987; Jalongo 2004). It has also been noted that, in order to maximize the child's engagement, the pictures must be clear and appropriate to the child's developmental stage (Styles and Arizpe 2001). One may ask at this point how color, as a crucial pictorial property, may be related to enjoyment. This question presupposes that we know what color is and how it relates to the quality of pictures.

For adults, color has been described as having three levels of meaning (Painter *et al.* 2013) in a way that that is analogous to how language has three levels of meaning, which may be termed metafunctions. Color may add realism to a real or imaginary construct (meaning through ideational metafunction), atmosphere, aesthetic pleasure, emotion, and characterization (meaning through interpersonal metafunction) to the interpretation of the associated text (Nikolajeva and Scott 2001; Painter *et al.* 2013). Colors may also act as codes or signposts for action repeated throughout the book (meaning through textual metafunction). Painter *et al.* (2013) note that ambience, which brings an emotional response, varies according to color and propose that these responses vary along three interlinked axes. The ambience of vibrancy, an exciting and energetic emotion, is created by use of bold, bright, and fully saturated colors. The desaturation of color (adding white) results in more muted color tones and a quieter ambience. The ambience of warmth, both emotional and physical, is elicited by the use of colors such as red, orange, and yellow, whereas coolness is evoked through colors such as blue, green, and aqua. The ambience of familiarity is evoked by the use of a full color palette, as is seen in "real life", whereas a restricted color palette is more abstract and stylistically removed from real life, and therefore can be used to evoke a dreamscape of fantasy worlds.

Children have to learn what colors mean. While there may exist innate aspects of color vision, colors also have cultural and social values. Hence, it cannot be assumed, without any further investigation, that adults and children will interpret color in the same way (Werner 2011). (Note that this is a sensible point when one asks to what extent children's and artists' views on color converge.)

Quite to the contrary, it has even been assumed that the color of pictures is not of interest to infants and, in order to be developmentally appropriate, pictures for young children should be achromatic in shades of gray (which may include black and white), termed grayscale. Note that some picturebooks employ either black and white alone or in combination with a single hue. Black and white are highly contrasting, exhibiting large differences in reflectance, hence both are easy to focus on and therefore attractive to infants. See, for instance, *Baby's My First ABC: 1, 2, 3 Soft Cloth Book* by Genius Baby Toy (Anon. n.d.) or the *Baby's Very First Black and White Library* series (2012) by Stella Baggot.

However, the evidence that infants may prefer black-and-white pictures over color pictures appears weak (Brian and Goodenough 1929; Johnson 1995). Even if it is true that in young infants the mechanisms in the visual system that process luminance contrast are more fully developed than those that process color, it does not necessarily follow that the artistic palette should be restricted to black and white. Indeed, colorful pictures can also achieve high levels of luminance contrast.

Werner (2011) has considered whether children might even reject black-and-white or grayscale pictures. She raises the issue that the visual task of being able to interpret black-and-white line drawings is more difficult conceptually than if there are colors, as all the visual cues for recognition must come from the black lines. The black lines that are ascribed to any object or figure in a picture must be differentiated from those lines that are ascribed to the background. If the groupings of lines are ambiguous, the child may have difficulty recognizing objects in the black-and-white pictures. Most ambiguous figure visual illusions only work as black-and-white line drawings. Painter (2008) also recognizes that color could be used by the artists of picturebooks to emphasize certain elements of a picture, assisting with segmentation of objects against a background. Therefore, it is questionable whether black-and-white or grayscale pictures are easier or more difficult for infants to interpret than their colored counterparts.

In summary, color may lack salience in picturebooks because the child has yet to develop the higher-level capacity to appreciate the aesthetics of color or the contribution of color to ambience (Painter 2008). The development of these higher-level skills may be linked to other skills such as color naming (Johnson 1977). On the other hand, the child's visual development may not have developed sufficiently to drive the higher-level functions. A failure to respond to color may be due to an immature input to the higher-level processing just as much as to a failure to process the information at the higher level.

Because of this uncertainty, it is worthwhile reexamining the issue of the significance of color in picturebooks for children. As studies have shown that older children tend to prefer color in their pictures (Rudisill 1952), we will report on an experiment designed to investigate the ages at which young preschool-aged children first show a preference for having color in book pictures. While the older children can tell us why they made a certain choice, the youngest infants cannot, so understanding the outcomes of such an experiment requires an understanding of how the visual system develops and how this may affect how color in picturebooks is perceived. Therefore, the next part of this chapter describes the techniques used by scientists to study the development of vision in young children, followed by a review of how color vision develops, a report on the experiment, and finally a discussion as to what has been learned.

Techniques used in the scientific study of visual development

Infants are certainly born with very poor form and color vision, but there are a number of difficulties in tracing the development of vision. In the early months, the techniques cannot rely on an infant's purposeful response. Researchers in the visual development of children rely on a few, well-established techniques. Visually evoked responses (VERs) are electrical activity produced by the eye or brain in response to visual stimuli. They are typically measured on the scalp or on the surface of the eye. In examining the transmission of information in the whole visual pathway, visually evoked cortical potentials (VEPs) are measured by electrodes placed on the scalp. The waveforms seen depend on the form of the stimulus and are analyzed in terms of amplitude and transmission time. These measures require only wakefulness in the infant. They measure primarily the processing of the information arriving at the primary visual cortex, and no higher-level processing.

Forced preferential looking (FPL) is a technique in which the infant is shown two stimuli. If the child cannot discern any difference in the two images, she or he will pay equal attention to the two. One stimulus might be a black-and-white grating and the other a gray of the same average luminance. If the infant can resolve the stripes of the grating, she or he will pay more attention to it. The spacing or contrast of the grating is changed to establish what the infant can or cannot resolve.

Another technique is that of optokinetic nystagmus (OKN). In this method, the striped stimulus is moved laterally across the field of view, typically on a rotating drum or drifting across a computer screen. There is a most compelling and involuntary tendency to move the eyes to follow the image. It is analogous to looking out of the side window of a traveling vehicle and following the moving scenery in a series of smooth fixation movements interspersed with a faster eye movement back to refixate. It is colloquially referred to as "train nystagmus". If the infant cannot resolve the detail of the image, she or he will not follow the movement. The contrast or spacing of the image is adjusted to establish the boundary between the ability and inability to follow the stimulus.

In later childhood through to adolescence, children are able to make verbal responses to the stimuli (seen/not seen; position of the stimulus – top/bottom/left/right, etc.), so the psychophysical and clinical methods appropriate to adults may be adopted, and studies of this age group are usually incorporated with the whole life span. A short attention span is often an issue with children, and the design of experiments that can hold the child's attention has been described (Abramov *et al.* 1984; Dain and Ling 2009). For the intermediate ages, adult psychophysical and clinical methods may not be entirely appropriate, but the electrophysiological methods may lack the precision to monitor the now more subtle changes in color vision. The methodological differences between VEP, FPL, and OKN techniques may contribute to the inconsistent results reported in the literature (Madrid and Crognale 2000; Suttle *et al.* 2002). The study of the development of vision may be inextricably linked to the development of other skills and abilities (Brown 1990). The changes observed in vision may be limited by the other skills needed to complete a test successfully. Apart from methodological differences, Brown (ibid.) emphasized the overall difficulties in investigating infant color vision, in that the limiting factor to the types of experiments that can be carried out on infants is the fact that we cannot ask them for answers. Older subjects can give verbal responses and feedback as to whether or not they can see something, whereas infants cannot.

Since the option to respond to the color information in picturebooks will not be available if color vision itself is insufficiently developed, it is important to understand the development of color vision itself.

Development of color vision

Color vision at the receptor (cone photoreceptor) level is trichromatic – that is, there are three cone types, popularly referred to as red, green, and blue cones.

The red and green cones also provide the basis to all daytime (photopic) vision, including fine form vision (visual acuity) and detection of movement. Rods provide low-light-level sensitivity (scotopic) vision that has no color vision, poor form vision and limited movement detection. By the time the information has reached the next layer of cells in the retina, the retinal ganglion cells, the information has been reprocessed in channels that signal redness–greenness and visual acuity (P-cells), blueness–yellowness (K-cells), and achromatic information such as movement (M-cells). P-cells are relatively more numerous in the central vision. so the central vision must be used to see objects in fine detail. Similarly, K-cells have their peak population para-centrally and M-cells are relatively more numerous in the peripheral retina. In examining the development of color vision, the description of the experiment and its results may be based in trichromatic terminology of red, green, and blue or in the opponent colors terminology of red–green, blue–yellow (sometimes called tritan, which is the term for those congenitally lacking the blue receptor), and achromatic or form vision (visual acuity). Since each of these involves different mechanisms and anatomies, it should not be assumed that they mature at the same rate.

Differences between preterm and postterm infants have been shown in both contrast and chromatic (red–green) sensitivity when age is counted from birth date (Bosworth and Dobkins 2009), but most of the differences disappear if the infant's age is calculated from due date instead. This indicates some development of color vision *in utero* for full-term babies. Neonates fixate longer on some, but not all, colored squares on white compared with a white square (Adams 1995; Adams *et al.* 1991, 1994). This ability is also size-dependent (Adams *et al.* 1990). It has improved by the time that the infants are 1 month old (Adams 1995).

At 3 weeks of age, infants demonstrate some chromatic discrimination. Some 3-week-old infants are able to discriminate long-wavelength lights (red spectrum), providing evidence of some sort of color spectral sensitivity functions and three functional cone types (as well as a functioning rod system for scotopic vision) (Teller and Bornstein 1987; Teller 1982–1983, Knoblauch *et al.* 1998). Infants have relatively broad spectral sensitivity curves that are similar to those of adults. The absolute sensitivity is, however, much reduced (Teller 1982–1983). The presence of three cone types indicates that infants have the *potential* to see the world in the three-color dimensions from about 1 month of age. Congenital red–green dichromats (lacking either the red or the green receptor) can be identified at this age (Bieber *et al.* 1998b).

Postreceptoral color mechanisms may be a limiting factor in infants. Using FPL and VEP methods, various research groups have studied the color-opponent processes of the infant visual system. It is generally agreed that by 2 months of age, infants have functioning red–green pathways (Peeples and Teller 1975; Hamer *et al.* 1982; Teller and Bornstein 1987; Kelly *et al.* 1997; Bieber *et al.* 1998a; Suttle *et al.* 2002; Dobkins *et al.* 2001), but there is more uncertainty about the blue–yellow pathway at this age.

While Varner *et al.* (1985) showed evidence of some blue–yellow discrimination in some 5-week-olds and most 8-week-olds, the investigators acknowledge that their data do not necessarily imply that by 8 weeks of age, infant color vision is adult-like. On the other hand, several studies have shown little blue–yellow color vision in infants even at 2 months of age (Teller and Bornstein 1987; Pulos et al. 1980; Suttle et al. 2002). By 3–4 months of age, however, infants show positive responses to blue–yellow stimuli, indicating the presence of a functional blue–yellow pathway of some kind (Suttle et al. 2002).

Through OKN techniques, utilizing eye movements to provide cues of the direction of motion of a colored grating, Teller (1998) reports that 2- and 3-month-old infants, but not 1-month-old infants, produce OKN to red–green gratings. In another study, Teller et al. (1997) show that blue–yellow stimuli do not elicit OKN in 2- and 4-month-old infants, again providing evidence that the blue–yellow system in infants develops at a slower rate.

Kelly and Chang (2000) show further improvements in color vision at 3–4 months of age. At 5 months (Dobkins et al. 2001) and 8 months (Morrone et al. 1993), and in comparison with the achromatic channel through the M-cell (achromatic) pathway, the chromatic P-cell pathway has been found to mature at a slower rate (Hammarrenger et al. 2007). While the human achromatic response to VEPs is mature by 3 months of age, the red–green and blue–yellow mechanisms continue to mature and do not appear adult-like even at 1 year of age (Madrid and Crognale 2000; Crognale 2002).

Banks and Bennett (1988) provide another explanation for poor color vision in infants. These researchers suggest that, rather than their having immature chromatic mechanisms, there are preneural factors, such as eye size and photoreceptor morphology, that may reduce overall visual sensitivity. Banks and Bennett (ibid.) also suggest that the improvements in color vision between 4 and 12 weeks of age may reflect visual efficiency development rather than maturing color vision. They point out, however, that infants who fail at blue–yellow discriminations may actually have a tritan (blue sensitivity) defect. It appears that at 1 year of age, VEP responses still differ greatly from those of adults, with continuing development of both pathways until later in life (Crognale 2002).

Visual evoked potentials in response to color have been shown to continue to develop from 2 years of age onwards, not reaching adult-like maturity until 12–13 years of age (Madrid and Crognale 2000; Boon et al. 2009). Knoblauch et al. (2001) agree that there is continuing development of color vision from infancy, having found that color discrimination thresholds improve by a factor of 30 from 3 months to adolescence. An adaptation of the Cambridge Colour Test (Cambridge Research Systems, Rochester, UK) for use with children showed thresholds for 2-year-old children that were only two (protan and deutan axes) to three (tritan axis) times higher than adults' (Goulart et al. 2008). These latter authors' data for the age range 5–7 years were consistent with those of Ling (2004).

Apart from cognitive factors, Teller and Bornstein (1987) propose that the reasons for differences in findings between adults and infants include sampling error, crystalline lens density (the crystalline lens yellows with age), or macular pigmentation differences and differences in receptor-type sampling. Electrophysiological studies have revealed that children's visual processing of colored images is less complex but much stronger in amplitude than adults', which suggests that immaturity of the neuronal populations which underlie color vision processing and perception or immaturity of interneuronal communications (Boon *et al.* 2009) may also explain the poorer color discrimination of children compared with adults.

What is clear is that children do not fully attain adult levels of color discrimination until at least their late teens (Verriest *et al.* 1962, 1982; Crognale *et al.* 1998, 2001; Knoblauch *et al.* 2001; Crognale 2002; Kinnear and Sahraie 2002; Ling 2004; Goulart *et al.* 2008).

Development of color contingent skills before the age of 5 years

While infants have been shown to be trichromatic from an early age, there needs to be evidence that they can make use of that ability in higher processing. Color vision-based skills such as color naming and color sorting require, but are not guaranteed by, a sufficiently developed color vision system (Bornstein 1985b). Infants as young as 4 months have been shown to perceive color categorically (Franklin and Davies 2004). At 5 months of age, infants do not show a preference for objects in their canonical, or "correct", colors. However, by 6 months of age infants start to prefer pictures of faces and fruit in their canonical colors, but no preference was demonstrated for correctly colored flowers (Kimura *et al.* 2010). Because flowers have lower color diagnosticity than faces and fruit, it was thought that this reflected maturation of the ability to recognize objects in their canonical colors. Despite blue being one of the most preferred colors by infants (Zemach and Teller 2007), the infants preferred the fruit and faces in their canonical colors, which included yellows and greens, known to be least attractive to at least 3-month-old infants (ibid.). This indicates that 6-month-old infants are using color appropriately in their recognition of objects.

Other clues as to whether children use color come from the development of ability in color naming, most of which takes place before the age of 42 months (Johnson 1977; Anyan and Quillian 1971). Thirty-six-month-old children sort by color (Williamson *et al.* 2010), and color sorting precedes color naming (Soja 1994). Two-year-old children can identify the appropriate color for objects (Macario 1991); thus, it appears that the ability to associate a color name, rather than color vision, limits performance (Braisby and Dockrell 1999; Davidoff and Mitchell 1993; Andrick and Tager-Flushberg 1986; Bornstein 1985b).

At the age of 3 years, children can complete a sorting test (in which colored objects have to be arranged into a series, most often of hue) sufficiently well to make it possible to identify those with more major color vision deficiencies (Sassoon and Wise 1970). At the age of 5 years, children can carry out a color sorting test, but not with the same precision as 12-year-olds (Ling and Dain 2008). The ability to undertake a sorting test seems to be limited more by the development of the concept of a series than by color vision (Dain and Ling 2009).

Salience of color and form

The work of Brian and Goodenough (1929) is often quoted. These authors show a tendency to sort object by color rather than by form, increasing up to the age of 3½ years. After this point, form becomes the preferred sorting dimension, to be 90 percent of the choices in adulthood. Suchman and Trabasso (1966) showed a similar shift of preference from color to form. Bornstein (1985a) showed that children have more difficulty learning color names than shape names. These "either/or" kinds of studies are not really relevant for picturebooks, since the choice will be for color *and* form, as there is no practical way of offering color-only pictures without form.

Development of other visual attributes

Other visual attributes such as contrast sensitivity, visual acuity, and form perception are also not fully developed at birth and continue to mature. Contrast sensitivity is the ability to differentiate between light and dark. High contrast sensitivity indicates a visual system that can differentiate between small differences in luminance, whereas low contrast sensitivity indicates that the visual system can only differentiate between large differences in luminance. Contrast varies depending on the angular size of the adjacent light and dark areas. The spatial contrast sensitivity function describes how well contrast is perceived for objects or gratings ranging from large and coarse to small and fine-detailed. Human infants best see objects and gratings that are about four to six times larger than the best that adults can see. Different methods of testing contrast sensitivity have revealed different ages at which contrast sensitivity is adult-like. Using static stimuli, which is how pictures in books would be seen, some studies have found contrast sensitivity is likely to be adult-like by 7 years of age (Ellemberg *et al.* 1999), whereas others suggest that it is not adult-like at even 7–8 years of age (Gwiazda *et al.* 1997; Scharre *et al.* 1990; Leat and Wegmann 2004).

Visual acuity, the ability to resolve fine detail, is mediated in the eye by the function of the fovea and then by the visual cortex in the brain. At birth, the fovea, the part of the retina used for fixation and viewing objects in the world around us, is immature and the individual cone photoreceptors relatively widely spaced. Grating visual acuity (the ability to see stripes in a stimulus or to be able to distinguish stripes from gray of equal average luminance) is estimated to be on average 20/640 Snellen equivalent visual acuity at about 3 weeks of age. It then improves, as shown in Table 4.1.

It should be noted that, while 20/20 is used colloquially to indicate normal vision, the average adult visual acuity is actually close to 20/15. On the basis of these values, it might be thought that children would be able to start to resolve the largest pictures in regularly sized picturebooks from about 2 months of age. By 13 months of age, they will be able to resolve the pictures with adult-like levels of resolution, provided the books are viewed at half the distance at which

Table 4.1 Vision as a function of age

Age	Visual acuity (Snellen)	Visual acuity relative to 20/20	Source
3 weeks	20/640	0.03	(Mayer *et al.* 1995; Salomão and Ventura 1995)
2.4 months	20/320	0.06	
3.6 months	20/160	0.13	
1 year	20/80	0.25	
13 months	20/40	0.50	
6 years	20/20	1.00	(Ohlsson and Villarreal 2005; Drover *et al.* 2008; Dobson *et al.*, 2009)
Adult (late teens and later)	20/15	1.33	(Drover *et al.* 2008)

an adult would view the images in order to double the retinal image size. Adults typically view books from a distance of 33–40 centimeters.

The ability to perceive shapes and the contours that define objects in pictures and ascribe meaning to those objects has been found to be present at 6 months of age (Baker *et al.* 2008). However, the infants' ability to do this was much more degraded by noise than in adults. This indicates that the clarity with which objects are represented is of greater importance for object recognition in 6-month-old infants than in adults. Form recognition requires the viewer to first observe areas of light and dark, perceive and recognize lines and contours, be able to complete boundaries and contour combinations and their relative spatial locations, followed by integration of all the above elements with visual memory to recognize and ascribe meaning to an entire object (Changizi 2010). Cortical area V4 in the brain is considered critical to global form perception and object recognition (Wilson and Wilkinson 1998; Rosa *et al.* 2012). From 6 months of age, infants are able to recognize two-dimensional forms that are consistent with or novel to their experience. In other words, infants of 6 months of age are likely able to resolve pictures in picturebooks, and they are likely to be actively recognizing the forms and shapes that they are viewing in the pictures.

When considering how a picture looks to an infant or child with immature vision, it must be kept in mind that contrast sensitivity, color vision, visual acuity, and form perception are still developing. A child with poor visual acuity will see the larger shapes that make up a picture but may miss the fine details. A child with poor contrast sensitivity is thought to see even high-luminance-contrast pictures as attenuated in contrast, so that high-, medium-, and low-contrast pictures may be viewed as medium-, low-, and zero-contrast pictures respectively (Legge 2007). A child with poor color vision may not appreciate the presence of color. In studies of people with visual impairment, it has been found that the most sensitive system is the system that most determines the visibility of a stimulus (Boucart *et al.* 2008). Therefore, for those with poor visual acuity and normal color vision, color contrast is a stronger cue for recognition of an object than for someone with good visual acuity and normal color vision.

Thus, how visible elements of a picture appear to a child will differ depending on the relative sensitivity of different visual functions in the child, functions that are each known to improve with age but perhaps at different rates. In principle, for a young child, visibility of the picture may be optimized by ensuring that the pictures:

- employ high luminance contrast to allow the forms in the picture to be detected;
- contain large shapes or shapes drawn with thick lines in consideration of the child's poorer visual acuity, thereby allowing the child to resolve the details of the picture;
- employ colors that have high color difference to allow variations in color to be perceived by the child;
- depict forms or situations that are within the experience of the child;
- depict forms or situations with minimal image degradation.

However, visibility and recognizability are not necessarily the same as preferences in picture characteristics (Zemach and Teller 2007). Zemach and Teller (ibid.) examined whether 3-month-old infants were attracted to specific colors when luminance and brightness were equalized, and whether this was related to their visibility, as indicated by measured detection thresholds for different colors. They found that visibility accounted for 34 percent of the preferences for color; color purity accounted for only 2.4 percent of preferences in their sample, which suggests that the remaining explanation must be an actual preference for the specific colors of blue, purple, and red. They speculated that at matched brightness and saturation, these colors are more "visually compelling" than greens and yellows.

Rudisill (1952) evaluated the preferences of older children, those who attended the first six grades (about 5–10 years of age) of school, for different kinds of illustrations of the same content, a child engaged in an interesting activity with an animal or toy, with and without color: (1) an uncolored photograph; (2) a colored photograph; (3) a colored drawing, realistic in form and color; (4) an outline drawing, realistic in form, outlined in color without regard for realistic effect; and (5) a colored drawing, conventionalized in form, decorative, but unrealistic in color. The colored photograph (2) was preferred over the uncolored photograph (1) by 70–86 percent of all the children. The realistically colored drawing (3) was preferred over the conventionalized colored drawing in the unrealistic colors (5) by 58 percent of the children in the youngest grade and 93 percent of the children in the oldest grade. The colored photograph (2) and the realistically colored drawing (3) were preferred over the outline drawing without realistic color (4) by most of the children, and the most favored picture was the more realistic and colorful of the two. If a picture was uncolored but otherwise more realistic, it was more preferred by the children. Rudisill concluded that if two pictures are identical in all other respects, most children of elementary or primary school age prefer a realistically colored to an uncolored picture, a finding that is very similar to other findings for 6- to 8-month-old infants (Kimura *et al.* 2010).

Although preferences do not necessarily have to be aligned with visibility and recognizability, the work of Rudisill and Kimura *et al.* appears to suggest that for infants and school-age children, this is one of their main criteria for liking a picture. Rudisill collected the reasons children gave for their choices and concluded that the children first sought to recognize the content of a picture, and so they prioritized and liked realism over whether a picture was colored or uncolored. Interestingly, Rudisill noted that none of the younger children were aware that (1) and (2) were photographs rather than pictures that they were viewing, so photographs and pictures were conceptually similar for the kindergarten children.

Collectively, the above studies would suggest that infants and school-age children should prefer correctly colored and realistic pictures in their picturebooks when these are depicting a scene within their experience. However, picturebooks are not designed to depict only what is familiar, thereby encouraging symbolic recognition; they are also intended to stimulate the imagination, to pique curiosity, and to expand horizons by depicting unfamiliar scenes (Apseloff 1987). One question of interest is when preschool-age children first begin to appreciate color in their picturebooks, which may include familiar or fantastical scenes, and whether this is related to their color discrimination ability, assuming that all else is the same. To this purpose, an experiment was developed.

Investigation of preferences for grayscale or color images

Method

Infants and young children of preschool age (<6 years) were recruited from childcare centers, a preschool, and community library children's events. Data were collected regarding the child's sex (male or female), date of birth, date of testing, location of testing, and family history of color vision deficiency. Children were tested for the presence of congenital color vision deficiencies, or deficient sensitivity in the red–green and blue–yellow color vision systems, using the pseudoisochromatic plates in *Color Vision Testing Made Easy* (Waggoner 1994) and plates 16 (medium red–green), 19 (strong red–green), 21 and 22 (medium blue–yellow) from the HRR Pseudoisochromatic Plate (4th edition, Richmond Products, USA) (Cole *et al.* 2006). A demonstration plate containing a symbol with both high luminance and chromatic contrast, and intended to be seen by all children, was used to gain an understanding of each child's gaze behavior for objects that are definitely seen. Another demonstration plate, which contained no symbols, was used to gain an understanding of each child's gaze behavior when they do not see an object. For the youngest children, the HRR plates were used in a forced preferential looking manner with the demonstration plate (4) that has no symbols. The plates were presented within a lightbox, constructed from a box 50×40×30 cm painted approximately Munsell N5 (average gray) lit with an 8-watt T5 tubular fluorescent tube lamp to ensure uniform presentation of colors of the cards at different testing sites. The correlated color temperature was 4,246 K, the CIE General Color Rendering Index, R_a, was 85.0, and the mean illuminance at the pictures was 554 lx (Optimum SRI 2000 Spectral Light Meter, Optimum, China). On the basis of their responses in the color vision screening, the children were classified as making no errors (score 0), making one major error (score 1), or making two or more major errors (score 2). If the child made one major error, for example failing to detect a stimulus using the FPL method, then they were assigned a score of 1. If they did not detect multiple stimuli using the FPL method or they made more than one error on the pseudoisochromatic plate tests, they were assigned a score of 2. The forced-choice preferential looking (FPL) technique was used to determine preferences for color in children's book pictures (Figure 4.1). The children were asked, "Which picture do you like better?" without the examiner drawing attention to the coloring or any of the features of the pictures. Thirteen gray cards were created: 1 blank and 12 with a children's book illustration sized 20 × 20 cm in color on either the left or the right side and in grayscale, containing identical luminance contrast and form information, but no color information, on the other side. The pictures were scanned in color, displayed in Adobe Photoshop, and printed on a laser printer. For the grayscale image, the Adobe Photoshop "mode" was changed from "RGB Color" to "Grayscale" and the image printed on the same printer. The colored pictures varied from those with a selection of highly saturated colors without shading and stylized shapes (including an illustration of the anthropomorphized rabbit Miffy standing under some colored flags from *Miffy* (2010) by Dick Bruna, pictures of horses galloping and a chick hatching from an egg from Lamaze's softbook *Discovery Farm* (Anon. n.d.) and a picture of a girl about to brush her teeth from Kathleen Amant's *Anna Brushes Her Teeth* (2008)) to minimal shading and still stylized shapes (including an illustration from the Ladybird series of books about *Peppa Pig* (Anon. 2009), showing Peppa and her friends running a race on a sports track, Iconix's *Pororo the Little Penguin* (n.d.) character flying an airplane, and people unloading their cars at a recycling depot from Jess Stokam's illustrations for *Recycling* (n.d.)). Some had realistic shapes with realistic colors, shading, and texture (Axel Scheffler's illustrations from *Pip and Posy: The Little Puddle* (2011) showing an anthropomorphized mouse playing at home and having a bath, and from *Pom-Pom, Tiddly-Pom* (2007) by Bonnie Worth et al., which is based on the Winnie-the-Pooh character showing the bear and his friends celebrating a birthday party), whereas others had a stylistically limited palette of colors for each illustration (Beatrix Potter's *Peter Rabbit* (2007) illustrations showing Peter Rabbit resting in a field of green radishes and a picture of a doorway in a garden of flowers). The more realistic illustrations tended to have higher levels of detail but the main shapes of all pictures were easily resolvable even with poor visual acuity. Half the pictures also included simple text within the picture. The stimuli were designed so that if an infant or child had not yet developed color vision, the two pictures would be perceived as identical in form and luminance contrast. Half of the pictures had the colored picture on the left and the grayscale picture on the right. The other half had the colored picture on the right and the grayscale picture on the left. The child's attention was first directed to the center of the blank card. The blank card was then removed to reveal one of the 12 test cards. The cards were presented in random order in the lightbox, which contained a peephole for the examiner to evaluate whether a child spent more time viewing the left or right when presented with the card stimulus (see Figure 4.1). For children who were verbal or liked to point, the gaze preference, stated preference, and pointing behaviors were observed and manually recorded. Only one child displayed inconsistent behaviors between gaze, stated preference, and pointing behaviors, and those data were excluded.

An extended gaze at one of the pictures was regarded as evidence for increased interest in that picture over the other picture, so was recorded as a preference (see Figure 4.1). Gaze length was determined by the examiner

Figure 4.1 A 4.3-year-old child observing one test card within a lightbox. Note that the test card shows the same picture, identical in both form and luminance contrast details, but one picture is in color and the other in grayscale.

counting out the number of seconds silently in their mind. As gaze behavior may be different for different children, each child's gaze behavior during the screening for color vision deficiencies was used to define normal gaze behavior when they could not see a target (control demonstration plate with no symbols) compared to when they could see a target (the demonstration plate, which is highly visible owing to the presence of both luminance and chromatic contrast of the symbol). Gaze behavior during the FPL testing procedure was judged by the examiner with reference to the known behaviors of each child as observed during the color vision screening procedure, as discussed previously. If the gaze switched from one picture to the other picture and back again for more than 10 cycles, no preference was recorded. If the examiner was unsure, the card was tested again later on. If a child preferred the colored picture for at least 9 out of the 12 cards, an overall color preference was recorded for the child. If a child preferred the grayscale picture for at least 9 out of the 12 cards, an overall grayscale preference was recorded for the child. If a picture type was preferred for 4, 5, 6, 7, or 8 times or there was no preference, then no preference overall was recorded for the child.

Results

One hundred eight children were recruited. However, only 94 children (50 males, 44 females) were tested (see Figure 4.2). The untested children were usually from the childcare centers and were infants (<1 year of age) or toddlers who required multiple daytime naps. The untested children were asleep during the testing visits, despite the researchers making several return visits. Nine boys and nine girls had a family history of color vision deficiency. It may be seen that none of the 3.5- to <4-year-old children made color vision errors. For the other age groups, errors were made. At these young ages, the errors could be due to immaturity of the color vision system but might instead be due to a congenital color vision deficiency, as some of the children had a family history of color vision deficiency. We could not differentiate between these two possible reasons for poor color vision using our testing protocol, as having a family history of color vision deficiency does not necessarily indicate that the child has a congenital color vision deficiency.

Fisher's Exact Test (see http://psychclassics.yorku.ca/Fisher/Methods/chap4.htm) $\chi = 18.550$, $p = 0.03$ indicated that there was a significant difference in color preferences by age group. Individual overall preferences for color were observed at all age groups, and this became almost unanimous after 4 years of age (Figure 4.2). The one child in the 4- to 4.5-year age group who did not prefer color was 4.1 years of age, on the younger side of the cohort. Age was weakly correlated with color preference (Spearman's rho = –0.40, $p < 0.001$) and number of errors on the color vision screening plates (Spearman's rho = –0.26, $p = 0.02$).

Color preference was not explained by color ability, indicated by the number of errors made during the color vision-screening test (Fisher's Exact Test

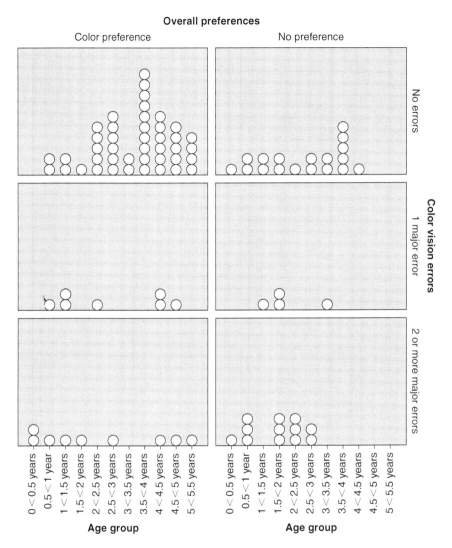

Figure 4.2 Overall preferences as a function of age group (6-month divisions) and color vision test errors (no errors, one major error, two major errors). A circle represents each child's data. Note that none of the children had an overall preference for grayscale pictures, so only the results for overall color preferences or no preferences are displayed here.

$\chi = 1.406$, $p = 0.51$). It may be seen that 18 children who made no errors on the color vision screening plates had no preference, and 16 children who made one or more major errors still preferred the colored pictures (Figure 4.2).

Out of those who exhibited an overall color preference, an examination of how strongly they exhibited the preference is depicted in Figure 4.3. It may be

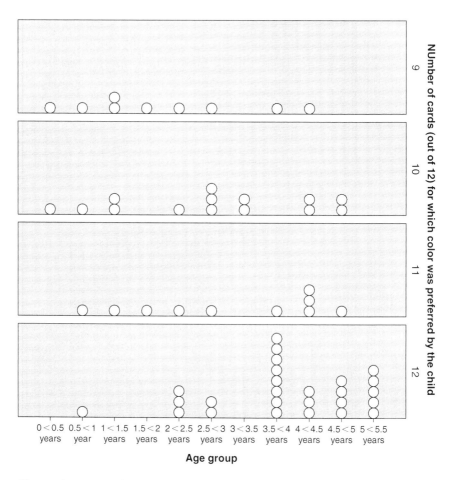

Figure 4.3 Strength of color preferences by age group.

seen that all the children aged 5–5.5 years preferred the colored picture for all 12 pairs. In the younger age groups, preferences for color were not as strong. What might children be appreciating when they express a preference?

Observations of the youngest infants during the testing process revealed that their decisions as to where to look were quick and decisive. They were either drawn to a picture or they were not. There was very little cycling of fixation between the color and grayscale versions of the picture. This suggests that the stimulus was highly salient and the gaze reflexive, so is unlikely to have been mediated by cognitive processes, such as making an executive decision to like one image over the other, or even recognition of the object, as such judgments should require more time to make. The level of saliency appeared to be similar to that which occurs during pop-out perception tasks. Pop-out tasks are visual search tasks where the preprocessing and precognitive processes can rapidly identify the potentially most meaningful object within the extent of the spatial field of attention on which to focus so that it can be recognized with the minimum of delay (Müller and Krummenacher 2006). The changing of fixation to the object is necessary because our best visual acuity is at the center of our visual field (where we are directly looking; try reading this word with your peripheral vision. It cannot be done, because our visual acuity becomes progressively and substantially poorer the farther away from the center of fixation). The most meaningful object should be distinguished in some way from the rest by form, luminance, or color for the pop-out effect to occur. If there is nothing in the visual field that pops out or draws the attention, for example if all objects look similar in some way, then we have no choice but to search serially, observing first one object then the next in sequence until we find the object of most meaning to us. Three-month-old infants have been observed to show the pop-out effect, so this may explain their results (Adler and Orprecio 2006).

Observation of the responses of the oldest children, aged 5–5.5 years, revealed that their decisions were also quick and decisive. The older children uniformly reported verbally that the reason for their preference was that the picture was colored, and all children volunteered this information without needing to be asked. The grayscale pictures did not appear to attract their attention (see Figure 4.3). Hayakawa *et al.* (2011) noted a similar effect in their study of visual search abilities of children of 4 to 6 years of age where they were drawn to colored images at the expense of content detection accuracy (the task was to detect pictures of snakes) to a much greater extent than were adults. If Hayakawa *et al.*'s findings explain the behavior of the oldest children tested in our study, then it is likely that the content of the grayscale images was not considered strongly by the children in making their preferences. This could be tested in future studies by comparing preferences between colored and grayscale pictures of different content. It appears that both the preprocessing and precognitive processes (their initial gaze behavior) and the cognitive processes (as evidenced by their verbal self-report of their preference) of children aged 5–5.5 years may be biased towards color compared with the other ages tested. Could the strong cognitive preference for color reflect a growing understanding of how color can add meaning to pictures (Nikolajeva and Scott 2001; Painter 2008) in this age group?

Observation of the middle range of children tested, about 3- to 4-year-olds, indicated that they usually weighed the decision of preference between the two versions of the picture much more carefully, as they took much longer to decide. Most children looked at each picture, perhaps more than once, before finally making a decision. This is also evident in the data shown in Figure 4.3, where many of the children sometimes select a grayscale picture over the colored picture. The children appeared to be looking at every aspect of both pictures before making a decision. Few volunteered why they liked a picture or stated that the colors affected their decision. For many of the children, it was very difficult for them to have to decide between the two pictures. One reason for this could be that their color vision may be such that the colors perceived may not appear that different from the grayscale image and it is a subtle distinction that requires a more careful evaluation as to whether a preference is, indeed, justified. It may also suggest that children are more interested in the narrative or content aspects of the picture, and color is secondary to the joy of appreciating the picture, which is not that different from how adults may view illustrations. For example, in Nikolajeva and Scott's discussion of the interaction between picture and text in picturebooks (2001), most of the discussion relates to the content of the pictures and their interaction, whereas color is regarded as having secondary effects on the interaction by adding atmosphere, mood, and characterization to the content. However, verbal language and color-naming skills are still developing within this age range, which does suggest that the children's interaction with colors is not cognitively adult-like (Anyan and Quillian 1971; Johnson 1995).

Other clues as to what the 3- to 4-year-old children may have been responding to when they made their preference include looking at the pictures for which the color preferences were lowest (66 percent of preferences) and highest (84 percent of preferences). Interestingly, the higher color preferences were elicited from the picture from *Pom-Pom, Tiddly-Pom* depicting the anthropomorphized bear Winnie-the-Pooh and his friends celebrating a birthday party together with a birthday cake, party hats, party food, and balloons, items that are expected to be colorful in real life so that the grayscale picture looked quite drab, un-party-like, and unrealistic by comparison. With reference to Painter's descriptions of ambience from color (2008), both the most-preferred and the least-preferred pictures had a similar color palette (familiarity), level of color saturation (vibrancy), and warmth (warmth), therefore it does not appear to be interpersonal metafunction that is important for these children. Instead, it appears that it is the ideational metafunction that is more important, as it would be more ideationally realistic if the birthday party scene were colorful in the experience of the children. It appears that Rudisill's (1952) thoughts that realism is appreciated by school-age children and the preferences for canonical color in infants (Kimura *et al.* 2010) may also be relevant in 3- to 4-year-old children. The lowest color preferences were elicited from the picture of a generic anthropomorphized brown mouse having a bath in a yellow bathtub, a scene which is probably outside the children's experiences and is not associated with a natural set of realistic colors. In addition, yellow is one of the least-favored colors in 3-month-old infants (Zemach and Teller 2007). For that reason, the colors in that picture do not assist with recognition, are not particularly well liked, and do not appear to be especially realistic or unrealistic. It is not possible to comment on whether the textual metafunction of color was important to these children, as whole books where color may be of importance as a symbolic thread throughout the book were not offered in this study design. Thus, if the 3- to 4-year-old children had age-normal color vision, which is still poorer than adult color vision, the variation in individual preferences for or against the colorful version of the picture may have been due to the fact that the colors were not perceived adequately by the children so that they appeared very similar to the grayscale version of the picture *or* that the colors were perceived adequately but the content or narrative of the picture was sufficiently interesting such that colors were unnecessary or not appealing enough to sway preferences.

In most of the age ranges tested, some of the children made errors on the color vision test plates, confirming that color perception was not adult-like in those children. However, color preference was not associated with the number of errors on the color vision test plates, indicating that some children with color vision deficiencies still preferred color, whereas other children who had normal color vision had no strong preference for color in their pictures. This tends to agree with Zemach and Teller's findings that preference for color or otherwise could not be fully explained by color detection thresholds.

Conclusions

This chapter has reviewed the ways in which pictures in picturebooks may be made more visible to the developing visual system of children and discussed the fact that high luminance contrast can coexist with color, so the addition of color does not necessarily have to result in a sacrifice of visibility, and may even aid in recognition. The chapter then presented an experiment to extend understanding of the preferences of preschool-aged children regarding color in their pictures. The results of the reported experiment tell us that preschool children interact with colored pictures in different ways at different ages. Once children can appreciate colors, they certainly interact with the color. The interaction may be an appreciation for color in some pictures but not in others. It is significant that none of the children showed an overall grayscale preference (i.e. not one child preferred the grayscale picture 9 out of the 12 cards), indicating that while not all the colored pictures were more attractive to the children, it is likely that they are noticing that there is color in a picture and that by the time they are 4.5 years of age they will cognitively recognize that they appreciate colored pictures. It also suggests that for younger children, color is appreciated if it adds to the story by increasing the realism of the scene depicted in the picture. However, our results suggest that the 4.5- to 5.5-year-old children may interact less with a book with grayscale rather than colored pictures, as color was highly salient and attractive for them. This finding is of importance if the pictures in picturebooks are to serve one of their functions, which is to engage preliterate children with literature (Apseloff 1987; Jalongo 2004; Kümmerling-Meibauer 2011).

In view of the fact that none of the 94 children showed an overall grayscale preference over color, and children preferring color were observed in every age group, even the youngest, it would be prudent for all picturebooks to employ color, as preschool children will interact with the color. The youngest will use color to aid in detection and recognition, the slightly older children will delight in how the colors make the pictures more lifelike and real, and the oldest preschool children will strongly appreciate color.

Acknowledgments

We appreciate the support of all the children and parents who volunteered for the study, the children's librarians at Randwick City Council Margaret Martin and Bowen libraries, and the directors and educators at the following organizations for their interest and support in the study: UNSW Early Years, House at Pooh Corner, Kanga's House, Tigger's Honey Pot, and Headstart Early Learning Centre Roseville. The authors also appreciate the work of Tammy Yi-Ting Hsu and Jolene Fong, who assisted with the data collection.

References

Primary sources

Amant, Kathleen. 2008. *Anna Brushes Her Teeth*. Newtown, NSW: Walker Books.
Anon. n.d. *Baby's My First ABC: 1, 2, 3 Soft Cloth Book*. Indian Trail (Charlotte), NC: Genius Babies.
Anon. n.d. *Discovery Farm*. Salford: Lamaze Toys.
Anon. 2009. *Let's Go!* (Peppa Pig). London: Ladybird Books.
Baggot, Stella. 2012. *Baby's Very First Black and White Library*. London: Usborne.
Bruna, Dick. 2010. *Miffy*. Richmond, Victoria: Hardie Grant Egmont.
Choi Jong Il. n.d. *Pororo the Little Penguin*. Seoul: Iconix Entertainment.
Potter, Beatrix. 2007. "Who Lives Here, Peter Rabbit?" In *Fun with Peter Rabbit*. London: Penguin.
Scheffler, Axel. 2011. *Pip and Posy: The Little Puddle*. London: Nosy Crow.
Stokham, Jess. n.d. *Recycling!* Belrose, NSW: Child's Play.
Worth, Bonnie, Jean-François Panayotopoulos, and John Kurtz. 2007. *Pom-Pom, Tiddly-Pom*. Chadstone, Victoria: Funtastic.

Secondary sources

Abramov, Israel, Louise Hainline, Joseph Turkel, Elizabeth Lemerise, Henry Smith, James Gordon, and Susan Petry. 1984. "Rocket-ship psychophysics: Assessing visual functioning in young children". *Investigative Ophthalmology and Visual Science* 25: 1307–1315.
Adams, Russell J. 1995. "Further exploration of human neonatal chromatic–achromatic discrimination". *Journal of Experimental Child Psychology* 60: 344–360.
Adams, Russell J., Daphne Maurer, and Heidi A. Cashin. 1990. "The influence of stimulus size on newborns' discrimination of chromatic from achromatic stimuli". *Vision Research* 30: 2013–2030.
Adams, Russell J., Mary L. Courage, and Michelle E. Mercer. 1991. "Deficiencies in human neonates' color vision: Photoreceptoral and neural explanations". *Behavioural Brain Research* 43: 109–114.
Adams, Russell J., Mary L. Courage, and Michelle E. Mercer. 1994. "Systematic measurement of human neonatal color vision". *Vision Research* 34: 1691–1701.
Adler, Scott A. and Jazmine Orprecio. 2006. "The eyes have it: Visual pop-out in infants and adults". *Developmental Science* 9: 189–206.
Andrick, Grex R. and Helen Tager-Flushberg. 1986. "The acquisition of colour terms". *Journal of Child Language* 13: 119–134.

Anyan, Walter R. and Warren W. Quillian. 1971. "The naming of primary colours by children". *Child Development* 42: 1629–1632.

Apseloff, Mary. 1987. "Books for babies: Learning toys or pre-literature?" *Children's Literature Association Quarterly* 12: 63–66.

Baker, Thomas J., James Tse, Peter Gerhardstein, and Scott A. Adler. 2008. "Contour integration by 6-month-old infants: Discrimination of distinct contour shapes". *Vision Research* 48: 136–148.

Banks, Martin S. and Patrick J. Bennett. 1988. "Optical and photoreceptor immaturities limit the spatial and chromatic vision of human neonates". *Journal of the Optical Society of America A* 5: 2059–2079.

Bieber, Michelle L., Kenneth Knoblauch, and John S. Werner. 1998a. "M- and L-cones in early infancy: II. Action spectra at 8 weeks of age". *Vision Research* 38: 1765–1773.

Bieber, Michelle L., John S. Werner, Kenneth Knoblauch, Jay Neitz, and Maureen Neith. 1998b. "M- and L-cones in early infancy: III. Comparison of genotypic and phenotypic markers of color vision in infants and adults". *Vision Research* 38: 3293–3297.

Boon, Mei Ying, Catherine M. Suttle, Bruce I. Henry, and Stephen J. Dain. 2009. "Dynamics of chromatic visual system processing differ in complexity between children and adults." *Journal of Vision* 9(6): art. no. 22.

Bornstein, Marc H. 1985a. "Colour-name versus shape-name learning in young children". *Journal of Child Language* 12: 387–393.

Bornstein, Marc H. 1985b. "On the development of color naming in young children: Data and theory". *Brain Language* 26: 72–93.

Bosworth, Rain G. and Karin R. Dobkins. 2009. "Chromatic and luminance contrast sensitivity in fullterm and preterm infants: Effects of early visual experience on magnocellular and parvocellular pathway processing". *Journal of Vision* 9: 1–16.

Boucart, Muriel, Pascal Despretz, Katrine Hladiuk, and Thomas Desmettre. 2008. "Does context or color improve object recognition in patients with low vision?" *Visual Neuroscience* 25: 685–691.

Braisby, Nick and Julie Dockrell. 1999. "Why is colour naming difficult?" *Journal of Child Language* 26: 23–47.

Brian, Clara R. and Florence L. Goodenough. 1929. "The relative potency of color and form perception at various ages". *Journal of Experimental Psychology* 12: 197–213.

Brown, Angela M. 1990. "Development of visual sensitivity to light and color vision in human infants: A critical review". *Vision Research* 30: 1159–1188.

Changizi, Mark. 2010. *The Vision Revolution: How the Latest Research Overturns Everything We Thought We Knew about Human Vision*. Dallas: Ben Bella Books.

Cole, Barry L., Ka-Yee Lian, and Carol Lakkis. 2006. "The New Richmond HRR pseudoisochromatic test for colour vision is better than the Ishihara test". *Clinical Experimental Optometry* 89: 73–80.

Crognale, Michael A. 2002. "Development, maturation, and aging of chromatic visual pathways: VEP results". *Journal of Vision* 2: 438–450.

Crognale, Michael A., John P. Kelly, A. H. Weiss, and Davida Y. Teller. 1998. "Development of the spatio-chromatic visual evoked potential (VEP): A longitudinal study". *Vision Research* 38: 3283–3292.

Crognale, Michael A., Jonathan W. Page, and Andrea Fuhrel. 2001. "Aging of the chromatic onset visual evoked potential". *Optometry and Vision Science* 78: 442–446.

Dain, Stephen J. and Barbara Y. Ling. 2009. "Cognitive abilities of children on a gray seriation test". *Optometry and Vision Science* 86: E701–707.

Davidoff, Jules and Peter Mitchell. 1993. "The color cognition of children". *Cognition* 48: 121–137.

Dobkins, Karen R., Christina M. Anderson, and John P. Kelly. 2001. "Development of psychophysically drived detection contours in L- and M-cone contrast space". *Vision Research* 21: 1791–1807.

Dobson, Velma, Candice E. Clifford-Donaldson, Tina K. Green, Joseph M. Miller, and Erin M. Harvey. 2009. "Normative monocular visual acuity for early treatment diabetic retinopathy study charts in emmetropic children 5 to 12 years of age". *Ophthalmology* 116: 1397–1401.

Drover, James R., Joost Felius, Christina S. Cheng, Sarah E. Morale, Lauren Wyatt, and Eileen E. Birch. 2008. "Normative pediatric visual acuity using single surrounded HOTV optotypes on the Electronic Visual Acuity Tester following the Amblyopia Treatment Study protocol". *Journal of AAPOS* 12: 145–149.

Ellemberg, Dave, Terry L. Lewis, Chang H. Liu, and Daphne Maurer. 1999. Development of spatial and temporal vision during childhood. *Vision Research* 39: 2325–2333.

Franklin, Anna and Ian R. L. Davies. 2004. "New evidence for infant colour categories". *British Journal of Developmental Psychology* 22: 349–377.

Goulart, Paulo R. K., Marcio L. Bandeira, Daniela Tsubota, Nestor O. Oiwa, Marcelo F. Costa, and Dora F. Ventura. 2008. "A computer-controlled color vision test for children based on the Cambridge Colour Test". *Visual Neuroscience* 25: 445–450.

Gwiazda, Jane, Joseph Bauer, Frank Thorn, and Richard Held. 1997. "Development of spatial contrast sensitivity from infancy to adulthood: Psychophysical data". *Optometry and Vision Science* 74: 785–789.

Hamer, Russell D., Kenneth R. Alexander, and Davida Y. Teller. 1982. "Rayleigh discrimination in young human infants". *Vision Research* 22: 575–587.

Hammarrenger, Benoit, Franco Lepore, Sarah Lippé, Mélanie Labrosse, Jean-Paul Guillemot, and Marie-Sylvie Roy. 2003. "Magnocellular and parvocellular developmental course in infants during the first year of life". *Documenta Ophthalmologica* 107: 225–233.

Hammarrenger, Benoit, Marie-Sylvie Roy, Dave Ellemberg, Mélanie Labrosse, Jacqueline Orquin, Sarah Lippé, and Franco Lepore. 2007. "Developmental delay and magnocellular visual pathway function in very-low-birthweight preterm infants". *Developmental Medicine and Child Neurology* 49: 28–33.

Hayakawa, Sessue, Noboyuki Kawai, and Nobue Masakata. 2011. "The influence of color on snake detection in visual search in human children". *Scientific Reports* 1: art. no. 80. doi:10.1038/srep00080

Jalongo, Mary Renck. 2004. *Young Children and Picture Books*. Washington, DC: National Association for the Education of Young Children.

Johnson, Carla J. 1995. "Effects of color on children's naming of pictures". *Perceptual and Motor Skills* 80: 1091–1101.

Johnson, Eric G. 1977. "The development of color knowledge in preschool children". *Child Development* 48: 308–311.

Jones, Rhian. 1996. *Emerging Patterns of Literacy: A Multidisciplinary Perspective*. London: Routledge.

Kelly, John P., Katja Borchert, and Davida Y. Teller. 1997. "The development of chromatic and achromatic contrast sensitivity in infancy as tested with the sweep VEP". *Vision Research* 37: 2057–2072.

Kelly, John P. and Suan Chang. 2000. "Development of chromatic and luminance detection contours using the sweep VEP". *Vision Research* 40: 1887–1905.

Kiefer, Barbara. 1995. *The Potential of Picturebooks: From Visual Literary to Aesthetic Understanding.* Englewood Cliffs, NJ: Merrill.

Kimura, Atsushi, Yuji Wada, Jiale Yang, Yumiko Otsuka, Ippeita Dan, Tomohiro Masuda, So Kanazawa, and Masami K. Yamaguchi. 2010. "Infants' recognition of objects using canonical color". *Journal of Experimental Child Psychology* 105: 256–263.

Kinnear, Paul and Arahs Sahraie. 2002. "New Farnsworth-Munsell 100 Hue Test norms of normal observers for each year of age 5–22 and for age decades 30–70". *British Journal of Ophthalmology* 86: 1408–1411.

Knoblauch, Kenneth, Michelle L. Bieber, and John S. Werner. 1998. "M- and L-cones in early infancy: I. VEP responses to receptor-isolating stimuli at 4- and 8-weeks of age". *Vision Research* 38: 1753–1764.

Knoblauch, Kenneth, Françoids Vital-Durand, and John L. Barbur. 2001. "Variation of chromatic sensitivity across the life span". *Vision Research* 41: 23–36.

Kümmerling-Meibauer, Bettina, ed. 2011. *Emergent Literacy: Children's Books from 0 to 3.* Amsterdam: John Benjamins.

Leat, Susan J., and Daniela Wegmann. 2004. "Clinical testing of contrast sensitivity in children: Age-related norms and validity". *Optometry and Vision Science* 81: 245–254.

Legge, Gordon E. 2000 *Psychophysics of Reading in Normal and Low Vision.* Mahwah, NJ: Lawrence Erlbaum.

Lewis, David. 2001. *Reading Contemporary Picturebooks: Picturing Text.* London: RoutledgeFalmer.

Ling, Barbara Y. 2004. "Development of colour vision in children". PhD thesis, University of New South Wales.

Ling, Barbara Y. and Stephen J. Dain. 2008. "Color vision in children and the Lanthony New Color Test". *Visual Neuroscience* 25: 441–444.

Macario, Jason F. 1991. "Young children's use of color in classification: Foods and canonically colored objects". *Cognitive Development* 6: 17–46.

Madrid, Marina and Michael A. Crognale. 2000. "Long-term maturation of visual pathways". *Visual Neuroscience* 17: 831–837.

Mayer, D. Luisa, A. S. Beiser, A. F. Warner, E. M. Pratt, K. N. Raye, and J. M. Lang. 1995. "Monocular acuity norms for the Teller Acuity Cards between ages one month and four years". *Investigative Ophthalmology and Visual Science* 36: 671–685.

Morrone, Concetta M., David C. Burr, and Ariana Fiorentini. 1993. "Development of infant contrast sensitivity to chromatic stimuli". *Vision Research* 33: 2535–2552.

Müller, Hermann J. and Joseph Krummenacher. 2006. "Visual search and selective attention". *Vision and Cognition* 14: 389–410.

Nikolajeva, Maria. 2003. "Verbal and visual literacy: The role of picturebooks in the reading experience of young children". In *Handbook of Early Childhood Literacy*, edited by Nigel Hall, Joanne Larson, and Jackie Marsh. 235–248. Thousand Oaks, CA: Sage.

Nikolajeva, Maria and Carole Scott. 2001. *How Picturebooks Work.* New York: Garland.

Nodelman, Perry. 1988. *Words about Pictures: The Narrative Art of Children's Picture Books.* Athens: University of Georgia Press.

Ohlsson, Josefin and Gerardo Villareal. 2005. "Normal visual acuity in 17–18 year olds". *Acta Ophthalmologica Scandinavica* 83: 487–491.

Painter, Clare. 2008. "The role of colour in children's picture books: Choices in AMBIENCE". In *New Literacies and the English Curriculum*, edited by Len Unsworth. 89–110. London: Continuum.

Painter, Clare, J. R. Martin, and Len Unsworth. 2013. *Reading Visual Narratives: Image Analysis of Children's Picture Books.* Sheffield: Equinox.

Peeples, David R. and Davida Y. Teller. 1975. "Color and brightness discrimination in two-month-old human infants". *Science* 189: 1102–1103.

Pulos, Elizabeth, Davida Y. Teller, and Stephen L. Buck. 1980. "Infant color vision: A search for short-wavelength-sensitive mechanisms by means of chromatic adaptation". *Vision Research* 20: 485–493.

Rosa, Marcello, Alexandra Angelucci, Janelle Jeffs, and John Pettigrew. 2012. "The case for a dorsomedial area in the primate 'third-tier' visual cortex". *Publications of the Rearch Society Bulletin* 280 (1750): 20121372; discussion 20121994, doi: 10.1098/rspb.2012.1372.

Rudisill, Mabel R. 1952. "Children's preferences for color versus other qualities in illustrations". *Elementary School Journal* 52: 444–451.

Salomão, Solange Rios and Dora F. Ventura. 1995. "Large sample population age norms for visual acuities obtained with Vistech-Teller Acuity Cards". *Investigative Ophthalmology and Visual Science* 36: 657–670.

Sassoon, Humphrey F. and James B. Wise. 1970. "Diagnosis of colour-vision defects in very young children". *Lancet* 295: 419–420.

Scharre, Janet E., Susan A. Cotter, Sandra S. Block, and Susan A. Kelly. 1990. "Normative contrast sensitivity data for young children". *Optometry and Vision Science* 67: 826–832.

Soja, Nancy N. 1994. "Young children's concept of color and its relation to the acquisition of color words". *Child Development* 6: 918–937.

Styles, Morag and Evelyn Arizpe. 2001. "A gorilla with 'Grandpa's eyes': How children interpret visual texts – a case study of Anthony Browne's *Zoo*". *Children's Literature in Education* 32: 261–281.

Suchman, Rosslyn G. and Tom Trabasso. 1966. "Color and form preference in young children". *Journal of Experimental Child Psychology* 3: 177–187.

Suttle, Catherine M., Martin S. Banks, and Erich W. Graf. 2002. "FPL and sweep VEP to tritan stimuli in young human infants". *Vision Research* 42: 2879–2891.

Teller, Davida Y. 1982–1983. "Scotopic vision, color vision, and stereopsis in infants". *Current Eye Reearch* 2: 199–210.

Teller, Davida Y. 1998. "Spatial and temporal aspects of infant color vision". *Vision Research* 38: 3275–3282.

Teller, Davida Y. and Marc H. Bornstein. 1987. "Infant color vision and color perception". In *Handbook of Infant Perception*, edited by Philip Salpatek and Leslie Cohen. 185–235. Orlando, FL: Academic Press.

Teller, Davida Y., Thomas E. W. Brooks, and John Palmer. 1997. "Infant color vision: Moving tritan stimuli do not elicit directionally appropriate eye movements in 2- and 4-month-olds". *Vision Research* 37: 899–911.

Varner, Denise, James E. Cook, Marilyn E. Schneck, Maryalice McDonald, and Davida Y. Teller. 1985. "Tritan discriminations by 1- and 2-month-old human infants". *Vision Research* 25: 821–831.

Verriest, Guy, R. Vandevyvere, and R. Van der Donck. 1962. "Nouvelles recherches se rapportant à l'influence du sexe et de l'âge sur la discrimination chromatique, ainsi qu'à la signification pratique des résultats du Test 100 Hue de Farnsworth-Munsell". *Révue d'Optique* 41: 499–509.

Verriest, Guy, Jean Van Laetham, and André Uvijls. 1982. "A new assessment of the normal ranges of the Farnsworth-Munsell 100-Hue Test scores". *American Journal of Ophthalmology* 93: 645–652.

Waggoner, Terrace. 1994. *Color Vision Testing Made Easy*. Gulf Breeze, FL: Home Vision Care.

Werner, Annette. 2011. "Color perception in infants and young children: The significance of color in picturebooks". In *Emergent Literacy: Children's Books from 0 to 3*, edited by Bettina Kümmerling-Meibauer. 39–54. Amsterdam: John Benjamins.

Williamson, Rebecca A., Vikraim K. Jaswal, and Andrew N. Meltzhoff. 2010. "Learning the rules: Observation and imitation of a sorting strategy by 36-month-old children". *Developmental Psychology* 46: 57–65.

Wilson, Hugh and Frances Wilkinson. 1998. "Detection of global structure in glass patterns: Implications for form vision". *Vision Research* 38: 2933–2947.

Zemach, Iris K. and Davida Y. Teller. 2007. "Infant color vision: Infants' spontaneous color preferences are well behaved". *Vision Research* 47: 1362–1367.

Part II
Co-constructed learning from picturebooks

5 Gesturing in joint book reading

Katharina J. Rohlfing, Angela Grimminger, and Kerstin Nachtigäller

Introduction

Reading to children is reported to be a valuable activity to promote children's language acquisition (e.g. De Temple and Snow 2003; Reese *et al.* 2010). Yet the quality of verbal behavior during book reading is considered to be more important than the frequency of reading (De Temple and Snow 2003). In a review, Reese and colleagues (2010: 107) summarize that the quality of reading is particularly effective when promoted within the context of the home: programs supporting parents in their reading techniques are "an effective way to enhance children's expressive, and in some studies, their receptive vocabulary". However, when we look at a parent reading to a young child (see Figure 5.1), what becomes apparent is the fact that the reading activity is not at all restricted to verbal behavior. In fact, both the parent and the child communicate with each other nonverbally to a great extent. It is thus surprising that to date, little is known about nonverbal behavior during joint book reading.

In our chapter, we will focus on hand gestures. To our knowledge, only two studies, those of Murphy (1978) and Rowe and Pan (2004), have been concerned with gesturing during joint book reading. Murphy (1978) analyzed pointing during book reading in 32 mother–child dyads, with the children being divided into four age groups: 9, 14, 20, and 24 months. She identified a form of routinized behavior in a book-reading situation, namely pointing and labeling, in all age groups. However, these routines served different functions with respect to children's age: while pointing with naming was predominantly used with younger children, pointing was very likely accompanied by questions with the 20- and 24-month-olds.

In Rowe and Pan's (2004) study, 68 low-income mothers and their 2-year-old children were visited at home during two activities: reading the book *The Very Hungry Caterpillar* and, afterwards, playing with toys for a total of 10 minutes. The video recordings were coded for verbal and nonverbal behavior. Coding of verbal behavior assessed the lexical items, the conversational function (eliciting or noneliciting), and the communicative intent (directing attention, discussing joint focus, or negotiating an immediate activity). In coding nonverbal behavior, the synchronous occurrence of pointing and speech was noted.

Figure 5.1 Mother and child gesturing to a picturebook. While the mother points to the whole picture, the child is pointing to specific parts of it. The pointing of the mother serves also a manipulative purpose, as the finger fixes the page and prevents the child from turning the pages.

Children's vocabulary development one year later, as assessed by the Peabody Picture Vocabulary Test–III (PPVT), was significantly related to the interaction during bookreading and toy play.

Rowe and Pan's (2004) study is valuable not only because it characterizes nonverbal behavior during book reading, but especially because it compares maternal behavior in these two situations: joint book reading and free play. The results revealed that even though mothers devoted only 18 percent of the time to book reading, the majority of maternal pointing gestures (54 percent) occurred during this activity. Controlling for the time spent in these two situations leads to even more insights, as mothers were found to produce 4.6 pointing gestures per minute when reading the book to their children and only 0.7 points during the free play. With respect to verbal coding, Rowe and Pan (ibid.) found that mothers discussed the joint focus of attention more often and children were more likely to respond to a maternal pointing gesture with a label during book reading. Children's receptive vocabulary one year later (assessed by the PPVT) was positively correlated with maternal pointing gestures per minute during book reading — but not during free play. The authors thus concluded that "[a]lthough dyads may spend relatively brief periods of time interacting around a book, this form of interaction appears to be one that is particularly facilitative of child vocabulary development, in part because of mothers' nonverbal communicative input to children". In the following, we will discuss why joint book reading constitutes a special form of interaction that is facilitative of children's vocabulary development. In our discussion, we consider two sources of evidence: research on joint attention on the one hand, and research on pragmatic routines on the other hand.

Joint attention refers to the phenomenon of interaction partners being simultaneously engaged and focusing on one another and the same external entity (cf. Baldwin 1995). This phenomenon has been recognized as a human capacity for social attention coordination (Mundy et al. 2007) and is an important prerequisite for effective communication in general (Zukow-Goldring 1996). Children engage in joint attention when they begin to point at the end of their first year (Liszkowski 2005). "For a point to communicate meaning it has to be embedded in a context which is construed by the interlocutors' relations towards each other and the environment" (ibid.: 136). Individual differences in joint attention skills among infants are considered to be related to subsequent language and cognitive development (Mundy et al. 2007). On their way to achieve social coordination and to follow gaze or pointing gestures, children require a lot of support from their caregivers (Bakeman and Adamson 1984). This support was also found to be related to later language skills (e.g. Tomasello and Farrar 1986). More specifically, individual differences in caregivers' joint attention organization were reported to be related to children's subsequent language skills. A study by Della Corte and colleagues (1983) found that children whose mothers coordinated their conversation more with the child's focus of attention outperformed other children in their lexical skills. A further study by Tomasello and Farrar (1986) revealed that children learned individual words better when they were provided within a joint episode (i.e. the object was labeled at the moment at which both interaction participants focused on it). Together these studies suggest that establishing a joint attentional focus to an external entity and coordinating it with an ongoing conversation facilitates language acquisition in children.

Coordinating a joint focus seems to be particularly pronounced in joint book reading (Murphy 1978), and we think that two factors are responsible for this: the expectation of interaction routines and the repeatability of the situation. In the following, we will consider both factors.

Yont and colleagues (2004) observed that different pragmatic contexts elicit different maternal interaction styles. More specifically, the speech of mothers and their 12-month-old children was different in the context of book reading compared to free play. This led the authors to conclude that during book reading, language was used as a conversational tool, while during toy play it functioned as an instrumental tool. Further focusing on verbal behavior, Gelman *et al.* (2005) report that pictures – rather than objects – elicit a higher proportion of generic and labeling phrases from mothers and their 2- to 3-year-old children. In this way, children receive information about the objects involved in the pictures as category members rather than individuals (see also Ganea and Canfield, this volume, Chapter 2). Rowe and Pan (2004) compared nonverbal behavior in two situations, free play and book reading, and found that during book reading, gestures are often used to discuss a joint focus of attention and to reinforce the verbal message. Snow and Goldfield (1983) observed that even with young children, book reading results in routines of conversations about which children and mothers share intuitions. It is important to recognize that both verbal and nonverbal behavior together contribute to these intuitions because they form a cultural action organization (Pellegrini and Galda 2003). Thus, applying the same pragmatic strategies (such as pointing to a picture and asking "what is this?"; see Example 2 in the "Results" section, p. 106) is not merely a form of scaffolding referent identification in the sense that the pointing gesture highlights the meaning (e.g. Booth *et al.* 2008). The pragmatic strategies also make the roles of the interactants more transparent, as the child will have specific behavioral expectations linked to a gesture: For example, a child will expect a label (Example 1) or a question (Example 2) when the caregiver is pointing. Growing experience with such strategies dictates her or his role in this joint activity, as the child will either give a word for or point to the referent in response to the *wh*-question.

Another factor contributing to the pragmatics of book reading is the repeatability of the situation. Nachtigäller and Rohlfing (2011a: 135) put the advantages of the pragmatics in the reading activity the following way: what appears to bring a facilitative effect for children's language acquisition is the fact that the depicted events are accessible in general, so other persons (adults, but also siblings) can refer to the exact same events. "In fact, children often demand to re-read the particular books many times, thus creating the recurrences" (Snow and Goldfield 1983: 553). The benefits of a repeating story on vocabulary learning has been shown in a study by Horst and colleagues (2011; see also Horst in this volume, Chapter 9), who found that children learned a new word better when it was embedded in a repeatedly read storybook rather than in different stories that were read three times. This finding suggests that the repeatability of a situation also promotes language learning and thus contributes to the quality of reading as an important factor in book-reading activities.

In sum, a lot is known about verbal behavior during a shared reading activity that is effective in language acquisition. However, little is known about nonverbal behavior in general, and hand gestures in particular, that might well support the acquisition of communicative skills.

Most studies investigating the effect of gestural behavior in the input on children's language learning used a freeplay situation. This is also the case in Rowe and Goldin-Meadow's (2009) longitudinal study. Children in the study were repeatedly videotaped during mother and child free-play situations, beginning when the children were 14 months old and continuing every 4 months until children were 42 months of age. The authors found that the mothers' gestural input at the age of 14 months mediated children's vocabulary skills at 54 months. Can a similar mediating role of gestural input during joint picturebook reading be found? In light of Rowe and Pan's (2004) finding for 2-year-olds, we hypothesize that for young children at the age of 14 months, the book-reading situation will also reveal a more crucial relation between maternal gestures and the child's subsequent vocabulary development than a free-play situation.

Another research gap that we want to address arises from the question of whether the content of the book has an impact on maternal gestural behavior. Previously, we found that mothers provided more (proto-)narratives to their children when two objects are depicted in relation to each other (e.g. a cup on a table) compared to when one object is depicted (e.g. a cup; Nachtigäller and Rohlfing 2011b). Continuing our research, we were interested in exploring the effect of different kinds of picture material on nonverbal behavior. To date, current research related to the topic of maternal behavior in book-reading situations considers either very specific picturebooks (e.g. *The Very Hungry Caterpillar* in Rowe and Pan 2004) or books in which children were shown a set of simple object pictures (Kümmerling-Meibauer and Meibauer 2005; Snow and Goldfield 1983). These "early-concept books", however, might trigger a very specific labeling routine, i.e. a caregiver indicating the picture to the child and labeling it (Example 1, pp. 106–107) or asking questions like "what is this?" (Example 2, pp. 107–108). Thus, investigations with other picture material (e.g. with more objects on one page) are necessary to verify whether some caregivers' practices in very specific picture compositions can be extended to book reading in general. Our hypothesis is that – as in the findings reported for verbal behavior (Nachtigäller and Rohlfing 2011b) – different picture materials will influence maternal nonverbal behavior.

Methods

The data for our investigation are drawn from a longitudinal study that extended over a period of 17 months.

Participants

In the longitudinal study, 18 mother–child dyads participated. For our analyses at the age of 14 months, we will report data from 17 dyads. However, for the longitudinal analyses we report data from only 11 dyads. The reason for this inconsistent procedure is the extensive coding that could not be finalized for all 17 participants as yet. Additionally, some video recordings had to be excluded because of experimental error.

In order to pursue the question of whether picture material can change the maternal gestural behavior, the participants were divided into two groups. Eight of the dyads participated in a "noun group" – that is, the book they were reading depicted single objects (e.g. a cup). Nine of the dyads participated in a "relation group", in which the book depicted objects in relation to each other (e.g. a cup on a table).

Procedure

Two research assistants visited the mother–child dyads at their homes. The mother and her child were asked to sit on the floor and to read a book together in a comfortable position. The book was designed with photographs (see the next subsection, "Materials"). There was no time limit for the reading activity.

Before reading the book, the dyads engaged in a free-play situation with toys that were provided in four bags, each containing three toy sets. The mother was instructed to play with her child as she would usually do and the experimenter left the room. After five minutes, the experimenter exchanged the toys by providing another bag with toys, and again left the room.

To videotape the situation, the camera was always positioned in front of the dyad. Subsequently, the recordings were coded using an XML-format program called MARTHA.

At all visits, we asked the mothers to fill out the language survey ELFRA (Grimm and Doil 2000), where parents check the words they think their child produces or comprehends. This survey is standardized, and thus a reliable method to obtain insights into the child's productive and receptive vocabulary development.

Materials

For the book-reading situation, we designed two picturebooks that consisted of 12–14 laminated pages, each showing a colored photograph. This way, we were able to carefully and systematically differentiate between two types of books, as follows.

In the noun group, the book depicted individual objects such as a cup or a swing (see Figure 5.2, top). However, it was important to us to show the

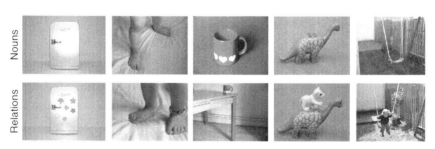

Figure 5.2 Examples of the pictures used in the books. The noun group (top) received a book depicting (single) objects; the relation group (bottom) received a book depicting two objects in relation to each other.

objects in a possible context. Thus, the swing, for example, is in the foreground while other objects can be seen in the background. The same is true for the baby feet. The book in the relation group consisted of pictures showing objects in relation, such as a cup on a table or a child on a swing (see Figure 5.2, bottom).

Overall, the chosen materials are quite typical of "early-concept books" (Kümmerling-Meibauer and Meibauer 2005) that display individual objects and events from the child's surroundings without any text. However, our pictures were not composed for a literary purpose, as their order was not related to a story. In fact, the order of the pictures was randomized for each visit.

For the free-play situation, mother–child dyads were provided with toys (such as magnets and a magnetic board, a doll with a necklace, a fishing rod, nesting cups, building blocks) that enabled a variety of activities. To make the situation comparable to that for the "relation group", we also provided toys that could be put in relation to one another. The toys were given in randomized order for each visit and each dyad.

Coding of nonverbal behavior

McNeill (1992: 25) characterizes a gesture as happening in three phases. The first phase is the preparation, in which "the hand rises from its resting place". The second, and main, phase is called "stroke", in which the gesture appears to be highly synchronized with speech. In the final retraction phase, the gesture returns to the rest position. These phases are important aspects in analyzing Examples 3–5 in the "Results" section.

Here we report on only one category of maternal nonverbal behavior: the gesture type *pointing*. What differentiates pointing from, say, iconic gestures is the fact that it refers to an immediate object or event. Iconic gestures, in contrast, can depict an object or event (e.g. moving a finger back and forth can depict how to cut bread). Iconic gestures have been found to be rare in input to children (Iverson et al. 1999). In contrast, manipulative gestures (Rohlfing 2011) are common in adults interacting with children. The purpose of manipulative gestures is to facilitate the child's own action and to achieve a goal. For example, if a child tries to turn the page, an adult might position the book in front of the child in order to facilitate the object's manipulation. Manipulative gestures are different from pointing gestures in that they are actions that can be perceived as communicative. Pointing, in contrast, can be defined as a gesture performed with an arm or hand that involves a pointing finger extension; it is communicative in its nature. In Figure 5.1, both the child and the mother are performing a pointing gesture. Pointing gestures were found to be the most common nonverbal behavior in the interaction with a child (Iverson et al. 1999). However, the types of gestures are not evident in every situation and thus cannot be identified easily for all cases. In Figure 5.1, while the mother performs a pointing gesture her pointing finger simultaneously fixates the page of attention: only when she takes the finger away can the page be turned. This way, the mother decides when to turn to the next object, and at the same time the child is prevented from turning the page, an activity that children find attractive at this age. Thus, the pointing finger serves a manipulative purpose here as well.

Results

Comparison of gestural behavior across two contexts: book reading and free play

Following Yont and colleagues (2004), who found that caregivers' input differs with respect to the context, we assumed that different gestural behavior can be elicited in book-reading compared to free-play situations. More specifically, we expected gestural behavior to facilitate the way caregivers refer to objects or events by fostering joint attention to the depicted event.

When looking at the quantity of pointing at the time when the children were 14 months old, we found a significant difference between the number of maternal pointing gestures used in free play ($M=0.01$, $SD=0.009$ gestures/words) and book reading ($M=0.05$, $SD=0.03$ gestures/words) when we controlled for the overall number of words that the mothers produced ($Z=-3.6$, $p<0.001$). The child's pointing behavior also differed significantly between these two situations: According to a Wilcoxon test ($Z=-2.7$, $p<0.01$), children pointed significantly more during book reading ($M=6.35$, $SD=5.94$) than in free play ($M=2.65$, $SD=4.24$).

In the following, we present five cases of pointing episodes that exemplify the quality of the nonverbal behavior and that we consider to be typical for – even though not limited to – the book-reading situation. We then discuss the value of these pointing behaviors as a strategy by whichto learn language. We further compare how common these episodes are in book-reading and free-play situations.

EXAMPLE 1: Pointing and labeling
In this example, the mother is reading a book that depicts single objects to her 18-month-old child. As can be seen in (1), she turns the page, looks at the picture (2), and (3) while pointing to the object, she provides a label, "Puppe" ("doll") for it. The child is following her actions with his gaze (1–3). The mother then looks at the child (4) and elaborates more on the picture by telling him that the doll is made not of plastic but of fabric. One can assume that she is not gazing at the picture while mentioning the fabric because she is referring to something that is not directly accessible – that is, it cannot be perceived via the picture directly.

This example is typical in two respects. First, mothers point to an object in the picture and label it. Murphy (1978) observed that for young children – particularly 14-month-olds – a pointing gesture is accompanied by naming the referent. The pointing gesture has been recognized as attracting attention even in very young children (Rohlfing *et al.* 2012). This way, the child's focus is likely

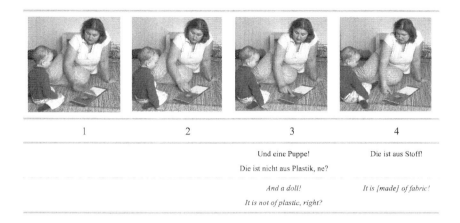

Figure 5.3 Pointing to and labeling depicted objects. The mother is clearly pointing to the body of the doll.

to be on the referent when she or he hears the label. Second, mothers then provide more information about the object by elaborating on it. This elaboration results in the child receiving not only a single label for an object but also hearing some utterances with the label and other words that are related to it semantically.

In comparison to free play, we found that mothers of 14-month-olds used 47.6 percent of their pointing to label objects on the pictures, while only 9.6 percent of pointing was used for the same activity during free play. According to a Wilcoxon test, this difference was statistically significant ($Z = -3.57$, $p < 0.001$). This finding strongly suggests that pointing and labeling is a pragmatic strategy very typical in book-reading situations with 14-month-olds.

EXAMPLE 2: Pointing and asking questions
Figure 5.4 shows a 23-month-old child with her mother in a book-reading situation. The age of the child (the fact that she is older than the children in other examples) is representative of this example. This is because mothers increasingly ask questions starting at around 18 months of age. A similar observation is made by Murphy (1978), reporting that "when mothers of 20- and 24-month-old infants point they are very likely to accompany the point with a wh-question". According to Murphy (ibid.: 376), these questions formulate a request to the child to demonstrate "either naming what the mother is pointing to [...]; describing some attribute of the referent [...]; or pointing to another aspect of the picture". It is by 20 months of age that Murphy observes infants starting to provide their own verbal labels. In our example, the mother turns the page (1) and, while pointing to the depicted object, she immediately asks the question "what is this?" (2). The girl answers by providing the correct label, as she says "table!" (3). The mother acknowledges this response by repeating the label and

| 1 | 2 | 3 | 4 |

Mother: "Was ist das?" Child: "Tisch!" Mother: "Ein Tisch!"
"What is this?" "table!" "A table!"

Figure 5.4 Pointing while asking questions and eliciting the names of objects from the child.

providing the indefinite article "a table"; she then moves on to the next picture (4). From this example, it becomes apparent that the picture and the pointing gesture serve a particular function: Together with the mother's question "what is this?", they elicit a label from the child. In this example, the child seems to comfortably know what her part in this routine is. As Murphy (ibid.: 379) puts it, for children aged 20 months and older, pointing is a well-established activity coordinated with speech and sophisticated in its use.

To answer the question of whether pointing in combination with asking questions is a pragmatic strategy typical for book reading, we compared maternal behavior to 14-month-old children in a free-play situation to the situation in which a book was read. We found that mothers asked questions about the objects and events on the pictures together with 11.8 percent of their pointing gestures, while only 2.6 percent of pointing was used for the same activity during free play. According to a Wilcoxon test, this difference was marginally significant ($Z = -1.8$, $p = 0.07$).

EXAMPLE 3: Pointing to relations
The next example relates directly to the findings reported by Murphy (1978) and Rohlfing (2011). Both authors identified multiple pointing gestures that are performed "without any break between them" (Murphy 1978: 375). While Murphy calls these discrete combinations of points "pointing string", Rohlfing (2011: 169) uses the term "pointing saccades". Murphy (1978: 379) observed this behavior during shared book reading and suggests that this pointing can indicate numerous components of a picture. Rohlfing (2011), however, identified this behavior in a task-oriented dialogue in which it is used towards young children with reference to two objects in a sequence, without the usual retraction phase (see the "Methods" section, pp. 103–106, for more details on different phases in gestural performance). Her semantic interpretation is that this

| 1 | 2 | 3 | 4 |

Mother: "und ein kleiner Löwe ist da drauf"   Mother: "auf dem Rücken steht er"

"and a little lion is on the top"   *"on the back, he is standing"*

Figure 5.5 Pointing to relations. The mother alternately points at the lion, which is on top of a dinosaur, and at the dinosaur's back to highlight the spatial relationship between those two objects.

behavior indicates a "togetherness" of the relationship between the two objects to young children (ibid.).

In our data from book readings, we found many pointing saccades in support of Murphy's observations. In Figure 5.5, the pointing saccade becomes visible by the fact that the pointing finger of the mother moves up and down along the page. More specifically, in (1) the mother of a 15-month-old child indicates the lion on top of a dinosaur. Then, without retracting her gesture, the mother pushes her index finger even more firmly against the book (2) and moves her gesture to the other object to indicate the relationship (3). After pointing out the other object, the dinosaur, she moves her gesture to the original object (4). This is a very typical pattern in our observations: in order to emphasize certain aspects (here, the relationship) even more, the mother says, "auf dem Rücken steht er" ("it is standing on the back") and puts more stress on her gesture, moving it dynamically to point out relevant features (the back of the dinosaur). Finally, the gesture returns to its origin – that is, where it was initiated. Against Murphy's (1978) assumption that such combinations of points indicate numerous components of a picture, we argue that by pointing repeatedly to particular components in the picture, a correspondence of those components is indicated. We do not argue that the mother intentionally draws the saccade. Instead, we think that separate gestures are responsible for the appearance of a pointing pattern "mainly because of the dynamics and incrementality of the verbal-gestural thinking that has brought them to life" (Rohlfing and Kopp 2007). It is likely that such patterns create a conceptual focus for the child and thus organize the child's attention.

EXAMPLE 4: Pointing to a group of objects
In the next example, the child, aged 18 months, leans forward to the picture, saying, "da" ("here"), and the mother points to the picture, which shows a

1	2	3	4
Child: "Da!" Mother: "Ein Kühlschrank!" *"Here!"* *"Fridge!"*	Mother: "Da kleben kleine Magnete dran" *"There are small magnets sticking to it"*		

Figure 5.6 With the pointing finger of her left hand, the mother points to a group of similar objects.

refrigerator with some magnets on it, and labels the object first "ein Kühlschrank" ("a refrigerator") (1). She then elaborates on the object by pointing out the single magnets on the refrigerator and saying, "Da kleben kleine Magnete dran" ("there are small magnets sticking to it") (2–4). The magnets are of different shapes (stars, squares, etc.) and the mother is pointing to the different magnets quickly in a sequence. Thus, one label refers to a category of different objects.

Without retracting her gestures, the mother points out a group of similar components (Murphy 1978) – that is, she organizes this category of things that the child needs to perceive as similar. This observation adds a "perceptual structure" (Zukow-Goldring 1996) to the findings by Gelman and colleagues (2005), who suggested that when referring to pictures, mothers highlight the object's membership to a category by pointing out similarities (see also Ganea and Canfield, this volume, Chapter 2).

EXAMPLE 5: Pointing to real objects
The mother of this 11-month-old child looks at the picture of baby feet in the book, but starts by referring to the baby's own foot. As can be seen in Figure 5.7, she takes the child's sock off and points to her foot first by saying, "Guck mal!" ("Look!") (1). Then she points at one foot on the picture and labels it "Da Füße!" ("There, feet!") (2). She then quickly returns to the child's foot by touching and petting it with her pointing finger (3). Finally, she tickles the child's foot (4) to let her feel the body part and says, "Killerfüße!" ("Tickle-Feet!"), and the child starts to laugh.

Overall, the mother puts a lot of effort into the situation, to let the child not only perceive the referent visually but also feel it by touch and, finally, positive

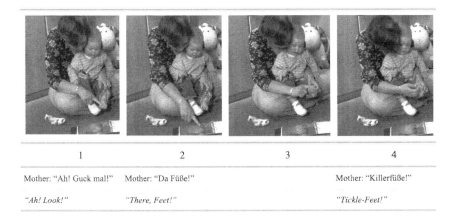

| 1 | 2 | 3 | 4 |

Mother: "Ah! Guck mal!"   Mother: "Da Füße!"   Mother: "Killerfüße!"

"Ah! Look!"   "There, Feet!"   "Tickle-Feet!"

Figure 5.7 Pointing to real objects. In this case (as in Figure 5.5), the child is sitting on the mother's lap. It seems that this position enables the mother to manipulate the child's body easily (taking the sock off), as she can use both hands for this action.

emotions. While the word "feet" is provided only once to both the real and the depicted body part (2–3), the pointing gesture is performed twice to each referent. The pointing pattern that emerges from the real to the depicted referent can also be seen as a form of trajectory linking the picture with the real world and indicating their correspondence.

In summary, extending the results presented by Murphy (1978), we found that particular multimodal strategies such as pointing and labeling, and pointing and asking questions, are more typical in book reading than in free play (Example 1 and 2). Examples 3–5 extend the findings reported by Rohlfing (2011), and suggest that pointing saccades are about semantic correspondence of the depicted and the pointed out entities.

Does maternal pointing at the age of 14 months mediate later language acquisition?

So far, we have shown that in book reading, mothers use specific types of behavior when pointing to depicted events or objects. A remaining question is whether this behavior relates to children's later language development. Consolidating previous findings, we hypothesized that for young children at the age of 14 months, the book-reading situation will reveal a more crucial relation between maternal gestures and the child's subsequent vocabulary development (assessed via ELFRA) than a free-play situation.

We found that maternal gestural behavior correlated positively with receptive ($r_s(9)=0.87$, $p<0.01$) and productive ($r_s(9)=0.74$, $p<0.05$) vocabulary when the children were aged 14 months. Accordingly, the more children speak and understand at the age of 14 months, the more the mothers will apply their pointing gestures in the interaction. In looking at the data longitudinally, we could not find such a significant correlation for children aged 11 months ($r_s(8) = 0.51$, $p = 0.25$). Further, when the children were 18 months old, their reported vocabulary and the gestural input ($r_s(8) = 0.08$, $p = 0.8$) were only marginally related to one another. Thus, we can confirm that the age of 14 months seems to be particularly related to maternal nonverbal input.

Of particular interest to us is, however, the question of whether there is a longitudinal effect that captures a relation between behavior in early interaction and the child's language acquisition at a *later* age. A regression analysis allowed us to determine what maternal behavior is predictive of children's reported vocabulary at the age of 24 months. We found that only the gesture–speech combination of the mother – that is, the number of words accompanied by gestures in the book reading (but not in the free play) at the child's age of 14 months – could explain 39 percent of the variance that we find in the productive vocabulary when the children are 24 months old: $F(1,8) = 5.125$, $p < 0.05$ ($\beta = 0.625$). Thus, maternal gestural behavior in combination with speech in early book-reading situations can be viewed as crucial for language development. This finding supports Rowe and Goldin-Meadow's (2009) findings suggesting that early multimodal interaction at the child's age of 14 months is related to the child's further language development. A crucial extension of the findings reported by Rowe and Pan (2004) is that it was not the gestural behavior during book reading on its own, but its combination with speech, that was predictive of children's language development ten months later.

Different picture material and maternal pointing behavior

In line with our previous research (Nachtigäller and Rohlfing 2011b), which showed that mothers were more likely to provide narrative structure to their children when more objects were presented in the book, our hypothesis for nonverbal behavior was that different picture materials will elicit different pointing behavior. We expected the "relation group" to gesture more than the "noun group", simply because more components are depicted in the relation book, and thus mothers have more possibilities to indicate something.

We performed a 3 (different age groups) × 2 (noun/relation book) ANOVA with repeated measures and found no significant effects of age or the book's content on maternal gestural behavior. Contrary to our expectation, in the noun group mothers seemed to gesture more ($M = 19.5$ in the relation book and $M = 23.7$ in the noun book). This finding might reflect individual differences rather than the effect of condition, which is supported by the fact that mothers in the "noun group" were gesturing more than mothers in the "relations group" even in the free-play condition ($M = 66.7$ in the noun group and $M = 40.6$ in the relation group). For children, the book content was also not significant: in both groups, children produced a similar number of gestures ($M = 4$).

With respect to the different pointing patterns introduced above (Examples 1–5), across the investigated ages we found significantly more saccades indicating similarities ($Z=-2.714$, $p<0.01$) or relationships ($Z=-1.912$, $p=0.056$) among the depicted objects in the "relations group" rather than the "noun group".

In summary, contrary to our expectations the relation book does not trigger more gestures. However, we found that the occurrence of some pointing patterns is influenced by the book's content. We can therefore conclude that while the book's content does not seem to influence gestural behavior of the dyad, it does trigger some specific types of pointing saccades.

Discussion

In this specific situation of reading a picturebook to a young child, both interactional partners are jointly focusing their attention on the book. This focus, in turn, seems to be structured by the caregiver in a specific way when compared to freeplay situations. Through recent studies, we are beginning to understand the potential parameters that are responsible for the effects that such a context has on language acquisition. While verbal input is under investigation in current research, little is known about how gestures contribute to language acquisition in this situation, even though they are visibly a part of an ongoing activity. Thus, we asked three questions: (1) what kind of gestural input plays a role in joint bookreading? (2) At what age are children particularly sensitive to a caregiver's nonverbal behavior? (3) Does the content of a book influence nonverbal behavior?

Pursuing question (1), we identified various forms of pointing that are typical for reading books to young children that might be particularly effective in enhancing children's vocabulary skills. We found that pointing in combination with labeling as well as asking questions was particularly common during book reading when compared to free play. While these strategies are well known (Murphy 1978), we also provided new observations. Concerning the semantics of pointing gestures, we argue that a deictic gesture does more than merely highlight the referent: by indicating various components of the pictures without being retracted, a pointing gesture can create an iconic pattern (Rohlfing and Kopp 2007). In our examples, the pattern captures the correspondence of the different components, as either a relationship or a category. Even though in our examples, we identify multimodal strategies that the mothers use, we cannot answer the question of how these strategies affect the language acquisition process in children. One possibility is that these strategies are a form of structuring the child's perception: they combine social signals that attract attention and thus facilitate the child's perception of the referent(s). Another possibility is that these strategies emerge as a product of routinized dialogical reading. In this case, they need to be established jointly by recurring opportunities for this activity. This provides the basis for the child to develop expectations about the interactants' roles, which is reflected by the fact that children pointed more in the book-reading situation than in free play.

With respect to question (2), and in line with previous studies (Murphy 1978; Rowe and Goldin-Meadow 2009), we found that maternal speech at the children's age of 14 months, when combined with nonverbal behavior during shared book reading – but not during free play – predicted children's later vocabulary development at 24 months. Thus, the combination of maternal gestural behavior with speech in early book-reading situations can be viewed as crucial for language development and should be considered in programs promoting "dialogical reading" (Whitehurst *et al.* 1988) to young children. The goal of dialogical reading as a specific method of reading picturebooks is to encourage the child to participate actively in a dialogue (see also the chapters by Blewitt and Reese in this volume, Chapters 6 and 10 respectively). Parents should become trained not only in verbal but also in gestural behavior and in how to adapt it to children's language capabilities.

Finally, question (3) investigated whether the nonverbal behavior of mothers differed with respect to the book's content. In our approach, we provided different books, one with single objects (e.g. a cup) and another that depicted objects in relation to each other (e.g. a cup on a table), to two different groups. As we could not find significant differences in the quantity of nonverbal behavior in mothers between the book material conditions, our results allow us to suggest that the activity in itself, more than the content of the book, is a valuable situation, in which mothers and children can jointly and multimodally participate in a dialogue. However, our conclusions are limited by the ages studied and the applied picture materials. Further research should address the effects of storybooks on parental multimodal behavior. Against the background of our previous research (Nachtigäller and Rohlfing 2011b), we further assume that a particular book content might influence narrative behavior more than gestural behavior, even though some qualitative differences could be observed in our study. Future and more detailed analyses of gesture–speech semantics are required to answer the questions of whether and in what form gestural behavior corresponds with narratives, whether causal, temporal narrative structures can be conveyed via gestures, and what forms of gestural behavior can help children grasp narrative aspects.

With our analyses, we contribute to the characterization of the pragmatic behavior in joint book reading, as it constitutes specific verbal and nonverbal maternal input on the one hand and children's interactional behavior on the other hand. Both should be acknowledged in theories of language acquisition as well as in programs promoting reading strategies. Both explain why book reading is a "positive activity in which to engage with young children" (Reese, this volume).

Acknowledgements

The research reported in this article was made possible by a Dilthey Fellowship from the Volkswagen Foundation to Katharina Rohlfing. Many thanks to all mothers and children who participated in this study.

References

Bakeman, Roger and Lauren B. Adamson. 1984. "Coordinating attention to people and objects in mother–infant and peer–infant interaction". *Child Development* 55: 1278–1289.
Baldwin, Dare A. 1995. "Understanding the link between joint attention and language". In *Joint Attention: Its Origins and Role in Development*, edited by Chris Moore and Philip J. Dunham. 131–158. Hillsdale, NJ: Lawrence Erlbaum.
Booth, Amy E., Karla K. McGregor, and Katharina J. Rohlfing. 2008. "Socio-pragmatics and attention: Contributions to gesturally guided word learning in toddlers". *Language Learning and Development* 4: 179–202.
Della Corte, Maria, Helen Benedict, and Diane Klein. 1983. "The relationship of pragmatic dimensons of mothers' speech to the referential–expressive distinction". *Journal of Child Language* 10: 35–43.
De Temple, Jeanne and Catherine E. Snow. 2003. "Learning words from books". In *On Reading Books to Children: Parents and Teachers*, edited by Anne van Kleeck, Steven A. Stahl, and Eurydice B. Bauer. 16–36. Mahwah, NJ: Lawrence Erlbaum.
Gelman, Susan A., Robert J. Chesnik, and Sandra R. Waxman. 2005. "Mother–child conversations about pictures and objects: Referring to categories and individuals". *Child Development* 76: 1129–1143.
Grimm, Hannelore and Hildegard Doil. 2000. *Elternfragebögen für die Früherkennung von Risikokindern*. Göttingen: Hogrefe.
Horst, Jessica S., Kelly L. Parsons, and Natasha M. Bryan. 2011. "Get the story straight: Contextual repetition promotes word learning from storybooks". *Frontiers in Psychology* 2: 1–11.
Iverson, Jana M., Olga Capirci, Emiddia Longobardi, and M. Cristina Caselli. 1999. "Gesturing in mother–child interactions". *Cognitive Development* 14: 57–75.
Kümmerling-Meibauer, Bettina and Jörg Meibauer. 2005. "First pictures, early concepts: Early concept books". *The Lion and the Unicorn* 29: 324–347.
Liszkowski, Ulf. 2005. "Human twelve-month-olds point cooperatively to share interest with and helpfully provide information for a communicative partner". *Gesture* 5: 135–154.
McNeill, David. 1992. *Hand and Mind: What Gestures Reveal about Thought*. Chicago: University of Chicago Press.
Mundy, Peter, Jessica Block, Christine Delgado, Yuly Pomares, Amy V. Van Heck, and Meaghan V. Parlade. 2007. "Individual differences and the development of joint attention in infancy". *Child Development* 78: 938–954.
Murphy, Catherine M. 1978. "Pointing in the context of a shared activity". *Child Development* 49: 371–380.
Nachtigäller, Kerstin and Katharina J. Rohlfing. 2011a. "Einfluss von erlebten und vorgestellten Ereignissen auf die Erzählweise in kindgerichteter Sprache". *Zeitschrift für Literaturwissenschaft und Linguistik* 162: 139–155.
Nachtigäller, Kerstin and Katharina J. Rohlfing. 2011b. "Mothers' talking about early object and action concepts during picture book reading". In *Emergent Literacy:*

Children's Books from 0 to 3, edited by Bettina Kümmerling-Meibauer. 193–208. Amsterdam: John Benjamins.

Pellegrini, Anthony D. and Lee Galda. 2003. "Joint reading as a context: Explicating the ways context is created by participants". In *On Reading Books to Children: Parents and Teachers*, edited by Anne van Kleeck, Steven A. Stahl, and Eurydice B. Bauer. 321–335. Mahwah, NJ: Lawrence Erlbaum.

Reese, Elaine, Alison Sparks, and Diana Leyva. 2010. "A review of parent interventions for preschool children's language and emergent literacy". *Journal of Early Childhood Literacy* 10: 97–117.

Rohlfing, Katharina J. 2011. "Meaning in the objects". In *Experimental Pragmatics/Semantics*, edited by Jörg Meibauer and Markus Steinbach. 151–176. Amsterdam: John Benjamins.

Rohlfing, Katharina J. and Stefan Kopp. 2007. "Meaning in the timing? The emergence of complex pointing patterns". In *Proceedings from Symposium on Language and Robots*. 79–82. Aveiro, Portugal, December.

Rohlfing, Katharina J., Matthew R. Longo, and Bennett I. Bertenthal. 2012. "Dynamic pointing triggers shift of visual attention in young infants". *Developmental Science* 15: 426–435.

Rowe, Meredith L. and Susan Goldin-Meadow. 2009. "Early gesture selectively predicts later language learning". *Developmental Science* 12: 182–187.

Rowe, Meredith and Barbara A. Pan. 2004. "Maternal pointing and toddler vocabulary production during bookreading versus toy play". Poster presented at 14th Biennial International Conference on Infant Studies, Chicago, May 5–8.

Snow, Catherine E. and Beverly A. Goldfield. 1983. "Turn the page please: Situation-specific language acquisition". *Journal of Child Language* 10: 551–569.

Tomasello, Michael and Michael J. Farrar. 1986. "Joint attention and early language". *Child Development* 57: 1454–1463.

Whitehurst, Grover J., Francine L. Falco, Christopher J. Lonigan, Janet E. Fischel, Barbara O. DeBaryshe, Marta C. Valdez-Menchaca, and Marie Caulfield. 1988. "Accelerating language development through picture book reading". *Developmental Psychology* 24: 552–559.

Yont, Kristine M., Catherine E. Snow, and Lynne Vernon-Feagans. 2003. "The role of context in mother–child interactions: An analysis of communicative intents expressed during toy play and book reading with 12-month-olds". *Journal of Pragmatics* 35: 435–454.

Zukow-Goldring, Patricia. 1996. "Sensitive caregiving fosters the comprehension of speech: When gestures speak louder than words". *Early Development and Parenting* 5: 195–211.

6 Growing vocabulary in the context of shared book reading

Pamela Blewitt

Children's literature and adults' reading to children contribute to every aspect of language growth, from vocabulary building to metalinguistic understanding. Reading to young children gives them exposure to new words and practice with grammatical forms and pragmatic conventions. Children's literature introduces them to the notion that language is a decontextualized symbolic medium – that is, a vehicle for representing concepts and experiences beyond the immediate context. This chapter focuses on how children's literature and adults' reading to children (shared reading) helps build children's vocabularies.

The importance of vocabulary growth in early childhood cannot be overstated, especially for children's success in school. Typically developing children show substantial individual differences in vocabulary size as early as 3 years old (Hart and Risley 1995; Weizman and Snow 2001). These differences remain fairly stable after age 5, and they predict children's reading comprehension and overall academic performance, especially after age 9 (Sénéchal and LeFevre 2002; Stanovich 1986; Storch and Whitehurst 2002). In most school systems, 9-year-olds are expected to have mastered the mechanics of reading so that they can use reading as a tool for learning. Having a good vocabulary makes learning from reading more efficient, giving children with larger vocabularies a learning advantage and explaining in part why early-emerging vocabulary differences begin to correlate with school achievement (e.g. Ouellette 2006).

The contribution that shared reading can make to early vocabulary growth is well documented. Children's literature provides exposure to new words and to familiar words in new contexts (e.g. DeTemple and Snow 2003; Dickinson *et al.* 2003). A host of experimental studies have verified that young children learn words from shared reading (e.g. Ard and Beverly 2004; Biemiller and Boote 2006; Blewitt *et al.* 2009; Elley 1989; Ewers and Brownson 1999; Hargrave and Sénéchal 2000; Justice 2002; Justice *et al.* 2005; Penno *et al.* 2002; Reese and Cox 1999; Robbins and Ehri 1994; Sénéchal 1997; Sénéchal and Cornell 1993; Sénéchal *et al.* 1995). And longitudinal studies of families have found that how much parents read to their very young children predicts the children's vocabulary by age 5, even when factors such as parents' education and children's intelligence are taken into account (e.g. Administration for Children and Families 2003; Raikes *et al.* 2006; Rodriguez *et al.* 2009; Sénéchal and LeFevre 2002).

This chapter begins with a brief examination of the processes involved in word learning and building a good vocabulary, followed by a review of evidence that young children grow their vocabularies at different rates, especially if we compare children from families of differing socioeconomic status (SES). The chapter then addresses the following question: given that reading to children is a valuable context for early vocabulary acquisition, are there extratextual strategies that adults can use when reading to young children that might enhance word learning from children's literature?

Research on the effects of shared book reading on vocabulary acquisition often targets children's learning of labels for objects. Therefore, much of this chapter specifically relates to the influence of adult reading strategies on children's acquisition of concrete nouns. Whether or not some of the findings generalize to other word types is yet to be established, although it seems likely that they do.

How vocabulary grows

Fast mapping

As Susan Carey elegantly demonstrated over 30 years ago, vocabulary expands in two ways (Carey 1978; Carey and Bartlett 1978). The first of these is called *fast mapping*. When children hear a new word, they are likely to associate its phonological form with a referent or with some aspect of the referential situation and then to store the phonological form in their lexical memory. This process helps children add new words to their vocabularies quickly, increasing the *breadth* of their vocabularies. Carey and Bartlett (1978) showed that young children may associate a word to superficial aspects of a referent with just one or two exposures. With concrete nouns, children tend to link the word to the initial referent's appearance. Figure 6.1 illustrates this simple associative process for the word *airplane*.

Much of the available research on how young children learn concrete nouns is about the fast mapping phase of word learning. Studies assess what happens

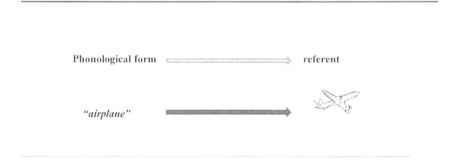

Figure 6.1 Fast mapping of a new word occurs when the phonological form of the word is associated with a referent, illustrated here using the word "airplane".

when children first hear a new word. For example, researchers have identified some interesting tendencies, which are often described as word learning biases or constraints (e.g. Hollich *et al.* 2000; Markman 1991; Merriman and Bowman 1989; Woodward and Markman 1998). If a speaker points to an object and says "Manty", a child is likely to assume that the nonsense word is a label for the whole object rather than for one of its parts. This tendency is called the "whole object bias". If a speaker points to a display of two or more objects and says "Where's the manty?", children usually select a novel object rather than one they can already label. This tendency is called the "mutual exclusivity bias", because children appear to assume that labels are mutually exclusive such that new names cannot apply to objects with known labels. Another line of research examines children's sensitivity to social cues that might establish a word's referent. For example, young children are likely to follow a speaker's direction of eye gaze to determine the referent of a new word (e.g. Akhtar *et al.* 2001; Baldwin 1991, 1993; Hollich *et al.* 2000). Overall, young children's word-learning biases and their sensitivity to social cues contribute positively to fast mapping, even though there is always the potential for errors.

Many of the measures that are used to document vocabulary growth are assessments of how children compare to others with regard to their vocabulary *breadth* – that is, the number of words they have in their mental lexicon. These measures only require that children have fast-mapped the words. For example, the Peabody Picture Vocabulary Test, now in its fourth edition (PPVT–IV; Dunn and Dunn 2007), is a widely used, standardized test of the size of a child's receptive vocabulary. It uses a multiple choice approach to determining whether children can identify appropriate referents of a word. For each test word that children hear, they must select a referent from four pictures. Children can correctly respond as long as they have superficially mapped the test word to a typical referent.

Slow mapping

Acquiring full understanding of a word's meaning and use requires a longer, second phase of learning called *slow mapping*. This time-dependent process corrects errors that might occur during fast mapping, and it builds a more nuanced and elaborated representation in the child's mental lexicon. With concrete nouns, for example, slow mapping includes identifying the appearance of multiple referents and sorting out critical perceptual properties from those that are simply characteristic or even serendipitous. It includes learning about the referents' functions: their actions, processes, and/or uses. It also involves learning the word's taxonomic place, such as the superordinate categories it is part of, and the subordinate kinds it includes, thus linking the word to other words and concepts and creating a network of semantic connections. Such meaning elaboration seems most likely to occur if children experience multiple exposures to a word with a range of referents in a variety of contexts. In Figure 6.2, you can see how the meaning of *airplane* is likely to expand and refine as children hear

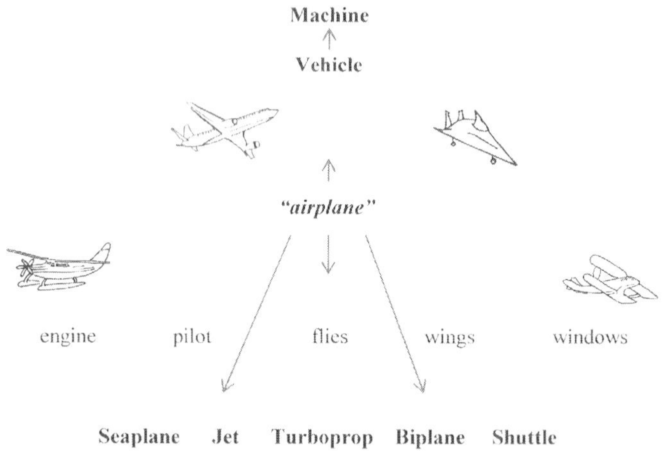

Figure 6.2 Slow mapping includes identifying typical functions, activities, parts, and perceptual features of a word's referents, as well as forming links to words and concepts that are taxonomically related, such as superordinate and subordinate categories. This figure illustrates some of the information that might be associated with the word "airplane" during slow mapping.

the word in new situations. Slow mapping can be thought of as increasing the *depth* of a child's vocabulary.

The slow mapping process is less often studied and less well understood than fast mapping. Measuring elaborated knowledge of a word is more difficult than determining whether a child can recognize or identify a word's referent. Most often, researchers ask children to define words, and then they count and/or categorize the correct units of information (or semantic features) that children provide. One of the problems with this kind of assessment strategy is that knowing "what to say" when asked to define a word is a skill in itself, one that seems to depend on children's exposure to good definitions and to practice (e.g. Snow 1990). The difficulty of measuring elaborated word knowledge is perhaps one reason that slow mapping is less often studied than fast mapping.

Social class and vocabulary

Vocabulary breadth

When researchers measure the relative size of young children's vocabularies, they usually find that children in higher socioeconomic groups perform better than lower-SES children (e.g. Hart and Risley 1995; Hoff 2003). For example, in two studies Blewitt and colleagues have used the Peabody Picture Vocabulary Test to compare children from blue-collar (lower-middle-income) families to those from more affluent, upper-middle-income families (Dolena and Blewitt 2009; Sorhagen and Blewitt 2010). Children were 3- and 5-year-olds from families in predominantly white suburban communities surrounding the large city of Philadelphia. In both studies, children from upper-income families showed a substantial advantage in overall vocabulary size compared to lower-income children, although all age and SES groups achieved at least average performance levels.

Many researchers have found that SES differences in vocabulary breadth are associated with variations in the amount and quality of language input children experience. Parents' language input to children predicts children's vocabulary size (e.g. Hart and Risley 1995; Huttenlocher *et al.* 1991; Tamis-LeMonda *et al.* 2006; Weizman and Snow 2001). Parents in lower-SES families tend to have fewer conversations with their young children, are less likely to respond to the content of their children's verbalizations, and expose their children to less language and fewer explanations of words overall than parents from higher-SES families (e.g. Hart and Risley 1995; Hoff 2003; Ninio 1980). As noted earlier, one of the contexts in which parents are likely to expose children to rich language input is shared reading. On average, parents in lower-SES families spend less time reading to their young children than parents in higher-SES families (e.g. Anderson *et al.* 1980; Bradley *et al.* 2001; Burns and Blewitt 2000).

Vocabulary depth

Very few studies have explored relative differences among children with regard to their slow mapping of words – that is, vocabulary depth. Do children with larger vocabularies (greater vocabulary breadth) also have more elaborated knowledge of the words in their vocabularies? Given the SES differences in language input to children, and given that repeated exposure to a word may be important for slow mapping, it seems likely that higher-SES children would tend to have more elaborated word meanings than lower-SES children, creating a second layer of advantage with regard to vocabulary.

Blewitt and colleagues report data that support this idea (Dolena and Blewitt 2009; Sorhagen and Blewitt 2010). For example, they assessed not only children's vocabulary breadth but also their vocabulary depth. The primary measure of elaborated word knowledge was a word-defining task. For this purpose, it was important to test words that children had at least fast-mapped so that the words were familiar. Appropriate test words were identified in pilot studies with young preschoolers from the same schools as those from which participants for the main studies were recruited. The pilot test mimicked the multiple choice procedure for measuring word comprehension used in the Peabody Picture Vocabulary Test. Children had to select the correct referent for a test word from a set of four pictured items. If all pilot participants responded correctly, the word was regarded as familiar, and it was eligible for inclusion as a test word in the word-defining task. The test words in each study included labels for artifacts and natural kinds, such as *airplane* and *horse*.

A good "Aristotelian" definition situates a word by mentioning a *superordinate category* – that is, a general class that subsumes the labeled concept, such as "An *airplane* is a machine..." A good definition also lists one or more criterial characteristics that might be perceptual features, parts, or functions, such as "An *airplane* is a machine with wings that flies through the air..." Finally, a good definition may list *subordinate categories* – that is, kinds subsumed by the labeled concept, such as "An *airplane* is a machine with wings that flies through the air, such as a jet".

Children in the studies by Blewitt and colleagues were asked to define test words for a very curious stuffed animal. The children's word definitions were not models of the classic, Aristotelian form, but many children could provide information that would be considered part of a definition for at least some of the words. For example, for *airplane* they might say "It flies", or "Wings", or "It can be a jet", or "You ride in it". Coders counted how many units, or individual pieces of information, children offered that matched what could be considered defining, and they coded the types of information. Among the types were *perceptual features* (shape, color, size, sound, taste, smell), *functional characteristics* (processes, uses or actions), *parts*, and *taxonomic associates* (superordinate and subordinate categories). There were social class differences in how much information children provided (see Figure 6.3).

Upper-middle-class children produced more units of information at each age level. Generally, at each level of SES, older children offered more information units than younger children, but for some kinds of information, lower-income

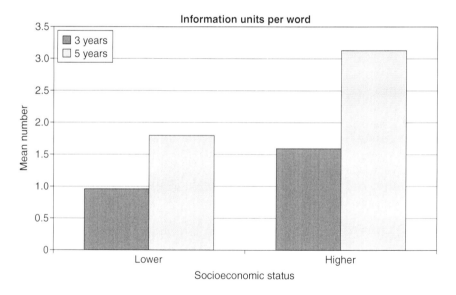

Figure 6.3 Mean number of information units of all types in 3- and 5-year-olds' definitions of familiar test words in Dolena and Blewitt (2009). Children were from lower- and upper-middle-class families.

5-year-olds seemed to have made little progress in their word knowledge relative to lower-income 3-year-olds. This was particularly true for taxonomic information – that is, superordinate or subordinate kinds. For children from lower-income families, 5-year-olds were no more likely than 3-year-olds to mention superordinate and subordinate categories in their definitions. Generally, preschoolers are unlikely to include taxonomic information in their definitions (e.g. Benelli *et al.* 1988; Watson and Olson 1987; Wehren *et al.* 1981), but it is notable in this study that although higher-SES 5-year-olds had begun to do so, lower-SES 5-year-olds had not.

Does this really mean that lower-SES preschoolers are not yet making taxonomic connections? Or could it mean that they just do not yet know the words that label the related taxonomic categories? Or, perhaps, does it mean that they have less experience with definitional form than higher-SES children and less awareness of what kinds of information it makes sense to include in a definition? Lower-SES children may be behind in all of these ways.

Sorhagen and Blewitt (2010) explored further the apparent taxonomic deficit in lower-SES children using a task they called the Indirect Assessment of Taxonomic Knowledge, adapted from Waxman and Hatch (1992). Its purpose was to elicit from children labels for an object at different taxonomic levels if they knew them. It was an attempt to bypass the problem that lower-SES children may be less familiar with good definitional form than higher-SES children. The hope was that if a child knew some superordinate or subordinate category labels, this task would draw that knowledge out. Children were shown a picture of a familiar object, such as a bird. They were asked a series of questions about the object's labels, always asking about incorrect labels. Using an *incorrect* label in a question was intended to prompt children to respond with a *correct* label at the same taxonomic level. First, children were asked a question using a "basic-level" label; this is the most common label for an object. For example, with a picture of the bird, children were asked "Is this a flower?" They nearly always responded with the correct, basic-level label: "No, it's a *bird*". Then children were asked a question using an incorrect superordinate category label for the object ("Is this a *plant*?") to elicit the correct superordinate label ("No, it's an *animal*"). Finally, children were asked a question using an incorrect subordinate label ("Is this an *eagle*?") to elicit the correct subordinate label ("No, it's a *robin*").

With this task, children produced more correct superordinate and subordinate words than they tended to give in their word definitions. More importantly, the lower-SES 5-year-olds showed signs of having begun to make taxonomic connections. Nonetheless, the lower-SES children were still significantly behind the higher-SES children.

As noted earlier, differences in the quantity and quality of language input to children are likely to contribute to social class differences in the depth of children's vocabulary, just as they contribute to differences in vocabulary breadth. In an unpublished study from my laboratory, Heefner (1994) identified a qualitative difference between lower- and higher-middle-class mothers' input to young children that may explain, in part, why lower-SES children lag behind in acquiring knowledge of taxonomic connections. Heefner asked mothers to define and explain unfamiliar labels to their 3-year-olds. From transcripts of their input, she counted the number of units of information mothers offered and found that lower-SES mothers provided less information overall than higher-SES mothers. Heefner also looked at mothers' teaching strategies. These were similar across SES in many ways, but some differences emerged. The chief difference was that higher-SES mothers produced proportionately more utterances that highlighted taxonomic information, emphasizing inclusion relations (e.g. "A *cardinal* is a red bird"; "Mommy's car and the school bus and a plane are all *vehicles*").

To summarize to this point, there are two kinds of social class differences in vocabulary growth, and these differences appear as early as age 3. First, vocabulary *breadth* tends to be greater for children from higher-SES families. Second, there are social class differences in children's vocabulary *depth* – that is, in how much elaborated knowledge children gain about words that they have learned. Studies by Blewitt and colleagues have also found variations in how adults define and explain words to children that may contribute to SES differences in children's elaborated word knowledge.

Growing vocabulary through shared reading

Shared reading is a context that provides children with opportunities to learn new words. The value of reading to young children has been recognized for a long time, and both parents and teachers are usually aware of at least some of the benefits (Mol and Bus 2011). But shared reading may be more or less effective for vocabulary growth, depending on adults' approaches to story reading. Even among parents who say they read to their children every day, there are differences that are likely to lead to different outcomes with regard to word learning. Some parents hastily and without expression or discussion read through a story at bedtime, eager to turn off the lights and get their children to sleep. Other parents seize on multiple opportunities during the day to share books with their children. Clearly, we would expect more learning for children of the latter parents by virtue of the quantity of exposure to books (e.g. DeTemple and Snow 2003). But even adults who read equally often to children may use reading strategies that are differentially effective for advancing vocabulary growth. Much of my research has been aimed at discovering what these strategic differences might be and documenting their effects on both the breadth and the depth of word learning in young children.

Most strategic differences appear in adults' extratextual talk, which is the conversation that they initiate about stories as they read to children. Many studies have documented that extratextual talk increases word learning from children's literature (e.g. Ard and Beverly 2004; Biemiller and Boote 2006; Blewitt *et al.* 2009; Elley 1989; Ewers and Brownson 1999; Justice *et al.* 2005; Penno *et al.* 2002; Sénéchal 1997). Adults have particular styles of extratextual conversation (e.g. Dickinson and Smith 1994; Haden *et al.* 1996). Some interrupt stories to talk; others wait until the story is over. Some ask children a lot of questions; others are more didactic. When they ask questions, some readers ask simple questions about words or story events; others ask more difficult questions that require children to make inferences or connections to non-story experiences.

Blewitt and colleagues (e.g. Blewitt and Langan 2014; Blewitt *et al.* 2009; Dolena and Blewitt 2009; Sorhagen and Blewitt 2010; Walsh and Blewitt 2006) typically test the impact of adults' reading strategies using experimental designs and a set of procedures with three features. First, storybooks are original, written and illustrated for the research. This is rather labor-intensive, but the benefit is that many features of the stories can be controlled: which new words are introduced (the *target words* for a study), how frequently and in what contexts words appear, and the availability of pictures illustrating target words. Illustrations are not sophisticated, but they are appealing, and children seem to find the stories interesting. Figure 6.4 presents two sample pages, with two target words

Sample pages from *Sammy's Day Out*

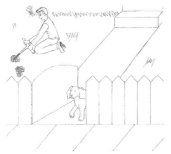

One sunny afternoon, when he was feeling particularly brave, Sammy decided to explore. While Jonny was using a **dibble** to dig holes and plant vegetables in the garden, Sammy slipped out of the yard and started on his way.

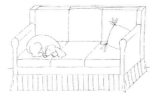

Sammy's family took him in the house where he curled up on his favorite spot on the ***davenport***. He fell asleep dreaming of his exciting day out.

Figure 6.4 *Sammy's Day Out* is one of the storybooks written and illustrated for use in shared reading research. These pages feature the unfamiliar target words "dibble" and "davenport."

(emphasized), from one storybook, *Sammy's Day Out*. The story describes the adventures of a curious dog named Sammy, who wanders away from his family and has a series of new experiences before returning home, weary but happy.

Second, target words are determined to be *unfamiliar* to preschool children through pilot work using the same multiple-choice format as described earlier for identifying familiar words. Three- to 5-year-olds from both lower- and higher-middle-class families are asked to point to a pictured referent of a test word from among four choices. If the success rate for all age and SES groups does not exceed chance (25 percent correct), a word is designated as unfamiliar to children in this age range.

Third, researchers read to children in one-to-one sessions on visits to their childcare centers or preschools. Usually three storybooks are read in a session. The target words are distributed among the storybooks such that each target word appears once in each of two stories. So, in a typical reading session children confront each target word twice in text.

Many of these studies have centered on whether asking different kinds of questions about target words differentially affects word learning. Asking questions during shared reading *does* improve children's word learning, and yet the *kinds* of questions do not seem to matter. Questions of many kinds promote word learning to a similar degree. For example, in one study (Walsh and Blewitt 2006) two types of question were compared: *eliciting questions*, which require children to respond using a new word from the story, and *noneliciting questions*, which repeat the new word but do not require the child to produce it. Every time a target word appeared in text, the reader followed up with a question. In the eliciting question condition the reader pointed to the referent in the accompanying picture and asked, "What is this?" If children did not produce the target word themselves, the reader answered the question correctly so that children would have another exposure to the word. In the noneliciting question condition, the reader asked a simple question about the pictured referent that provided exposure to the target word, such as "What color is the *dibble*?" In a third condition, the reader asked no questions about target vocabulary, so that children did not get extratextual exposure to new words. In all conditions, children participated in three reading sessions over the course of six weeks, and in each session they heard the same three storybooks. In the final session, fast mapping was measured by using the familiar multiple-choice format for assessing word comprehension. As each target word was presented, the 3-year-old participants had to select the correct referent from a set of four pictures. (Slow mapping was not measured in this study.) Asking questions improved children's word learning compared to reading stories without asking questions. However, one question type was not more helpful than the other.

Blewitt *et al.* (2009, Experiment 1) explored whether asking questions at different levels of difficulty makes a difference for word learning. As noted earlier, some adults tend to ask simple questions, such as "What color is the *dibble*?" in their extratextual talk, and others are likely to ask more cognitively demanding questions. More demanding questions usually require children to make inferences or connections that are not immediately obvious from story or picture, such as "Why do you think a *dibble* might be good for digging holes?" or "Would you like to sleep on a *davenport*?" In one condition, children heard only "low-demand" questions; in a second condition, children heard only "high-demand" questions; and in a third condition they heard no questions at all. The procedures were similar to those of Walsh and Blewitt (2006), and so were the results: asking questions benefited performance on the multiple-choice test of fast mapping, but the kind of question did not make a difference. Justice (2002) reported similar results when she compared the benefits of low and high demand questions.

If the kinds of questions readers ask about new words in stories are not important for the fast mapping of words, what is important about extratextual talk? Certainly, the fact that extratextual talk may provide additional exposure to new vocabulary, giving children repeated opportunities to learn, is valuable. But asking children questions about new vocabulary seems to have a greater effect than simply repeating novel words in extratextual talk. For example, Sénéchal *et al.* (1997) compared two story-reading conditions. In one, they repeated the target words after the words appeared in text. In the other condition, they asked children to point to a referent of the target word, what they called "active responding". Children performed better on measures of fast mapping in the question condition, even though they had been exposed to the target words equally often.

Blewitt and Langan (2014) hypothesize that asking questions, regardless of type, is an adult reading strategy that promotes children's active interest and involvement in the story-reading experience, encouraging children's attention to the story, to the conversation that surrounds it, and to the new words in the story. They call this *child engagement* and suggest that an adult's ability to promote child engagement using extratextual talk is the key to its benefits for word learning. This general quality of the adult's reading style is more important than the particular questions he or she asks. There is more to facilitating child engagement than just asking questions. Adult *verbal responsiveness*, referring to how an adult responds to children's actions or speech, may be an especially important ingredient of many adults' extratextual talk. Adult verbal replies qualify as "responsive" if they have three characteristics: they are *prompt*, meaning temporally contiguous; they are *contingent*, meaning they are related to children's behavior and focus of attention; and they are *appropriate* – that is, positively connected to children's behavior (e.g. Tamis-LeMonda *et al.* 2006). Imagine a child is building a structure with blocks. She places a final block, and says "Done!" An immediate adult response of "That is a fine tower!" would be verbally responsive, but "Don't knock it over and make a mess!" would not be. The latter might be prompt and contingent, but verbally responsive replies are also appropriate. They are supportive and often add constructive information. Blewitt and Langan argue that verbal responsiveness promotes child engagement. Appropriately responding to a child's behavior or verbalizations helps assure that adult and child share a joint focus of attention. The adult's interest, positive regard, and informative feedback are also powerful motivators, helping sustain children's attention and interest.

Observations of mothers' interactions with infants and young children outside of the shared reading context have established that adults' verbal responsiveness is associated with children's vocabulary acquisition. For example, Tamis-LeMonda and her colleagues (2001) have found that toddlers with more verbally responsive mothers reach vocabulary milestones (e.g. first 50 words produced) more quickly than toddlers with less verbally responsive mothers, and that verbal responsiveness is more predictive of children's vocabulary growth than how much mothers speak to their children (Bornstein *et al.* 1999).

Blewitt and Langan (2014) found evidence of a direct causal link between adults' verbal responsiveness and children's word learning in the book-reading context. They introduced 3-year-olds to six target words in three storybooks, and children heard all of the stories in each of two reading sessions, about a week apart. At the end of the second session, they used the multiple-choice comprehension test to measure fast mapping of the new words, and a word-defining task to assess slow mapping. Three-year-olds were assigned to one of three reading conditions, each with different extratextual input about target words. The intent was to use extratextual speech to provoke a different level of child engagement in each condition. In the *low engagement* condition, the reader pointed to a pictured referent and repeated a target word each time it occurred in the text, with statements such as "There's the *dibble*!" In the *moderate engagement* condition, the reader attempted to increase child engagement by asking the child to point to the pictured referent, using questions such as "Can you find the *dibble*?" Whatever the child's response, the reader just quietly and in a neutral tone said "Okay". In the *high engagement* condition, the reader asked the same questions but attempted to increase children's engagement by being verbally responsive, enthusiastically saying "That's right!" when the child pointed correctly, or "Good try, but it's this one" if the child was incorrect.

Only in a negligible number of cases did children make errors in responding to questions. This was a very easy task for them. Therefore, in the high engagement condition the reader said "That's right!" nearly all of the time. Also, in all conditions the reader repeated the target words with equal frequency, so there were no differences in the number of times adults exposed children to the words. The reader interacted warmly with the children and read with expression in all conditions. The differences among these three conditions were only in the degree of effort to engage the child by prompting with questions and by varying adult responsiveness.

The effects of the engagement manipulations were quite strong in this brief intervention. Figure 6.5 demonstrates that children learned more about the target words with each increase in engagement. They chose correct referents for more of the words on the comprehension test, and they were able to provide more information about the words on the definition test. Asking questions alone (moderate engagement condition) improved performance, and being verbally responsive (high engagement condition) improved performance even

Growing vocabulary and shared book reading 129

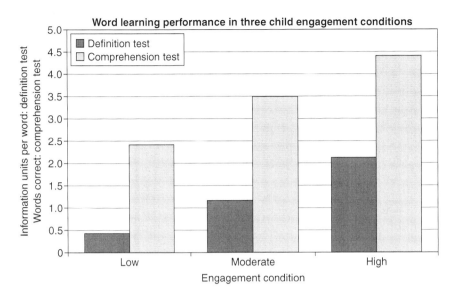

Figure 6.5 According to Blewitt and Langan (2014), 3-year-olds performed better on tests of six target words when the reader used strategies to promote child engagement.

more. Both fast mapping (comprehension test) and slow mapping (definition test) were helped by increases in child engagement. With regard to fast mapping as measured by the multiple-choice comprehension test, increasing children's engagement was more helpful for some words than for others. Specifically, it helped children learn synonyms.

Some background is necessary here to understand the implications of this result. Generally, there is a *synonym effect* in word learning. When task demands are high, children have more difficulty learning synonyms for familiar object labels than learning nonsynonyms (Liittschwager and Markman 1994; Piccin and Blewitt 2007). *Nonsynonyms* are names for unfamiliar objects – that is, objects for which children have no label yet. For example, *davenport* is a synonym. Although it is an unfamiliar label to most young English-speaking children, its referents can also be called *sofa* or *couch*, words that are likely to be quite familiar to preschoolers. The word *dibble* is a nonsynonym, unfamiliar to most young children, and it labels objects that do not have another, more familiar name. One reason for the synonym effect may be that children pay less attention to synonyms than to nonsynonyms, perhaps reserving their cognitive resources for learning labels for objects that they cannot already name (see Piccin and Blewitt 2007).

Blewitt and Langan (2014) found that children performed better overall on target words that were nonsynonyms than on those that were synonyms, as others have found. However, the synonym effect was attenuated at higher levels of child engagement, such that children performed as well on synonyms as they did on nonsynonyms in the most engaging condition. This finding supports the view that synonyms are usually more difficult to learn because children are less likely to pay attention to them spontaneously. Efforts to increase children's engagement, therefore, have more impact on learning synonyms because they encourage children to attend to words they otherwise might ignore.

The Blewitt and Langan (2014) study provides evidence that extratextual speech designed to increase children's engagement affects their word learning. It also illustrates that when extratextual speech meets the criteria of *verbal responsiveness* – being prompt, contingent, and appropriately positive and meaningful – children are likely to be more engaged.

Another study can also be interpreted as demonstrating the value of crafting extratextual input that is responsive to children, especially in the sense that the input is appropriately meaningful to them (Blewitt *et al.* 2009, Experiment 2). In this study, children were assigned to one of three different reading conditions. In the first, children were asked low-demand questions about unfamiliar target words. In the second, they were asked high-demand questions, and in the third, called the "scaffolding-like" condition, children were asked both low- and high-demand questions. In all conditions, children listened to three storybooks in each of three reading sessions so that they heard each target word six times in text. Each presentation of a target word was followed by a question, and each of the six questions was different. In the "scaffolding-like" condition, four of the questions, including the first three (two-thirds of the questions) were low demand. The fourth and the sixth questions were high demand. In real scaffolding, adults responsively adjust their questions on the basis of children's behavioral and verbal cues to their current level of understanding (Wood 1980; Wood and Middleton 1975). In this simulation of scaffolding, the researchers assumed that children did not know the new words at all at the beginning of the study, and therefore started with easy, low-demand questions. After the children had had several exposures to the target words, more demanding questions were introduced, on the assumption that children had made the association between the word and its referent and were ready to learn more. One week after the last reading session, children were tested both for fast mapping, using the multiple-choice procedure, and for slow mapping, using a word-defining task.

There were no significant differences among the three conditions in how children performed on the fast-mapping measure. The kinds of questions, and whether or not they were mixed, did not seem to affect how likely children were to associate a word with its referents. But there were differences in children's word definitions among conditions, with children in the scaffolding-like condition able to give more information about the target words than children in the other two conditions. This suggests that children in the scaffolding-like condition made more progress with slow mapping of target words than children in the other two conditions.

It may be that asking the right kinds of questions at the right times especially benefits slow mapping, because it helps children to maintain their engagement.

Low-demand questions (such as "Where is the *dibble*?") provide opportunities to link the new word to a referent, but they do not provide any other defining information. Asking only low-demand questions *after* fast mapping has occurred, therefore, does not provide information or prompt thinking that would elaborate word meaning. Conversely, high-demand questions do prompt such thinking. For example, a question about how an artifact functions (such as "Why is the boy using the *dibble* to dig holes?") could help a child to generate and store important functional information with the word (see Booth 2009; Kemler Nelson *et al.* 2008). However, asking high-demand questions *before* fast mapping has occurred may be confusing and is likely to cause children's attention to flag. Children may stop processing questions effectively, so that even after they have fast-mapped a word, they are unable to benefit from the deeper processing that high-demand questions should be able to encourage. Thus, children's slow mapping can be helped by more cognitively demanding questions, but only after children have formed an association between the phonological form of the word and a referent. Fundamentally, when adults sensitively adjust the level of their questions to how much children know, they are demonstrating a kind of verbal responsiveness that maintains children's engagement with the new words, with the story, and with the extratextual conversation.

Summary and conclusions

For many adults and young children, shared reading is a delightful way of spending time together, exploring and learning about life beyond their immediate experience. Children's literature often immerses the adult and child in a rich language environment that supports every aspect of the child's language acquisition. And it contributes in multiple ways to children's interest in, and preparation for, academic tasks, especially reading. Children's vocabulary growth is a critical benefit of early shared reading, one that is an important part of the contribution shared reading makes to children's later academic success. This chapter specifically focuses on two phenomena that are pertinent to how shared reading influences children's vocabulary: first, individual differences in young children's vocabulary growth and the environmental factors that correlate with these differences; and second, the effects of adults' reading strategies on children's word learning. Specifically, we have examined the extratextual strategies that seem to be most effective for children's vocabulary growth, at least with regard to concrete nouns.

Overall, findings support the claim that using extratextual talk to increase child engagement boosts children's word learning from shared reading. Asking children questions to encourage their attention to new words is helpful; being verbally responsive by responding promptly, contingently, and appropriately, with supportive feedback to children's contributions, is helpful; and scaffolding extratextual talk such that, for example, questions are sensitively tuned to the child's level of current knowledge is helpful.

Many adults spontaneously implement these extratextual child engagement strategies, but others may not. A large body of research demonstrates that lower-SES parents often engage in less conversation and provide less overall language input to young children than higher-SES parents, and these input differences appear to contribute to less vocabulary breadth for lower-SES children than for higher-SES children. Blewitt and colleagues (Dolena and Blewitt 2009; Sorhagen and Blewitt 2010) have also found that there are SES differences in the depth of children's vocabulary – that is, how elaborated their word knowledge is, with lower-SES children again lagging behind higher-SES children. Shared reading can help level the playing field for lower-SES children, and child development advocates encourage parents to read to young children as one way to help redress the language input differences that children experience (e.g. Rodriguez *et al.* 2009; Sénéchal and LeFevre 2002). Evidence is clear that even in lower-SES families, more shared reading from infancy onward predicts larger vocabularies by the time children enter school (e.g. Raikes *et al.* 2006). Research also indicates, however, that the amount of extratextual talk that surrounds early shared reading may be at least as important as the reading itself (e.g. Roberts *et al.* 2005). Encouraging parents from all walks of life to share reading in a relaxed environment, with time to talk and to use the extratextual strategies that promote child engagement, is likely to promote vocabulary growth most effectively.

One final note. Although this chapter is focused entirely on processes that affect word learning, it may be that the strategies that are most helpful to word learning have broader benefits. Any process that engages the child's interest in the story and the conversation that surrounds it is likely to enhance many aspects of language growth, as well as encouraging children's longer-term interest in, and enjoyment of, literary activities.

References

Administration for Children and Families (ACF). 2003. *Head Start FACES 2000: A Whole-Child Perspective on Program Performance. Fourth Progress Report.* Washington, DC: Author.

Akhtar, Nameera, Jennifer Jipson, and Maureen A. Callanan. 2001. "Learning words through overhearing". *Child Development* 72: 416–430.

Anderson, Alonzo B., William H. Teale, and Elette Estrada. 1980. "Low-income preschool literacy experiences: Some naturalistic observations". *Quarterly Newsletter of the Laboratory of Comparative Human Cognition* 2: 59–65.

Ard, Lisa M. and Brenda L. Beverly. 2004. "Preschool word learning during joint book reading: Effect of adult questions and comments". *Communication Disorders Quarterly* 26: 17–28.

Baldwin, Dare A. 1991. "Infants' contribution to the achievement of joint reference". *Child Development* 62: 875–890.

Baldwin, Dare A. 1993. "Infants' ability to consult the speaker for clues to word reference". *Journal of Child Language* 20: 395–418.

Benelli, Beatrice, Luciano Arcuri, and Gianni Marchesini. 1988. "Cognitive and linguistic factors in the development of word definitions". *Journal of Child Language* 15: 619–635.

Biemiller, Andrew and Catherine Boote. 2006. "An effective method for building meaning vocabulary in primary grades". *Journal of Educational Psychology* 98: 44–62.

Blewitt, Pamela and Ryan Langan. 2014. "Learning words during shared book reading: The role of extratextual talk that increases child engagement". Manuscript submitted for publication.

Blewitt, Pamela, Keiran M. Rump, Stephanie E. Shealy, and Samantha A. Cook. 2009. "Shared book reading: When and how questions affect young children's word learning". *Journal of Educational Psychology* 101: 294–304.

Booth, Amy E. 2009. "Causal supports for early word learning". *Child Development* 80: 1243–1250.

Bornstein, Marc H., Catherine S. Tamis-LeMonda, and Maurice Haynes. 1999. "First words in the second year: Continuity, stability, and models of concurrent and lagged correspondence in vocabulary and verbal responsiveness across age and context". *Infant Behavior and Development* 22: 67–87.

Bradley, Robert H., Robert Corwyn, Harriet Pipes McAdoo, and Cynthia Garcia Coll. 2001. "The home environments of children in the United States. Part I: Variations by age, ethnicity, and poverty status". *Child Development* 72: 1844–1867.

Burns, Matthew L. and Pamela Blewitt. 2000. "Parent's book reading: Does quantity or quality predict social class differences in children's vocabulary?" Poster presented at the annual meeting of the Eastern Psychological Association, Baltimore, March.

Carey, Susan. 1978. "The child as a word learner". In *Linguistic Theory and Psychological Reality*, edited by Morris Halle, Joan Bresnan, and George A. Miller. 264–297. Cambridge, MA: MIT Press.

Carey, Susan and Elsa Bartlett. 1978. "Acquiring a single new word". *Papers and Reports on Child Language Development* 15: 17–29.

DeTemple, Jeanne and Catherine E. Snow. 2003. "Learning words from books". In *On Reading Books to Children: Parent and Teachers*, edited by Anne Van Kleeck, Stephen A. Stahl, and Eurydice B. Bauer. 271–319. Mahwah, NJ: Lawrence Erlbaum.

Dickinson, David K. and Miriam W. Smith. 1994. "Long-term effects of preschool teachers' book readings on low-income children's vocabulary and story comprehension". *Reading Research Quarterly* 29: 105–122.

Dickinson, David K., Alyssa McCabe, and Louisa Anastasopoulos. 2003. "A framework for examining book reading in early childhood classrooms". In *On Reading Books to Children: Parents and Teachers*, edited by Anne Van Kleeck, Stephen A. Stahl, and Eurydice B. Bauer. 95–113. Mahwah, NJ: Lawrence Erlbaum.

Dolena, A. L. and Pamela Blewitt. 2009. "Social class differences in the 'slow mapping' of word knowledge in young children." Poster presented at the Biennial Meetings of the Society for Research in Child Development, Denver, April.

Dunn, Lloyd M. and Douglas M. Dunn. 2007. *Peabody Picture Vocabulary Test*. 4th edition. San Antonio, TX: NCS Pearson.

Elley, Warwick B. 1989. "Vocabulary acquisition from listening to stories". *Reading Research Quarterly* 24: 174–187.

Ewers, Cynthia A. and Shelley M. Brownson. 1999. "Kindergarteners' vocabulary acquisition as a function of active vs. passive storybook reading, prior vocabulary, and working memory". *Journal of Reading Psychology* 20: 11–20.

Haden, Catherine A., Elaine Reese, and Robyn Fivush. 1996. "Mothers' extratextual comments during storybook reading: Stylistic differences over time and across texts". *Discourse Processes* 21: 135–169.

Hargrave, Anne C. and Monique Sénéchal. 2000. "A book reading intervention with preschool children who have limited vocabularies: The benefits of regular reading and dialogic reading". *Early Childhood Research Quarterly* 15: 75–90.

Hart, Betty and Todd R. Risley. 1995. *Meaningful Differences in the Everyday Experiences of Young American Children*. Baltimore: Brookes.

Heefner, Amy Stuart. 1994. "Maternal labeling strategies and children's interpretations at multiple hierarchical levels in two socioeconomic groups." Unpublished Master's thesis, Villanova University, Villanova, PA.

Hoff, Erika. 2003. "The specificity of environmental influence: Socioeconomic status affects early vocabulary development via maternal speech". *Child Development* 74: 1368–1378.

Hollich, George J., Katy Hirsh-Pasek, Roberta M. Golinkoff *et al.* 2000. *Breaking the Language Barrier: An Emergentist Coalition Model for the Origins of Word Learning*. Monographs of the Society for Research in Child Development 65, no. 3, serial no. 262.

Huttenlocher, Janellen, Wendy Haight, Anthony Bryk, Michael Seltzer, and Thomas Lyons. 1991. "Early vocabulary growth: Relation to language input and gender". *Developmental Psychology* 27: 236–248.

Justice, Laura M. 2002. "Word exposure conditions and preschoolers' novel word learning during shared storybook reading". *Reading Psychology* 23: 87–106.

Justice, Laura M., Joanne Meier, and Sharon Walpole. 2005. "Learning new words from storybooks: An efficacy study with at-risk kindergartners". *Language, Speech, and Hearing Services in Schools* 36: 17–32.

Kemler Nelson, Deborah, Kelly O'Neill, and Yvonne M. Asher. 2008. "A mutually facilitative relationship between learning names and learning concepts in preschool children: The case of artifacts". *Journal of Cognition and Development* 9: 171–193.

Liittschwager, Jean C. and Ellen M. Markman. 1994. "Sixteen- and 24-month-olds' use of mutual exclusivity as a default assumption in second-label learning". *Developmental Psychology* 30: 955–968.

Markman, Ellen M. 1991. "The whole-object, taxonomic, and mutual exclusivity assumptions as initial constraints on word meanings". In *Perspectives on Language and Thought: Interrelations in Development*, edited by Susan A. Gelman and James P. Byrnes. 72–106. Cambridge: Cambridge University Press.

Merriman, William E. and Laura L. Bowman. 1989. *The Mutual Exclusivity Bias in Children's Word Learning*. Monographs of the Society for Research in Child Development 54, no. 3–4, serial no. 220.

Mol, Suzanne E. and Adriana G. Bus. 2011. "To read or not to read: A meta-analysis of print exposure from infancy to early adulthood". *Psychological Bulletin* 137: 267–296.

Ninio, Anat. 1980. "Picture-book reading in mother–infant dyads belonging to two subgroups in Israel". *Child Development* 51: 587–590.

Ouellette, Gene P. 2006. "What's meaning got to do with it: The role of vocabulary in word reading and reading comprehension". *Journal of Educational Psychology* 98: 554–566.

Penno, Julie F., Ian A. Wilkinson, and Dennis W. Moore. 2002. "Vocabulary acquisition from teacher explanation and repeated listening to stories: Do they overcome the Matthew effect?" *Journal of Educational Psychology* 94: 23–33.

Piccin, Thomas B. and Pamela Blewitt. 2006. "Resource conservation as a basis for the mutual exclusivity effect in children's word learning". *First Language* 27: 5–28.

Raikes, Helen, Barbara Alexander Pan, Gayle Luze, Catherine S. Tamis-LeMonda, Jeanne Grooks-Gunn, Jill Constantine, Louisa Banks Tarullo, H. Abigail Raikes, and Eileen T.

Rodriguez. 2006. "Mother–child bookreading in low-income families: correlates and outcomes during the first three years of life". *Child Development* 77: 924–953.

Reese, Elaine and Adell Cox. 1999. "Quality of adult book reading affects children's emergent literacy". *Developmental Psychology* 35: 20–28.

Robbins, Claudia and Linnea C. Ehri. 1994. "Reading storybooks to kindergartners helps them learn new vocabulary words". *Journal of Educational Psychology* 86: 54–64.

Roberts, Joanne, Julia Jurgens, and Margaret Burchinal. 2005. "The role of home literacy practices in preschool children's language and emergent literacy skills". *Journal of Speech, Language, and Hearing Research* 48: 345–359.

Rodriguez, Eileen T., Catherine S. Tamis-LeMonda, Mark E. Spellmann, Barbara A. Pan, Helen Raikes, Julieta Lugo-Gil, and Gayle Luze. 2009. "The formative role of home literacy experiences across the first three years of life in children from low-income families". *Journal of Applied Developmental Psychology* 30: 677–694.

Sénéchal, Monique. 1997. "The differential effect of storybook reading on preschoolers' acquisition of expressive and receptive vocabulary". *Journal of Child Language* 24: 123–138.

Sénéchal, Monique and Edward H. Cornell. 1993. "Vocabulary acquisition through shared reading experiences". *Reading Research Quarterly* 28: 361–374.

Sénéchal, Monique and Jo-Anne LeFevre. 2002. "Parental involvement in the development of children's reading skill: A five-year longitudinal study". *Child Development* 73: 445–460.

Sénéchal, Monique, Eleanor Thomas, and Jo-Ann Monker. 1995. "Individual differences in 4-year-old children's acquisition of vocabulary during storybook reading". *Journal of Educational Psychology* 87: 218–229.

Snow, Catherine E. 1990. "The development of definitional skill". *Journal of Child Language* 17: 697–710.

Sorhagen, Nicole and Pamela Blewitt. 2010. "Elaborated word knowledge in young children: The influence of social class and vocabulary size". Poster presented at the Conference on Human Development, New York, April.

Stanovich, Keith E. 1986. "Matthew effects in reading: Some consequences of individual differences in the acquisition of literacy". *Reading Research Quarterly* 21: 360–407.

Storch, Stacey A. and Grover J. Whitehurst. 2002. "Oral language and code-related precursors to reading: Evidence from a longitudinal structural model". *Developmental Psychology* 38: 934–937.

Tamis-LeMonda, Catherine S., Marc H. Bornstein, and Lisa Baumwell. 2001. "Maternal responsiveness and children's achievement of language milestones". *Child Development* 72(3): 748–767.

Tamis-LeMonda, Catherine S., Tonia N. Cristofaro, Eileen T. Rodriguez, and Marc H. Bornstein. 2006. "Early language development: Social influences in the first years of life". In *Child Psychology: A Handbook of Contemporary Issues*, edited by Lawrence Balter and Catherine S. Tamis-LeMonda. 79–108. New York: Psychology Press.

Walsh, Bridget A. and Pamela Blewitt. 2006. "The effect of questioning style during storybook reading on novel vocabulary acquisition of preschoolers". *Early Childhood Education Journal* 33: 273–278.

Watson, Rita and David R. Olson. 1987. "From meaning to definition: A literate bias on the structure of word meaning". In *Comprehending Oral and Written Language*, edited by Rosalind Horowitz and S. Jay Samuels. 329–353. The Hague: Brill.

Waxman, Sandra R. and Thomas Hatch. 1992. "Beyond the basic: Preschool children label objects flexibly at multiple hierarchical levels". *Journal of Child Language* 19: 153–166.

Wehren, Aileen, Richard DeLisi, and Marjoree Arnold. 1981. "The development of noun definition". *Journal of Child Language* 8: 163–175.

Weizman, Zehava O. and Catherine E. Snow. 2001. "Lexical input as related to children's vocabulary acquisition: Effects of sophisticated exposure and support for meaning". *Developmental Psychology* 37: 265–279.

Wood, David. 1980. "Teaching the young child: Some relationships between social interaction, language, and thought". In *The Social Foundations of Language and Thought*, edited by David Olson. 280–296. New York: W. W. Norton.

Wood, David and David Middleton. 1975. "A study of assisted problem solving". *British Journal of Educational Psychology* 66: 181–191.

Woodward, Amanda L. and Ellen M. Markman. 1998. "Early word learning". In *Handbook of Child Psychology*. Vol. 2: *Cognition, Perception, and Language*, edited by Deanna Kuhn and Robert S. Siegler. 371–420. New York: John Wiley.

7 Distributed cognition in early literacy

Lesley Lancaster and Rosie Flewitt

"What are you afraid of, Tame"?
   "The ghost," he says, his eyes changing.
   "What are you frightened of, Patchy?"
   "The alligator."...
   I try out "ghost" and "kiss" on the ones who can't learn to read. I print them on the low wall blackboard where they can touch them and Lo ... here are these stallers reading overnight!...There must be more words like this, analogous to these two; captions of other instincts, desires, resentments, horrors and passions.
   I can't help noticing all this strange writing that they do. It must be the beginning of composition; the first wall between one being and another; the putting of thoughts for someone else into written words instead of speech or touch; the graduation of talkers and touchers into writers ... But I didn't start it: they began themselves ... For there's magic in the minds of Little Ones and my fingers get sticky with it.

(Sylvia Ashton-Warner 1958)

Introduction

Sylvia Ashton-Warner's fictionalized account of teaching "Little Ones" in a remote New Zealand town during the 1940s describes the intense relationship between very young children's early explorations of reading and writing, and their social and emotional lives. The "imported vocabulary" that was supposed to supply them with all the necessary tools to learn to read and write failed to provide the means to interrogate their own lives; these tools were not infused with the "passions" and "magic" required to build bridges between written inscriptions and the social, emotional, and bodily lives of the children. Deacon (1997) points to the counterintuitive nature of early symbolic learning, with the learning of symbol systems requiring an approach that postpones commitment to seemingly obvious associations in order that the underlying architecture can be noticed. It is not the technical detail contained in the "imported vocabulary" and the like that is the starting point for engagement with symbolic principles, but those features of life experience that are significant, intriguing, or even commonplace (if Ashton-Warner's Little Ones are anything to go by) that provide a meaningful and grounded, superordinate framework for their attempts to engage with the symbolic principles that inform the writing systems used by those around them (Lancaster 2013). At the heart of this process, however, is an uncomfortable division between what seemingly happens in the mind and what happens in the world. Edwin Hutchins (1995: 354) has pointed out that early in the development of cognitive science, culture, history, context, and emotion were set aside as problems to be addressed once a good understanding of cognition had been achieved. However, the achievement of such an understanding remains elusive and the reintegration has yet to happen. The setting up of boundaries between an isolated mind "inside" the body, and a social, corporeal, and cultural world "outside" was from the outset unlikely to succeed, Hutchins suggests, as it "creates the impression that individual minds operate in isolation and encourages us to mistake the properties of complex sociocultural systems for the properties of individual minds" (ibid.: 355).

For many decades, the notion of cognition as a separate faculty has had a profound impact on educational policy and practice (Pea 1993: 47), and it continues to influence approaches to understanding learning, including, as we have suggested, how children come to understand symbolic systems such as writing, drawing, and number. One drawback of this position has always been that if intellectual abilities are considered as being "inside" the mind, it is difficult, if not impossible, to observe them. Rather, they have had to be inferred indirectly from evidence that is at best often only hypothetically relevant. In the case of reading and writing for example, it might be relatively easy to observe whether a child is or is not able to read or write, but much less easy to observe the processes by which this accomplishment is or is not achieved. A solution generally adopted to get round this problem has been to hypothesize what the cognitive processes might be, and then attribute achievement or lack of achievement to the presence or absence of these processes within the minds of individual children. The outcomes of such hypotheses have then been used as a basis for more general judgments about children's literacy attainment. This approach means that reading and writing are removed from the context in which they happen in order to facilitate their description (Meek 1988), and the extent to which the resultant descriptions actually explain the process of literacy learning remains unproven.

Another significant outcome of the separation of mind from social and cultural activity with regard to literacy is the marginalization of text in the process of learning to read and write. From the "cognition as separate" standpoint, a written text is seen as the material outcome of the activity of an individual mind, or as evidence of the imaginative construction of an individual creative intellect. Text is viewed as an object bound and contained in its material form, removed and quite distinct from the mind that gave rise to it. Furthermore, text is considered primarily as an instantiation of written language, as a "bounded linguistic artefact" (Hanks 1989: 99), with language considered as the prime mode for the communication of meaning; and if literacy is construed as a linguistic process involving the decoding and encoding of linguistic signs, then by extension the texts used in the teaching and learning process need to privilege language above everything else, irrespective of what other semiotic modes might be deployed. In classrooms, texts are thereby often downgraded to act as no more than linguistic tools used to teach children about the relationship between letters and sounds – a variant of Ashton-Warner's "imported vocabulary" problem. As Geertz points out, when "the study of inscriptions is severed from the study of inscribing" and 'the study of fixed meaning is severed from the social processes that fix it", then the possibility for understanding texts and the social phenomena that give rise to them are infected by a double narrowness: "Not only is the extension of text analysis to nonwritten materials blocked, but so is the application of sociological analysis to written ones" (2000: 32).

Distributed cognition and text in action

In this chapter, we pursue an alternative, distributed view of cognition with respect to literacy and text. We view cognitive development as being integrally intertwined with culture, history, location, and emotion, and start from Pea's premise that "the 'mind' rarely works alone" (1993: 47). People think and act in conjunction and partnership with others (Salomon 1993: xiii), with the cognitive load shared and distributed not just between those participating in actions in real time, but also between past and present participants, through the use of symbolic tools that have been developed through human history. Hutchins (1995), as part of an extended psychological and anthropological study of ship navigation "in the wild",[1] examines the historical development of navigational tools and associated computational systems. Navigation is performed by a team of people, with what happens in their individual minds "part of a larger computational system" (ibid.: xv) that incorporates work done by past generations of navigators. "External", physical computational symbols and systems carry the cognitive load and allow for complex computations that cannot be performed by individual minds alone. Over time, this has resulted in "a way of thinking [that] comes with these techniques and tools" (ibid.: 115), and associated changes to culture and technology. This case exemplifies three features of the distribution of cognition during social and representational activity that are significant in children's early engagement with cultural practices such as writing: the use of external tools to do things that the mind cannot manage alone (this includes the production of texts); the participation of others – adults and peers – who share the cognitive load; and the integrity of the physical environment to the process.

We aim to show how cognition is distributed as adults and children under the age of 4 engage with texts, and how interpersonal, bodily, and material interactions between adults and children drive this distributive process. We focus on how children and adults share access to knowledge and systems through multimodal (Flewitt 2008; Lancaster 2012), multimedia interactions, as well as to the various tools and devices that are present in the material settings of text production and interpretation. To illustrate how these theorizations of cognition and text unfold in the everyday experiences of young children, we draw briefly on evidence from our own research conducted over the past decade (Lancaster and Roberts 2006; Lancaster 2007; Flewitt, 2003, 2008). Through this work, we have made some attempt to reintegrate the cognition of young children with the historical, bodily, and emotional settings from which it arises. To do this, we have used a multimodal, analytic framework, an approach derived from semiotics and discourse analysis that takes account of all modes used in the course of communication and representation, and which views language as part of a communicative ensemble (Jewitt 2009: 14). It is a particularly important approach when working with children, who are still developing as language users, providing a more delicate and a fuller picture of children's representational intentions than can be achieved by concentrating on language alone. Meaning is distributed across modes, including bodily modes, with each making a partial contribution to the interpretation and representation of texts. This requires fine-grained transcription, microanalysis, and thick description. Geertz (2000: 4) points out that specialized microstudies can generate "the theoretically more powerful"; theory building on the small scale has the capacity to go more deeply into things, demanding a concentration on "very densely textured facts" (ibid.: 28). Coherent and theoretically consistent generalisations often need, initially at least, to be made within, rather than across, studies. Of particular relevance in the case of a study of very young children is the way in which the small scale can, potentially, provide access to the conceptual world of the subject or subjects concerned; as Geertz says, "in some extended sense of the term, to converse with them" (ibid.: 24).

In these studies, we have focused on how children under the age of 4 create and interpret signs and texts, and examined the interactions that mediate this cognitive and semiotic activity, showing how these phenomena are distributed between individual actors, social, material, historical, and psychological environments, as well as symbolic and technological artifacts that include preexisting, established, human-devised systems such as drawing, writing, and number. We consider the nature of the texts produced and interpreted by children of this age, and the extent to which they are an element of the "passion" and "magic" that drive early symbolic learning. To this end, we will review and clarify our definitions of text further in the light of the theoretical framework that we have adopted. We will examine these definitions in the context of how young children interpret and express meaning through signs, and consider the extent to which young children's interpretations can be regarded as text reading, and their graphic productions can legitimately be regarded as texts, prior to an ability to understand and produce conventional inscriptional systems.

Text unbound

Titon's definition of text as "any humanly constructed object" (1995: 434) moves the discussion away from a dominant linguistic view towards a much more inclusive, multimodal interpretation of the term, and incorporates a diversity of objects such as "a painting or a building or pots" (ibid.: 434). It also raises the possibility of text as being something immaterial, consisting of "an action or event", as involving human agents rather than objects (ibid.: 434) – in other words, text as social action. Sylvia Ashton-Warner highlights this in her description of the children's passionate interest in "whatever's happening and to whomever it is happening" as "the stuff that Meaning is made of" (1958: 171). In this way, text becomes more extensive, unbound, and necessarily distributed between objects, agents, and events. However, this very open definition of text is indeterminate: it offers neither constraints nor riders, arguably making it problematic, at a theoretical level at least, to distinguish text from nontext and to differentiate text itself from the social and material environment that gave rise to it. Hanks (1989: 95) provides a similarly open and inclusive explanation of text in his suggestion that it is "any configuration of signs", but with the important proviso that this must be "coherently interpretable by some community of users". So, a measure of social agreement and shared understanding is required before an action, event, or object can be referred to as a text, though this understanding may vary from one community of users to another. This important distinction has particular significance when one is considering whether the texts produced by very young children should be regarded as such (Lancaster 2013), and it offers a more inclusive definition that allows children of this age to be "enfranchised" as interpreters and producers of texts.

Such an inclusive and interpretative view of text is further exemplified by Kress and Van Leeuwen's conception of "practically lived texts". These include "the everyday practices of 'ordinary humans'", as well as more "conventionally text-like objects" (2001: 24). As an example of a practically lived text, they discuss the "discourse, design, and production" (ibid.: 11) of young children's bedrooms, and their photographic representation in a home design magazine. Within the space of each bedroom, there are furniture, fittings, pictures, drapes, clothes and toys, each of which can be construed as signs or texts that signify meanings of their own but also contribute to the totality of the room as a text with multiple meanings. While these are extended, complex texts, nevertheless they are still physically bound by the walls of the room but, at the same time, as practically lived texts they are subject to constant change over time. People go in and out of them, do things, move things, add things and take things away. This ongoing state of production is distributed between the various agents, objects, and events associated with the child whose room it is, and with other members of the household. Furthermore, the representation of the rooms in the magazine reveals a complex and recursive relationship between the symbolic and material dimensions of these texts. It could be argued that the photographs in the magazine are more "conventionally text-like" than the room is: the notion of a text as visual artifact is more familiar than the concept of a text as lived event. However, the images in the magazine reveal the network of relationships between the material and the symbolic, and between the text, the text maker, and the text reader (for further discussion, see Toren 1993: 473). The room is constructed according to current thinking about children's bedrooms; it is photographed by a magazine because it typifies certain fashions in relation to childhood and design. These photographs may then be subject to critique and replication, potentially transforming future design, enabling a continuous process of reflection and representation. This latter point is central to the whole notion of what texts are: wherever the line is drawn in terms of their physical or material boundaries, texts are ultimately ways in which people frame social experience and cultural practice in order to be able to engage with, examine, and reflect on them. They are at the heart of what Deacon calls "this unique human mode of reference, which can be termed *symbolic reference*" (1997: 42).

Distributed text

Clearly, this view incorporates numerous different genres of text with different permutations of people, objects, tools, and signs involved in their creation, depending on the nature and purpose of the text. In the case of an artifact such as a book, the more conventional position of regarding it as the unique product of an individual mind might seem more practically and theoretically acceptable. The sheer physical containment and portability of a book supports this sense of its being a closed and complete reflection of the mind of the author, particularly in the case of a work of fiction or poetry. It is not easy to access consistent and reliable information about how fictional texts are conceived of and produced, in spite of the production of extensive bodies of literary criticism. Moreover, writers rarely explain their own work to any great extent, and indeed for them to do so is likely to militate against the very suspension of disbelief that they may be trying to achieve. Of course, what a writer writes is indeed driven by a personal creative desire; as the writer and illustrator Maurice Sendak puts it, "all books ... came from my original creative soul, self, whatever ... and I just think of them as terrific inventions that came upon me and dominated my life until I finished them" (Gross 2011).

Yet this is far from the whole story. The author is instrumental, working with widely distributed and disparate resources derived from emotional, physical, material, and social encounters with different actors at different times and in different places – resources that might be remembered, seen, heard, touched, felt, or disregarded. These influences are never lodged absolutely inside or outside the mind, but move freely across boundaries. The writer or artist has sometimes been described as a *bricoleur* (Kress 2010; Chandler 2007), picking up things that are lying around, combining, refashioning, and adapting them as required. Lévi-Strauss (1966), who originated this use of the term, contrasts the *bricoleur* with the engineer, with the latter procuring and refining all the necessary tools and materials required in advance of production. This is a distinction that does not always stand up to scrutiny, however, and is challenged by Lincoln (2001) in her discussion of the researcher as *bricoleur*. She extends the concept in ways that are highly applicable to the type of *bricolage* that an author engages in. The *bricoleur* is not the crude and unsophisticated operator that Lévi-Strauss describes; rather:

This bricoleur looks for not yet imagined tools, fashioning them with not yet imagined connections ... searching for the nodes, the nexuses, the linkages, the interconnections, the fragile bonds ... It works the margins and liminal spaces ... knitting them together, forming a new consciousness.

(ibid.: 693–694)

Kress points to the way in which young children's sign making also employs principles of bricolage, "using the best, most apt available form for the expression of a meaning" (1997: 17). For its producer, a text provides a brief stopping place for particular collections and combinations of these things, providing "material anchors" (Hutchins 2005) whereby diverse and divergent meanings can be held together in ways that allow them to be contemplated and interpreted.

Typically, the material anchors that Hutchins refers to have been shaped by human-devised systems that have been "produced in and shaped by social activity which has regularity and recognizability for members of a social group" (Kress 2010: 147). It is these inscriptional systems that enable expression of the "creative soul" referred to by Sendak, and of the "passions" and "magic" of Ashton-Warner's Little Ones, allowing them to be disseminated within a material form that can be understood by human populations across time and space. The combination of fixity and flexibility that characterizes systems of inscription and calculation has meant that that they have been able to play a central role in the evolution and maintenance of human culture (Donald 1991; Lewis-Williams 2002). As Hutchins points out, "In an external representation, structure can be built up gradually – a distribution of cognitive effort over time – so that the final product may be something that no individual could represent all at once internally" (1995: 96). What we are talking about here is a process that does not occur just in the minds of individuals (Tribble and Sutton 2012: 592), or in any one place or time in history, but is part of a much wider cognitive ecology involving a network of mutual dependence and interactions. The suggestion that representational structures are built up through cognitive effort distributed over time provides some explanation of how the learning of highly complex inscriptional systems can be conflated into a period of approximately seven years, and by the youngest and least experienced members of human societies.

Early reading and understanding of texts

We now turn to the first of two examples relating to how young children's understanding of text and textual structures is distributed during early reading and writing, and how their interpretation of inscriptional systems is informed by their personal, social, and cultural experience. In this first illustration, we focus on a young child's reading of a picturebook, a multimodal text specifically produced for children and combining the modes of layout, images, and words to convey meanings. These data are taken from video ethnographies of young children's communicative strategies at home and in a preschool playgroup in southern England (Flewitt 2003), in a small-scale study funded by the Economic and Social Research Council. Here, we consider how young readers often share their reading of picturebooks with an adult or peer, and in doing so also employ the modes of speech, gaze, facial expression, and body movements to interpret texts. We argue that, rather than being simply optional adornments to the "real" reading of words, the combined use of multiple modes is integral to the cognitive processing involved in interpreting meaning from texts, as are the involvement of other actors, the material and historical settings, and established semiotic systems in the form of writing, drawing, and number. We begin with an example involving Jake, a 3-year-old boy who was one of four young children observed over the course of their first year in a rural preschool playgroup and at home, with a view to investigating the different ways the children drew on diverse communicative modes to express themselves in the different settings (see Flewitt 2005, 2006).

Jake's post-banger

A few weeks after his third birthday, Jake was at home in the kitchen with his mother, who was baking. He had been playing with a toy farm on the floor at the far end of the kitchen while she cooked, and they had been chatting on and off as they each pursued their own activity. After a while, Jake moved over to a box of toys and books at the side of the room, silently selected a large, illustrated children's nonfiction book about farm machinery, and climbed onto a comfortable sofa. Farming, farm machinery, and farm animals were his favourite topics; he lived on a small farm and had grown up surrounded by agricultural activity. He studied the book closely and silently, with his gaze lingering for extended periods on different illustrations, turning the pages carefully after every few minutes. One particular page featuring a John Deere tractor captured his concentration, and he started to compare this page with a previous one he had been studying, turning the page carefully over and back. He then began to talk to his mother, as shown in the extract reproduced in Table 7.1.

In the introductory description and the extract shown in the table, we have a fairly typical example of a young child, who might be described as an "emergent" reader (Gillen and Hall 2013), interpreting meaning from a picturebook. Motivated by his interest, Jake took the initiative to choose and then initially to study a book silently on his own. After a while, he ran into a "problem" and began comparing two different images (L1–4): one of a tractor with a digger, and one that he expected to have a "post-banger" (that is, an additional piece of tractor equipment to drive in posts for fences), but which he couldn't see. We might argue that at this moment, Jake is reading a "practically lived text" in the sense that it incorporates his interest in tractors and farm machinery, and his knowledge of the material objects associated with them. Furthermore, he recognized, as Pea (1993: 47) suggests, that he might not be able to work out this conundrum on his own, and he reached out to his mother for assistance (L1–4).

Table 7.1 Talk between Jake and his mother

1	Jake:	*(on sofa, pointing at illustration in book)* dat post one mum
2		*(gaze to book)* is dat a post one mum? *(studies picture)* dat not post
3		one *(gaze to different picture, points)* digger *(moves finger towards*
4		*picture, gaze to book)* look digger dere
5	Mum:	*(no response, busy at other end of kitchen)*
6	Jake:	*(looks through pages in book, gaze to book)* I couldn't see digger
7		on dis tactor an look is it *(turning page)* here? *(opens page)* yes
8		*(smoothes page open and studies it)*
9	Mum:	*(out of view, baking)* was that is that a John Deere tractor?
10	Jake:	yeh *(intake of breath, points to picture, gaze from book to Mum,*
11		*pointing at picture)* I can see a grid here
12	Mum:	*(glancing over)* it is yep
13	Jake:	*(turning page, lilts as he speaks, gaze to book)* john de-er
14	Mum:	*(taking cakes from rack)* an where's the um post banger?
15	Jake:	*(glances up at Mum, gaze to book, turning pages)* it hant got post
16		banger *(opening page. pointing to picture)* look *(pushing page open)*
17	Mum:	careful of the pages
18	Jake:	see *(glances up, points to picture)* look it hant got post one on *(gaze*
19		*to Mum)*
20	Mum:	*(walking towards Jake)* it has hasn't it?
21	Jake:	*(studies picture closely)*
22	Mum:	what? it hasn't got a post you mean? it has I can see a post
23	Jake:	*(studies picture closely)* can't (?)
24	Mum:	*(approaches Jake, points to book)* this post *(points to other picture*
25		*higher on page)* and that *(moves hand from top to bottom, replicating*
26		*dropping action, moves away)* it drops down doesn't it? *(pointing)* like
27		daddy's
28	Jake:	*(gaze to pictures)* yeh tis like daddy's *(sighs, studies another picture)*

When his mother did not respond (L5), he filled in her conversational turn by rephrasing his problem more fully, and in so doing appeared to find a partial solution to his problem (by finding a different illustration with a different digger) (L6–8). Still busy with her baking, his mother asked for clarification and encouraged Jake to look more closely at the pictures in the book (L14). Their shared life together at home meant that she had high expectations of Jake's specialist knowledge and vocabulary.

If we study the very distinct patterns of interaction that make up this seemingly natural maternal response to a son's inquiry, we can see evidence of a distributive process. At this point in the exchange, the mother believed she could use words to prompt Jake to resolve his problem without the need for her to break away from her baking. She does this by encouraging him to use memory, inference, and reason to generate meaning from an external symbolic representation (the multimodal text on the book page). Jake studied the text again, this time employing further aids to sharpen his own focus, such as pointing to the illustration as he spoke, smoothing out the page (L15–16), and finally lifting his gaze to his mother as a signal to enlist her help (L18–19). Still encouraging his independent problem solving, the mother walked towards him, reassuring him that what he was looking for was indeed there to be found, while also verbalizing his problem (L20, L22). She then pointed to an illustration elsewhere on the page which he had overlooked (L24 and L25), and used embodied action to show the key ingredient of movement between the two illustrated objects that tapped into Jake's memory of lived experience. This enabled Jake to make the connection between his expectation of what a post-banger should look like and how it was represented on the page (L25–26). She then added a further key ingredient of familiarity ("like daddy's", L27), and Jake's problem was finally resolved (L28).

The page of Jake's text contained multiple illustrations with labels and very short written sections, which were distributed around the page in a spatial rather than linear design. The dominant mode on each page was illustration: clearly drawn, full-color illustrations on a glossy page. For Jake, reading this text involved mobilizing resources on the page (the layout and illustrations), his own cognitive and physical resources (memory of his lived experience to aid his interpretation of the images; pointing and straightening the page to heighten his focus), and distributed resources which he accessed by enlisting the fine-tuned help of his mother. His mother in turn used multiple resources to support Jake's reading: verbal encouragement to keep trying; reassurance that a resolution was there to be found; words to prompt him to apply his personal experience of post-bangers, and finally body movement to help him to apply his knowledge. This extract can therefore be viewed as an instantiation of how cognitive processes such as early book reading occur in social environments and are dependent on interpretative relationships between what is materially available and the social and semiotic systems familiar to others in those environments. It illustrates Geertz's (2000) suggestion that social processes are integral to the interpretation of textual meaning, to Levinson's (2006) assertion that interaction provides an essential framework for early engagement with symbolic representation, and to Hutchins' (1995) suggestion that intellectual work is dispersed across minds, bodies, and physical settings.

A Mickey Mouse ecology

This extract exemplifies a set of activities that is a habitual part of the life of Jake and his mother. Gibson would describe this as a "niche" (1986: 128) within their daily routines – specifically, a "representational niche". The book and the interpersonal interactions between mother and son are the central elements in this, with other elements being the immediate physical setting in which these take place, and the farm environment beyond the house; all are part of the cognitive effort involved in Jake's interpretation of what he sees. Jake is not reading in a conventional sense, but is examining the relationship of certain images to the social and material world that he inhabits. Far from simply reflecting the limitations of a young child not yet able to decode print, this reveals his profound understanding of the underlying architecture of symbolic reference, and of what reading is all about. As with Ashton-Warner's "Little Ones", desires and passions are his starting point. In spite of its traditional material form, there is free movement across boundaries in this text; nothing is lodged absolutely inside its covers, a point that Jake understands only too well.

The symbolic architecture that Jake is already using continues to inform the ways in which readers and writers read and generate texts into adulthood. The same kind of free movement and unrestricted relationship between "inside" and "outside" the mind applies, even though the more extensive levels of knowledge and experience that adults bring to processes result in a more complex ecology. Sendak, for example, describes aspects of his work, particularly his picturebooks for young children, as involving an accumulation of objects, experiences, and interactions, some personal, some associated with other people, which merge and collide without respect for boundaries of time or physical reality. In an introduction to a 1988 reissue of *Mickey Mouse Movie Stories*,[2] he discusses the enormous significance of Mickey Mouse to his personal and creative life. One of the stories in this reissue "was the first book given to me by my doting elder sister. I literally treasured it to death". Sendak was about 6 at the time, and the physical and inscriptional structure of the book provided opportunities for that combination of sensual, emotional, and symbolic engagement that is so often typical of young children's relationship with material objects. As well as giving physical and affective solace, the book also provided Sendak with a material anchor for a confluence of objects, events, and relationships that were distributed across time and place: "This book encapsulated my passion for Mickey, movies, New York City, and the strange, dark, doomy Thirties that, for me, were lit only by Mickey's bright, beaming smile on the screen" (1988: viii).

Mickey Mouse the Mail Pilot was a story that had a particularly enduring influence on Sendak: "What most enthralled me … was the picture on the front cover of Mickey in his airplane: a magnificently utilitarian vehicle that bent and twisted with dough-like pliancy … I had to have that … plane!" He goes on to say that 37 years later he gratified that childhood wish by putting his own hero, Mickey, into an actual dough plane in his picturebook *In the Night Kitchen*, symbolically refashioning and transforming the plane into something operating at a new level of consciousness. A central requirement of the mental activity of this is a substantial suspension of disbelief. Sharkey and Sharkey (2006) point out that suspending disbelief allows for choices to be made, with people choosing to act as if something is real even if it is not: "I know this is an inanimate object, but I am going to act as if I believe it to be a living being". Similarly, people can feel real emotions about the lives of fictitious people, in the full knowledge that they are unreal (Mullarkey 2007). Suspension of disbelief is also required on the part of the reader and the inscriber with respect to the relationship between the physical world and its graphic image, and in an acceptance that events, real or otherwise, past or future, can have a parallel, two-dimensional, inscribed reality.

The suspension of disbelief provides the author with seemingly limitless opportunities to cross the boundaries of material and existential reality in order to explore Lincoln's "liminal spaces". The idea that Mickey Mouse, a character in a comic and film that is not only fictional, but a fantastic, talking cartoon character, could be personally and creatively significant in the life of a young child transcends what should be plausible. However, this counterintuition not only is accepted by the author in the course of making "not yet imagined connections", but is agreed across the social and cultural communities of those who are likely to read the author's work. For Sendak, layers of culture and conflict that were significant features of his childhood are embedded in his stories, along with people, objects, events, and relationships associated with different historical and psychological phases of his life; and they have been transformed in ways that defy the generally accepted constraints of physical and social reality. Such combinations of the social, material, and symbolic provide the opportunities to "touch down" fleetingly with collocations of memories and experiences, distributed across time and place in enduring material and structural forms.

Distributed cognition

This very brief discussion of one children's author suggests that the production of text is a widely distributed process in which the mind of the individual author plays a unique, but only partial, role. Hutchins (1995) suggests that intellectual work is dispersed across minds, bodies, and physical settings, as well as across the various external tools and devices that are used in its support. The production of "external" representations involves cognitive "work" involving memory, decision making, inference, reasoning, and learning. These processes are also distributed across time (Hutchins 2004), and their representational outcomes endure as tools for following generations to use, develop, and refine. Sendak did not have to develop new systems of writing and drawing, or the technology and artifacts that are associated with them, in order to communicate the insights of his "creative soul" to other people. Furthermore, the cognitive resources that he drew on were to be found not just in his head but also in the sociocultural surround, in language, the environment, in history, and in "other people and the legacies of previous generations;... in the rules by which we live; and elsewhere" (Nickerson 1993: 230).

Compositional processes similar to those that Sendak has referred to have also been observed in children's early inscriptive activity, where the production of intentional, meaningful signs and texts from early infancy suggests that cognitive processes are distributed from the outset (Rączaszek-Leonardi et al. 2013). Gaskins (2006: 279) makes the point that rather than starting from a position of no symbolic engagement and then being "taught" about inscription systems once they start formal education, by the end of their first year infants have already learned culturally motivated patterns of expressing inner experiences. These are dependent on socially structured interactions that are distributed between participants, objects, and settings, and are culturally diverse in character. Trevarthen (1995, 2004) also points out that individualistic "all-in-the-mind" theories of learning do not effectively explain the origins or evolution of human symbolic behavior. It requires a participatory consciousness, he suggests, with infants learning from communities of people, and from systems and artifacts that have been invented by such communities over time. Similarly, Kress points to the need for a more generous understanding of cognition than "the sparse understanding we have now" (1997: xviii), and one that can account for how young children engage in complex forms of sign making and interpretation, in diverse representational environments.

Early sign and text making

The second section of data that we are going to look at is from a small study[3] that examined whether children under the age of 3 are able to make meaningful signs and texts, and associate the making of marks with the representation of personal meanings (Lancaster and Roberts 2006; Lancaster 2007). All ten children involved in the study were between 18 months and 2 years of age at the outset, and it took place in the homes of the children, with family members present. The project focused specifically on graphic marking, and the children's production of signs and texts. It considered the different kinds of objects and experiences that the children chose to represent, and the strategies and systems they used to convey meanings. The children also incorporated other modes of meaning into their signs and texts: for example, they sometimes used bodily action to convey part of the meaning of a sign or text, particularly where active, verb-like meanings were involved. None of the children was able to draw, write, or represent numbers in conventional ways, but they already recognized differences between these systems (Karmiloff-Smith 1992) and were able to produce signs that had features that were drawing- or writing-like, or that represented quantity.

A significant feature of the evidence from the study was the continuous interactivity between children and adults around the children's sign- and text-making activity. This played a particularly important role in a situation where the children were using graphic signs that, while intentional and meaningful, were not yet part of a conventional system. For example, the meaning of a mark was commonly instantiated using a combination of language, gesture, and gaze, with the child typically pointing or touching the mark deictically to single it out from others on the page, then stating what it was while holding the gaze of the adult, who then repeated the meaning as given by the child. This kind of bodily, communicative ensemble was similar to that used by Jake and his mother. The establishment of meaning was thus distributed between the communicative modes used by the child, the graphic mark, and the language of the adult. The mark could then be drawn into a local, public arena as a sign or text with an agreed meaning that could be referred to subsequently. Extrapolating more widely from this, it could be said that cognition was distributed between the bodily and mental activity of the actors, the environment (incorporating place, time, events, and objects), symbolic tools, technological artifacts, and texts.

Mike's plane

Mike was 28 months of age at the time when this episode was recorded in the small family kitchen. Mike's mother, Ellie, was sitting at the kitchen table, which was covered with paper and crayons, and Mike was squatting on a chair next to her. The family had very recently returned from a holiday abroad. The highlight for Mike, as reported by his mother, was planes: flying in them, being in the airport and watching them, and then talking incessantly about them following his return. The different visual, physical, and material experiences of planes were remembered and revisited in his mind, and continuously reviewed and transformed through play, talking with his parents, looking at images of planes on television or in magazines, and so on. The initial plane event had thus been extended and distributed beyond its original physical and affective environment through a cumulative sequence of mental and symbolic activities. In this respect, different time frames and events had been assembled into a symbolic resource that could be drawn on, added to, or modified during further semiotic activity.

This short marking episode, totalling only 30 seconds, could also be described as a representational niche, exemplifying as it does a habitual activity within this household between Mike and his mother. In spite of the shortness of its duration, it divides into three distinct parts that could be broadly described as preparation, representation, and instantiation. At the start of the first part, Mike picks up a black crayon in his left hand (he is left-handed), scans the space in front of him, then picks up an orange crayon in his right hand. He then directs his gaze towards a piece of brown A4 paper on the table in front of his mother and starts to climb onto the table. His mother watches him and laughs, collaborating with his desire to move into a physical position that will provide maximum bodily ease and comfort when marking. As he does this, he moves his gaze onto the black crayon and makes an "oo" noise, at the same time dropping the orange crayon onto the table. This suggests a positive anticipation of what he is going to do with the black crayon and arguably provides evidence of representational intention and mental planning – a specific desire and purpose in terms of what he is proposing to do. He then takes a couple of steps across the table towards the piece of A4 paper, which his mother is now resting her hand on, and squats in front of it, moving the black crayon down towards the page. Ellie simultaneously slides the page to the left into a landscape position in front of him (doubtless to give him more physical space to move his left arm freely) and Mike settles in front of it, cross-legged. The physical space in which he is going to work is now established, and the requisite tools assembled and arranged. This process of physical and bodily organization, and management of tools, takes 12 seconds, a little longer than the other two parts of the episode.

Almost without pause, Mike moves the black crayon onto the bottom left-hand side of the page and, going from right to left, makes a short line followed by a zigzag formed of five loops and six upright points. As he starts marking, his mother leans forward to look over his right shoulder so that she can see what he is doing. After completing the zigzag, he lifts the pen off the page and moves it

Distributed cognition in early literacy 151

towards and above the right end of the zigzag, making four equidistant dots that rise above and to the right of it (Figure 7.1). The marking is swift and unhesitating, suggesting clear and premeditated purpose. He then lifts the pen off and away from the page, resting it on his left knee, indicating that he has completed what he intended to do. This second part is the shortest part of the episode, amounting to just seven seconds. The third part of the episode is concerned with establishing and instantiating the meaning of the sign that Mike has made. Ellie moves the page to the right to enable her to see it better, and they both focus their gaze on the marks that Mike has made, while Ellie asks him, "What's that?" Mike replies, without any pause, "It's an aeroplane, Mummy". There is a slight stress on the word "aeroplane", suggesting a degree of surprise on Mike's part that his mother does not immediately realize what the sign means. She repeats what Mike has said – "It's an aeroplane" – thus confirming and instantiating the meaning of the marks. She follows this with a further development to the interpretation of the marks: "Going high in the sky".

Mike has in common with Jake an interest in very large, mechanical moving objects, and with Sendak an interest in things to do with planes. All are confronted by issues, albeit slightly different ones, concerning the representation of these objects. In spite of being very young, Jake and Mike already know that material reality, past or present, real or imagined, can have a parallel, inscribed reality. They are already working within a symbolic framework that enables them to suspend disbelief consciously and sufficiently to accept that the large, material moving objects in which they are so interested can also have a

Figure 7.1 Mike's plane.

two-dimensional reality. Two further problems arise for Mike as he anticipates inscribing. The first is a matter of reduction that goes way beyond a question of size. His experience of planes already extends across boundaries of time and place, and includes personal physical and material knowledge, awareness of represented objects and images associated with planes, and movement into new realms of thinking about them through discussion with his parents. From all this, he has to choose what is criterial about them, and decide how this can be visually represented. The second concerns the potential of his current graphic repertoire to allow him to achieve his ends, and the technical tools that are available to him to do this.

Mike's swift production of a two-part sign belies the complexity of these decisions. His visual and material knowledge of planes came initially from looking at them through the viewing windows in the airport, where their size and shape would be particularly striking to a young child. He had also traveled inside a plane, where, apart from during taking off and landing, the physical experience is often one of feeling constrained and confined rather than of moving freely through the earth's atmosphere thousands of meters above the ground. The first of Mike's signs suggests something of these contrasting experiences. He uses a zigzag pattern that is linear in construction and shape, arguably suggesting the extent and length of a stationary plane; the rounded loops of the zigzag contrast with the linearity, suggesting the circular mass of the plane as a container. However, this is not a drawing in any conventional sense of the term, and any iconicity associated with the marks that Mike has made derives more from gestalt structures (Johnson 1987) and generic associations between mark forms and physical and bodily characteristics.[4] The second sign is seemingly more transparent in its meaning. The positioning of the dots denotes the upward direction of flight, and Mike's slow and equidistant placing of them suggests the plane rising into the sky. This sign is also not associated with any conventional system, but relies on metaphoric associations between criterial features of the plane, and the structure and organization of the graphic marks. The spatial configuration of these two signs, and the sequential manner in which Mike produces them, suggest a text whose semantic boundaries extend well beyond its material extent and is distributed among the objects, events, and narratives that gave rise to it.

Conclusion

In this chapter, we have attempted a reintegration of cognition with the social and cultural activity that surrounds young children's earliest participation in reading, writing, and other graphic activities. We have looked at evidence that indicates that bodily, emotional, historical, and interpersonal engagement with such systems is integral to how children connect with them, and to how they reach an understanding of the underlying symbolic infrastructure that supports them – in other words, how graphic marks begin to become meaningful to them. At the center of all this are the texts that inspire children to interrogate their own lives, and the texts that they produce as a means of representing their lives to others: their "instincts, desires, resentments, horrors and passions". We have suggested that a wider definition of text than that provided by traditional definitions is needed to explain how it is that very young children can engage intentionally and meaningfully with representational worlds well before they have the capacity to engage at a systemic level with conventional inscriptional systems. It also defines text as something that is more than just the material outcome of the activity of an individual mind. In our discussion of evidence from the studies that we have been involved in, we have identified the involvement of a network of interactive and distributive relationships between adults and children, and the texts, tools, objects, and activities that characterize the particular representational niche that they inhabit. This network appears to effect a distribution of cognitive work between these different elements that enfranchises and enables young children to act as creative and independent interpreters and producers of texts, and to work with abstract graphic concepts during early mark-making and reading activities. As Ashton-Warner reminds us, though, "But I didn't start it: they began it themselves".

Notes

1 Hutchins' use of this expression is a reference to human cognition in its natural habitat, as opposed to its study in laboratory conditions.
2 The original *Mickey Mouse Movie Stories* was published in 1934.
3 Economic and Social Research Council RES-000-22-0599, Grammaticisation in Early Mark Making: A Multimodal Investigation.
4 Young children often differentiate between small and large people or things by using small or large marks respectively (see Ferreiro and Teberosky 1983).

References

Ashton-Warner, Sylvia. 1958. *Spinster*. London: Virago.
Chandler, Daniel. 2007. *Semiotics: The Basics*. London: Routledge.
Deacon, Terrence. 1997. *The Symbolic Species*. New York: W. W. Norton.
Donald, Merlin. 1991. *The Origins of the Modern Mind*. Cambridge, MA: Harvard University Press.
Ferreiro, Emilia and Ana Teberosky. 1983. *Literacy before Schooling*. London: Heinemann Educational Books.
Flewitt, Rosie S. 2003. "Is every child's voice heard? Longitudinal case studies of 3-year old children's communicative strategies at home and in a preschool playgroup". Unpublished PhD thesis, School of Education, University of Southampton. Available at: http://eprints.soton.ac.uk/184047/.
Flewitt, Rosie S. 2005. "Is every child's voice heard? Researching the different ways 3-year-old children communicate and make meaning at home and in a preschool playgroup". *Early Years: International Journal of Research and Development* 25(3): 207–222.
Flewitt, Rosie S. 2006. "Using video to investigate preschool classroom interaction: Education research assumptions and methodological practices". *Visual Communication* 5(1): 25–50.

Flewitt, Rosie S. 2008. "Multimodal literacies". In *Desirable Literacies: Approaches to Language and Literacy in the Early Years*, edited by Jackie Marsh and Elaine Hallet. 122–139. London: Sage.

Gaskins, Suzanne. 2006. "Cultural perspectives on infant–caregiver interaction". In *Roots of Human Sociality*, edited by Nicholas J. Enfield and Stephen C. Levinson. 279–298. Oxford: Berg.

Geertz, Clifford. 2000. *Local Knowledge: Further Essays in Interpretive Anthropology*. 3rd edition. New York: Basic Books.

Gibson, James J. 1986. *The Ecological Approach to Visual Perception*. Hillsdale, NJ: Lawrence Erlbaum.

Gillen, Julia and Nigel Hall. 2013. "The emergence of early childhood literacy". In *The Sage Handbook of Early Childhood Literacy*, edited by Joanne Larson and Jackie Marsh. 2nd edition. 3–17. London: Sage.

Gross, Terry. 2011. Transcript of *Fresh Air* interview with Maurice Sendak. NPR (formerly National Public Radio).

Hanks, William F. 1989. "Text and textuality". *Annual Review of Anthropology* 18: 95–127.

Hutchins, Edwin. 1995. *Cognition in the Wild*. Cambridge, MA: MIT Press.

Hutchins, Edwin. 2004. "Distributed cognition". In *International Encyclopedia of the Social and Behavioral Sciences*, volume 4, edited by Neil Smelter and Paul B. Baltes. 2068–2072. Amsterdam: Elsevier.

Hutchins, Edwin. 2005. "Material anchors for conceptual blends". *Journal of Pragmatics* 37: 1555–1577.

Jewitt, Carey. 2009. "An introduction to multimodality". In *The Routledge Handbook of Multimodal Analysis*, edited by Carey Jewitt. 2nd edition. 14–27. London: Routledge.

Johnson, Mark. 1987. *The Body in the Mind*. Chicago: University of Chicago Press.

Karmiloff-Smith, Annette. 1992. *Beyond Modularity: A Developmental Perspective on Cognitive Science*. Cambridge, MA: MIT Press.

Kress, Gunther. 1997. *Before Writing: Rethinking the Paths to Literacy*. London: Routledge.

Kress, Gunther. 2010. *Multimodality*. London: Routledge.

Kress, Gunther and Theo Van Leeuwen. 2001. *Multimodal Discourse*. London: Arnold.

Lancaster, Lesley. 2007. "Representing the ways of the world: How children under three start to use syntax in graphic signs". *Journal of Early Childhood Literacy* 7(2): 123–154.

Lancaster, Lesley. 2012. "Multimodal communication: multimodality and literacy". In *Encyclopedia of Applied Linguistics*, edited by Carole Chapelle. Chichester, UK: Wiley-Blackwell.

Lancaster, Lesley. 2013. "The emergence of symbolic principles: The distribution of mind in early sign making". *Biosemiotics* 7: 29–47.

Lancaster, Lesley and Mark Roberts. 2006. Grammaticisation in Early Mark Making: A Multimodal Investigation, End of Award Report: RES-000-22-599.

Levinson, Stephen C. 2006. "On the human interaction engine". In *Roots of Human Sociality*, edited by Nicholas J. Enfield and Stephen C. Levinson. 39–69. Oxford: Berg.

Lévi-Strauss, Claude. 1966. *The Savage Mind*. Chicago: University of Chicago Press.

Lewis-Williams, David. 2002. *The Mind in the Cave: Consciousness and the Origins of Art*. London: Thames & Hudson.

Lincoln, Yvonna S. 2001. "An emerging new *bricoleur*: Promises and possibilities – a reaction to Joe Kincheloe's 'Describing the Bricoleur'". *Qualitative Inquiry* 6(6): 693–705.

Meek, Margaret. 1988. *How Texts Teach What Readers Learn*. Stroud, UK: Thimble Press.

Mullarky, John. 2007. "Life, movement and the fabulation of the event". *Theory, Culture and Society* 24(6): 53–70.

Nickerson, Raymond S. 1993. "On the distribution of cognition: Some reflections." In *Distributed Cognitions: Psychological and Educational Considerations*, edited by Gavriel Salomon. 229–261. Cambridge: Cambridge University Press.

Pea, Roy D. 1993. "Distributed intelligence and designs for learning". In *Distributed Cognitions: Psychological and Educational Considerations*, edited by Gavriel Salomon. 47–87. Cambridge: Cambridge University Press.

Rączaszek-Leonardi, Joanna, Iris Nomikou, and Katharina J. Rohlfing. 2013. "Young children's dialogical actions: The beginnings of purposeful intersubjectivity". *IEEE Transactions on Autonomous Mental Development* 5(3): 210–221.

Salomon, Gavriel. 1993. "No distribution without individuals' cognition: A dynamic interactional view". In *Distributed Cognitions: Psychological and Educational Considerations*, edited by Gavriel Salomon. xi–xxi. Cambridge: Cambridge University Press.

Sendak, Maurice. 1988. *Introduction: Mickey Mouse Movie Stories*. New York: Harry N. Abrams.

Sharkey, Noel and Amanda Sharkey. 2006. "Artificial intelligence and natural magic". *Artificial Intelligence Review* 25: 9–19.

Titon, Jeff T. 1995. "Text". *Journal of American Folklore* 108(430): 432–448.

Toren, Christina. 1999. "The significance for childhood cognition for a comparative anthropology of mind". *Man* 28(3): 461–478.

Trevarthen, Colwyn. 1995. "The child's need to learn a culture". *Children and Society* 9(1): 5–19.

Trevarthen, Colwyn. 2004. *Learning about Ourselves, from Children: Why a Growing Human Brain Needs Interesting Companions*. Edinburgh: University of Edinburgh.

Tribble, Evelyn B. and John Sutton. 2012. "Minds in and out of time: Memory, embodied skill, anachronism, and performance". *Textual Practice* 26(4): 587–607.

8 Affective interaction during classroom picturebook reading

Eleni Moschovaki and Sara Meadows

Introduction

There is an enormous amount of psychological and educational research related to book reading. Much of the research has focused on the impact of book reading on the development of early literacy concepts and the development of oral language skills (Scarborough and Dobrich 1994; Bus *et al.* 1995; Blok 1999; Fletcher and Reese 2005; Mol *et al.* 2008, 2009; Lepola *et al.* 2009; Reese *et al.* 2010; Stamou 2012; Barr 2013) and some on young children's cognitive engagement (Moschovaki and Meadows 2005; Hammett Price *et al.* 2009, 2012). There is evidence that the affective quality of home book reading rather than its cognitive aspects predicted children's later motivation to read (Sonnenschein and Munsterman 2002) and children's reading outcomes (Bingham 2007). Much less research has examined the affective features of book-reading interaction with young children.

According to the transactional theory, in book reading meaning is constructed by the transaction of the readers' prior knowledge and experiences and the text (Rosenblatt 1978). In reading aloud, there is an interaction between the child, the reader, and the text. The reader acts as a mediator between the implied reader and the actual one. The reader overrides the text and uses a variety of strategies (voice intonation, gestures, etc.) to make the task of reading interesting and adapt the text to the child's level of understanding (Cochran-Smith 1994). Thereby, text representations have considerable impact on children's cognitive and affective engagement.

Rogoff (1990) uses the notion of intersubjectivity, which refers to the shared meaning constructed by two or more individuals during social interaction and requires both affective and cognitive attunement. People seem unaware of how swiftly they track others' emotions and how that influences their own subjective emotional experience. The ability to feel into others' emotions is realized through the process of emotional contagion. This process consists of three stages: mimicry, feedback, and contagion (Hatfield *et al.* 1994). A great deal of research has documented that people automatically mimic and synchronize their movements with the facial expressions, voices, and postures of others. Infants, for example, are able to imitate facial expression at birth (Field *et al.* 1983) and display movement synchrony (Berghout-Austin and Peery 1983). Similar findings are found with preschoolers in natural settings, and this reciprocal process of imitation seems to foster social interaction (Grusec and Abramovitch 1982). On the other hand, parents also mimic their children and catch their emotions (Malatesta and Haviland 1982). It has been argued that mimicry affects one's own emotional experience, as evidence suggests that people tend to feel emotions consistent with the expression they adopt. Researchers postulate that such feedback produces an effect on the autonomous nervous system. Recent findings in neuroscience uncovered mirror neurons which are fired not only when an action is performed but also when we observe others engaging in a similar action. People often come to feel a pale reflection of their companion's actual emotion, and as a consequence people tend to catch one another's emotions (Hatfield *et al.* 2014). This is even more evident in young children who have not yet developed regulation processes in response to affective states (Bugental *et al.* 1995).

On the other hand, social referencing describes how the emotional cues of the adult assist babies and young children in the interpretation of ambiguous or unfamiliar events. There may be innate mechanisms for social referencing, for example mirror neurons, and it is known to be a powerful cue for learning from early in infancy (Meadows 2010). The availability of emotional social referencing may be one source of the better learning infants and children show from interaction (including over picturebooks) as compared with other media (e.g. Barr 2013). Such emotional messages not only facilitate children's understanding but also influence their emotional stance towards the particular events (Thompson 2006). Therefore, teachers' emotional expressions serve to alert, to interest, to motivate children in relation to the events of the picturebook they share and assist them to comprehend the text. Both concepts (intersubjectivity and social referencing) emphasize affect as an essential dimension of interpersonal communication. To date, book-reading research with young children has not examined the affective dimension of such interaction and how that unfolds sequentially in time. The description of the affective strategies teachers use during the reading aloud of children's picturebooks will clarify their impact on young children's affective reactions and vice versa. Such a description is important in view of the fact that such strategies make books and reading attractive, especially for those children with limited home reading experiences.

Research on home story reading has shown that parents adopt different book-reading styles according to book genre. When parents use information books and expository texts, the interaction is usually more extended than for fiction books and narrative text (Sulzby and Teale 1987; Bus and Van IJzendoorn 1988, Mason *et al.* 1989; Pellegrini *et al.* 1990). Other research has pointed out that discussion around expository texts lasts longer compared to storybook discussion, parents' utterances are longer, with greater vocabulary diversity, and they engage their children in more high-cognitive-demand discussion (Hammett Price *et al.* 2009). Teachers presenting information books use texts more selectively and engage children in more discussion, in contrast to less discussion and the reading of the whole text in storybooks (Hammett Price *et al.* 2012). Therefore, it is expected that both teachers' affective representations of the text and children's affective reaction will vary according to book and text genre.

This chapter presents the outcomes of our own research in relation to the affective dimension of picturebook reading. It describes the methodology of the study, the affective strategies teachers use with a variety of book genres, young children's affective reactions, and the relationship between them. The final section reviews research on book-reading styles and young children's developmental outcomes, and discusses the implications for future research and practice. A full account of the statistical analysis can be found elsewhere (Moschovaki *et al.* 2007).

Methodology

Participants

The research study took place in Greece in 1994–1995. Twenty teachers from different kindergarten schools volunteered to participate. The schools were located in two islands of the northeastern part of the Aegean Sea, namely Chios and Mytilini. All teachers had considerable teaching experience (mean experience 12.6 years). Children were of mixed ages from 3.5 to 5.5 years old and all attended the book-reading session. The Greek curriculum adopts an emergent literacy approach reading is a recommended language activity and is very popular in Greek kindergarten schools.

Materials

Teachers were given the same four picturebooks covering a variety of book and text genres.

Information picturebook with expository text

The book selected is *Fire* (1992) by Rius and Parammon. It is a minimal expository text (13 sentences) which describes the features and uses of fire. Illustrations follow each page and complement the text. The text, for example, mentions fire as bad, while the picture shows a fire in the jungle.

Information picturebook with narrative text

Life Underground (1994) by Rius and Parammon is an information book with a narrative text (26 sentences). It gives information about life under the earth's surface through the discussion of a baby rabbit with its father. The text has dialogues, and the book's illustrations followed the text, presenting in great detail life underground (roots, tunnels, ants, burrows, etc.).

Fiction picturebook with an unfamiliar format

Winnie the Witch (1990) by Paul and Thomas is a descriptive narrative text with no dialogue (50 sentences). Winnie is portrayed as a good yet eccentric witch who lives with her cat, Wilbert, in a black castle. The witch faces many misfortunes as she cannot distinguish her black cat from the black background. In the end, she solves her problem by transforming her castle into a colorful one. The illustrations depict the witch and the castle with great detail and artistry. They follow or complement the text on every page. The book is considered to be in a format unfamiliar to Greek children, as research has shown that the majority of their home book-reading experiences are related to traditional fairy tales (Kitsaras 1993).

Fiction picturebook with a familiar format

The Three Little Wolves (1993) by Trivizas and Oxenbury contains an extensive narrative text which follows the line of the traditional fairy tale "The three little pigs" (156 sentences). The big bad pig destroys the house of the three little wolves, which is built of brick, cement, and steel, until he becomes a friend of the three little wolves. The text is repetitive, with numerous rhymes, funny names, and dialogues. The illustrations follow the text on each page. This particular book is considered to be in a format that is familiar to preschool children.

Procedures

Teachers were instructed to read the picturebook as they usually would. Each book was read on a different day and all sessions were tape-recorded. After each book session, the first author kept notes on the presentation style and gestures of reenactment that each teacher applied during the reading of the text. Teachers had not previously presented any of the four books, since previous research has shown that when children are familiar with a text, they are more actively involved (Goodsitt *et al.* 1988; Beals *et al.* 1994). Additionally, the children were asked if anyone had these particular books at home. Only one child knew the story of *The Three Little Wolves*, as he had a copy of it at home, therefore almost all the children were unfamiliar with these particular picturebooks. In total, we collected 80 book-reading sessions.

There was considerable variation among teachers on the duration of each book reading session (see Table 8.1). The book-reading interaction in *Fire* lasted from 9 to 31 minutes, in *Life Underground* from 10 to 41 minutes, in *Winnie the Witch* from 13 to 43 minutes, and in *The Three Little Wolves* from 18 to 64 minutes. There were also significant differences in the presentation style among information and fiction books. For both information books, teachers adopted an interactive style. The majority of teachers read each page and immediately discussed its content with the children. Six teachers read the whole of the text without discussion and then carried on with the discussion of each

Table 8.1 Number of children, duration of stories, and presentation style of each story session

T	Fire			Life Underground			Winnie the Witch			Three Little Wolves		
	NoC	D	PS	NoC	D	PS	NoC	D	PS	NoC	D	PS
1	18	17	R/IN	19	20	R/IN	17	25	PO/W	11	28	PO/W
2	15	19	R/IN	21	15	R/IN	16	19	PO/W	22	49	PO/W
3	17	13	R/IN	17	26	R/IN	16	23	IN	16	26	PO
4	20	19	IN	19	33	IN	15	26	IN	14	34	PO
5	14	20	R/IN	14	23	R/IN	15	23	PO/W	14	64	PO/W
6	13	31	R/IN	10	29	R/IN	13	20	PO/W	13	25	PO/W
7	11	30	IN	11	16	IN	14	16	IN	11	29	PO
8	10	22	IN	14	15	IN	11	18	IN	12	23	PO
9	17	29	IN	17	22	IN	14	18	PO/W	18	38	PO/W
10	17	09	IN	15	14	IN	14	15	IN	14	23	PO
11	15	25	IN	14	41	IN	18	35	PO/W	12	36	IN
12	12	30	IN	11	27	IN	10	43	IN	12	62	IN
13	11	12	IN	12	10	IN	11	14	PO/W	11	28	PO/W
14	20	25	IN	16	24	IN	15	28	IN	20	31	PO/W
15	14	19	IN	11	15	R/IN	13	13	PO/W	12	29	PO/W
16	14	28	IN	15	27	IN	11	21	IN	13	27	PO/W
17	14	24	R/IN	15	16	IN	10	21	PO	16	21	PO
18	10	23	IN	09	23	IN	08	19	IN	08	18	PO
19	14	25	IN	13	30	IN	14	26	PO/W	14	32	PO/W
20	15	20	IN	15	15	IN	16	20	ST	12	48	PO/W

Notes
T: teacher; NoC: number of children who attended the session; D: duration of session in minutes; PS: presentation style.
IN: interactive style (extensive discussion during book reading); R/IN: reads first, interactive style afterwards; PO: performance oriented with simultaneous presentation of pictures; PO/W: performance oriented without picture presentation – pictures were presented at the end; ST: storytelling without pictures.

page. For the fiction books, there was considerable variation. In the unfamiliar fiction book (*Winnie the Witch*), ten teachers read the whole text without showing the book illustrations, and discussion followed at the end, during the presentation of the book illustrations. Nine teachers read the text while showing the pictures of the book and discussing them. Only one teacher did not read the story; instead, she did storytelling without pictures. In *The Three Little Wolves*, 11 teachers presented the whole text without illustrations, seven teachers read each page accompanied by the book illustration, and only two adopted an interactive style (extended discussion during book reading). In both fiction books, teachers who read the whole text first discouraged extensive discussion during the reading of the text. Such discussion occurred afterwards and focused on analyzing heroes' actions, perceptions, goals, and/or retelling the story. Thus, book-reading styles are not consistent but vary according to book genre.

Teachers' use of affective strategies

Teachers' affective strategies included utterances with intonation, dramatization, and personal involvement strategies.

Intonation

Voice intonation refers to the prosodic dimension of book reading and includes variation in pitch level of voice, speed of reading, and its rhythmic vocal quality. It has been suggested that text features influence the degree of the reader's involvement (Chafe 1982). Tannen (1985) mentions strategies such as rhythm, repetitions, dialogues, etc. which assist readers to become involved with the fictional world. Egan (1988) describes techniques that oral poets used in order to enchant their audience, such as rhyme, rhythm, metre, repetition, redundancy, particular types of story scripts, and the use of highly vivid or sense-based images, and argues for their educational value in education in early childhood. During the reading aloud of dialogues, rhyming sentences, and questions, teachers alter their pitch accent. Therefore, the following features were coded as intonation:

- Dialogues.
- Sentences with rhyming (e.g. "If you don't let me in I'll huff and I'll puff and I'll blow your house down!").
- Questions (e.g. "The other day, while they were skipping in the garden, what do they see?").
- Pausing with the purpose of stressing a story point (e.g. "Then, they found worms ... roots ... potatoes ... and ants ... that were digging the ground.").
- Prolonging the end of sentences, a popular storytelling technique (e.g. "Winnie was living in her black house with her cat, who was also black. That is how everything starteeeeeeed."). Prolonging words in order to emphasize their semantic meaning, such as length, size, duration (e.g. "They went on digging and they found the roots of a huuuge tree and the roots of a plant that seemed like an onion.")
- Whispering or raising the voice (pitch of voice) in order to stress words or attract children's attention (e.g. "It wasn't long before Rouni Rouni the sneaky bad pig appeared. He said: 'Little wolves, scared wolves, let me come in. *Not a whisper was heard. They were trembling like leaves because of their fear.*'") The teacher read the last two sentences in a whispering tone of voice in order to stress the fear the three wolves were feeling. Similarly, when Winnie the Witch casts her spells ("Abracadabra"), teachers increased the tone of their voice and stressed it accordingly.
- Reading slowly (speed of reading) in order to emphasize the minimal text in *Fire*. The text was expository and the slow speed of its reading helped the children memorize it (e.g. "Small, when it lights ... big, when it flames up ... terrible, when it spreads ... It is bad, when it burns ... but good when it warms.").

Figure 8.1 illustrates the proportion of utterances with intonation used by teachers across the four picturebooks. Eight stories were coded by a second person, and the interobserver reliability in coding utterances with intonation was 90.8 percent. The highest proportion of utterances with intonation (16.7 percent) occurred for *The Three Little Wolves*, since the text had numerous dialogues, questions, and rhyming features. The proportion of intonation for *Winnie the Witch* is 8.4 percent, for *Life Underground* 5.5 percent and for *Fire* 3.6 percent.

Dramatization

The dramatization category includes reenactment of the dialogues by voice alterations, and reenactment of scenes. The use of dramatization also depends on the characteristics of the texts. If the text has lots of dialogue, teachers adopt a different tone of voice according to who is speaking. Such a strategy assists children to understand who is speaking. In texts with no dialogue, some teachers create dialogues in order to make the reading of the story more attractive, as the following extract demonstrates.

TEACHER 18: *Winnie the Witch*
T: "Aaaa miaou, miaou", shouted Wilbert, her cat. "Be careful where you sit, you sat on me!" "What can I do," said Winnie the Witch, "since you are black and with all these black things I can't see you at all!" And poor Wilbert was in great pain, wasn't he?"

In addition, some teachers reenact scenes with gestures. For example, when Winnie cast her spell she waves her wand five times, and some teachers moved their hand five times.

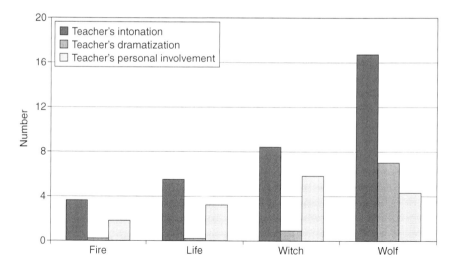

Figure 8.1 Teacher's affective strategies during book reading.

The highest proportion of dramatization occurred for *The Three Little Wolves* (7 percent), with much less for the other three books (*Winnie the Witch* 0.9 percent, *Life Underground* 0.2 percent, and *Fire* 0.2 percent; see Figure 8.1). Interrater reliability in coding utterances with dramatization was 98 percent.

Personal involvement

The personal involvement category refers to all utterances and paralinguistic cues whereby teachers demonstrated:

- Expression of personal interest (e.g. T: "Let's see, children, I'm very curious what else they may have found under the earth.").
- Expression of pleasure and/or excitement (e.g. for the house of flowers, "Oh look, children, isn't it beautiful?"); laughing when reading the text or at something a child said.
- Expression of empathy and/or sorrow (e.g. "Look, children, poor him [the colorful cat]. All the birds are making fun of him!" [sad voice]).

During the coding of the data, both language content and voice intonation were considered. The proportion of personal involvement comments for *Winnie the Witch* was 5.8 percent, for *The Three Little Wolves* 4.3 percent, for *Life Underground* 3.2 percent, and for *Fire* 1.8 percent (see Figure 8.1). Interrater reliability in coding utterances in this category was 88.2 percent.

A book effect was found in relation to teachers' use of affective strategies. Significant differences appeared between the fiction and information books and between the two fiction books, but not between the expository and the narrative text of the information books (Moschovaki *et al.* 2007).

Children's affective engagement

Children's affective engagement refers to reactions of personal interest, pleasure, excitement, empathy or sorrow that have been triggered either by the text or by the emotional reactions of the participants. The coding of children's affective reactions included three categories: language play, dramatization, and personal engagement.

Language play

The language play category includes all spontaneous utterances where children were playing with language, repeating funny words or engaging in rhyming play. Children have an intuitive disposition to playing with language. Researchers cite examples of games with nonsense verses and rhymes, during which children become very excited (Chukovsky 1971; Cook 2000; Crystal 2001). Such behaviors indicate that children are able both to perceive them and to like them. During picturebook reading, it became evident that text features encouraged children's language play. The author of *The Three Little Wolves* included funny names (e.g. Zip Zip Zoro, Popo Libopo, Fingo Mingo), rhymes (e.g. Rouni Rouni the sneaky bad pig – in Greek it rhymes), nicknames (e.g. Dromi Dromaki), rhyming dialogues (e.g. "Little wolf, scared wolf, open the door, open it to me" – in Greek it rhymes). The rhyming dialogues are repeated four times in the text of the *The Three Little Wolves* and prompted children's simultaneous participation in the reading of the text, a behavior called chiming. Children gained satisfaction from the recitation of the rhyming phrases and from the funny names, which were repeated with evident pleasure.

Moreover, the double meaning of words prompts children's language play. In the following episode, children play with the meaning of the Greek word *faki*, which has two meanings: "lentils" and "flashlight".

TEACHER 7: *Fire*.[1]
T: What's the use of the candle?
C1: When there is a blackout.
T: When there is a blackout.
C2: Miss, and big candles can do.
C3: And flashlights.
T: Flashlights [*faki*] use batteries, don't they?
C4: And the lentils [*faki*] we eat (all the children laugh).
T: Miss, can I say something?
T: Yes, Stelio.
C4: Give me lentils; I'm hungry! (all the children laugh).

In *Life Underground*, the reading of the compound words Lagoudobabas (father rabbit) and Lagoudomama (mother rabbit) had considerable appeal to many children, who responded with laughter.

The highest proportion of children's language play occurred for *The Three Little Wolves* (4.9 percent), with much less for the other three books (*Winnie the Witch* 1.6 percent, *Life Underground* 0.3 percent, *Fire* 0.3 percent; see Figure 8.2). Interrater reliability in coding utterances in this category was 97.3 percent.

Dramatization

All children's reenactments of scenes or events that occurred during the book-reading session were coded as dramatization (e.g. casting magic spells – "abracadabra"; blowing the house down).

Children engaged in dramatizations for *The Three Little Wolves* (4.3 percent) and for *Winnie the Witch* (1.6 percent), but much less for the two information books (*Life Underground* 0.1 percent, *Fire* 0.4 percent; see Figure 8.2). Interrater reliability in coding utterances in this category was 100 percent.

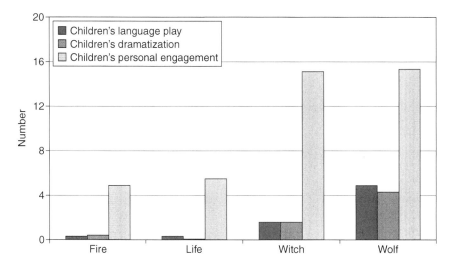

Figure 8.2 Children's display of affective engagement.

Personal engagement

The personal engagement category covers children's personal comments or paralinguistic cues that occurred as a spontaneous reaction to the text or the pictures and demonstrated the following:

- expression of personal interest (e.g. "What happened?");
- expression of pleasure or laughing (e.g. "Serves her right!");
- expression of excitement (e.g. "Oh no, he will blow it down!");
- expression of empathy and/or sorrow (e.g. "I feel sorry for the rabbits.").

The proportion of personal engagement utterances for *The Three Little Wolves* was 15.3 percent, for *Winnie the Witch* 15.1 percent, for *Life Underground* 5.5 percent, and for *Fire* 4.9 percent (see Figure 8.2). Interrater reliability in coding utterances in this category was 88.6 percent.

As with teachers' affect, a book effect was apparent in regard to children's affective engagement. Significant differences appeared between the information and the fiction books and between the two fiction books, but not between the narrative and the expository text of the information books (Moschovaki *et al.* 2007).

Two coding examples of book interaction can be found in the appendix (pp. 173–174).

Teachers' affective strategies when reading children's picturebooks and young children's affective reactions

The data were coded as sequences of utterances in order to examine how teachers' affective representation and young children's affective reactions unfold sequentially in time. The data were analyzed using the program SDIS and GSEQ (Bakeman and Quera 1995). The analysis of the data was done in two ways. First, we applied sequential analysis of teachers' affect followed by children's affect and the reverse using the data as a whole; second, we performed the same analysis separately for each book in order to examine the effects of book and text genre on the interactive patterns of discussion.

As expected, a strong bidirectional relationship emerged between teachers' affective behavior and children's display of affective engagement. Therefore, teachers' affective representation of the text influences children's affective behaviour, and children's affective expression reinforces teachers' use of affective strategies.

The strongest relationship emerged between teachers' comments of personal involvement and young children's display of personal engagement. This relationship was bidirectional: teachers' commenting and paralinguistic cues (laughter, exclamations, etc.) prompted children's reactions of personal interest, excitement, enjoyment, or sorrow, while children's display of personal engagement evoked similar reactions on the teacher's part. The following episode demonstrates such an interaction (Moschovaki *et al.* 2007: 414) in relation to one of the fiction books.

TEACHER 10: *The Three Little Wolves*
T: He blew it up with dynamite! (sad voice).
C1: But why don't they go to their mother? (with empathy).
T: But their mother told them they should build a house by themselves. Look, fire, children! Dynamite is a very bad thing. He destroyed this house as well.
C2: They must be dead now! (sad voice).
T: They are desperate! (sad voice).

The teacher demonstrates her sadness while attracting children's attention to the illustration of the blowing up of the house. Her feelings of sadness were transmitted to the children, who became very concerned and displayed their empathy with the misfortunes of the three little wolves. Similarly, a child's emotional reaction can be followed by emotional feedback on the part of the teacher, as the following episode points out.

TEACHER 20: *Life Underground*
T: (showing the illustration) Look! What are the hunters holding?
C1: Guns! (with excitement).
T: Guns. Why are they holding guns?
C1: To kill the rabbits.

T: Only rabbits?
C2: No.
T: Birds and other animals.
C3: It is a pity to kill animals!
T: It is a pity, they also want to live.
C3: I feel sorry for them.
C4: Once someone ran over a cat.
T: Oh, he must have done it by mistake, he shouldn't have done it.
C4: I cried.

In this example, a child initially expresses sorrow for the killing of animals, which triggers the teacher's emotional reaction and in turn prompts another child to share an emotional personal experience. Similar findings were replicated in relation to all four books, and thus the particular relationship does not depend on book and text genre.

A bidirectional relationship also appeared between teachers' dramatization and children's dramatization. In particular, teachers' voice reenactment of the text was usually followed by children's imitations of such reenactments. This relationship was found for both fiction books and for *Life Underground*. The content of the text played a significant role in affecting the extent of such reenactments. The highest proportion of dramatization took place for *The Three Little Wolves* (see Figures 8.1 and 8.2). The fact that the author of the text had included a lot of dialogues encouraged many teachers to adopt a more dramatic style of presentation by reenacting the dialogues using different voices. In addition, the author incorporated in the text reenactment of scenes, such as the blowing down of the house and the smelling of the house made of flowers. Some of the teachers prompted children to engage in reenactment, but in most cases children engaged spontaneously, as the following episode demonstrates.

TEACHER 3: *The Three Little Wolves*
T: (reads) He blew strongly like wind, fierce like a windstorm, with force like a typhoon he blew. Something like this: Fououououououou! Fououououououo!
CS: Fououououououou! (children imitate the teacher).

On the other hand, the transitional probability of children's dramatization followed by teachers' dramatization reached a significant level only in *Winnie the Witch*. The following episode presents such a case.

TEACHER 16: *Winnie the Witch*
T: (reads) One day, Winnie stumbled on Wilbert, turned over three times and fell on a rose bush.
C: Does it have thorns?
T: Yes.
C: Ouch, ouch, I'm in pain.
T: Ohhh, I'm in pain (imitates), that's what she would say (laughs).

Given that children's dramatization followed by teacher's dramatization was significant for only one of the four books, it seems that such an interaction occurs only rarely.

Furthermore, a strong relationship was found for teachers' intonation followed by children's language play. The transitional probability was significant in the two fiction books and the narrative book. Moreover, teacher's dramatization followed by children's language play was significant only in the two fiction books. Particular text features such as rhyming, funny names, nicknames, and compound words which were either read or reenacted by the teachers prompted children's language play as the following example illustrates.

TEACHER 11: *The Three Little Wolves*
T: (reads) "Certainly," said the kangaroo, whose name was Zip Zip Zoro.
CS: Zip Zip Zoro (laughing).

As with dramatization, the majority of language play took place in *The Three Little Wolves*. Almost all groups chimed or repeated rhyming phrases during the reading of the text – for example, Rouni Rouni the sneaky bad pig (in Greek it rhymes). Children displayed their satisfaction as they frequently laughed at the hearing of such sounds. As in other research, children's pleasure in language play was replicated in our study. It is interesting, though, that children's language play preceding teachers' intonation was significant only in the narrative text *Life Underground*. Additionally, the transitional probability of children's language play followed by teacher's dramatization was not significant in all four books. Therefore, children's language play does not influence teachers' use of intonation and dramatization during text reading.

A strong relationship also occurred for teachers' intonation followed by children's personal engagement. When each book was examined separately, this finding was replicated in the two fiction books and the information book with the narrative text. The content of the story had the greatest impact here. Apart from text features, children were excited by the misfortunes of the heroes in the two fiction books and expressed their feelings in various ways. Moreover, in *Winnie the Witch*, a fiction book with no dialogue, some teachers created their own dialogues or paraphrased parts of the book. The particular technique assisted children to become more engaged, since it attracted their attention and facilitated text comprehension. An example of such an adaptation is given below. The original text contained the following: "When Wilbur sat on the carpet with his eyes open, Winnie could see him. But when Wilbur closed his eyes and went to sleep, Winnie couldn't see him at all. So she tripped over him" (Paul and Thomas 1990: 9–10).

The following episode illustrates how the particular excerpt was presented by a teacher to her class (Moschovaki *et al.* 2007: 415).

TEACHER 13: *Winnie the Witch*
T: (reads) When Wilbur sat on the carpet with his eyes open, Winnie could see him because his green eyes were shining. But when Wilbur went to sleep on the carpet, Winnie couldn't see him on the black carpet since he was black.
C: Not again!
T: What did she do? She fell on him, she didn't see him and tripped over him. The Witch fell down and the cat was in pain with the witch oooover him (prolongs the ending).
CS: She fell down (laughing).

For the narrative text *Life Underground*, the majority of teachers showed the illustrations during text reading or immediately after reading each page. Children's reactions were related to the fate of the rabbit when hunters appear, and to the illustrations, as the following example points out.

TEACHER 12: *Life Underground*
T: (shows illustration) They started digging from here and made this enooormous tunnel and here is the house.
C: How big it is! (with amazement).

The teacher prolongs the word "enormous" in order to emphasize the length of the tunnel.

It is interesting, though, that children's personal engagement followed by teacher's intonation was significant in all four books. Thus, children's reactions influence teachers' text presentation, prompting them to bring text to life through voice intonation and paraphrasing in order to make the text more appealing to their audience.

The outcomes of this study illuminate the reciprocal processes of social interaction with a focus on affect between teachers and preschool-age children. Teachers' comments indicating personal interest, enjoyment, sorrow, and excitement were transmitted to the children, who reacted accordingly, and children's personal engagement comments prompted similar reactions on the teachers' part. Similarly, teachers' dramatization prompted children's reenactments. The use of voice intonation prompted children's personal engagement and, notably, children's demonstration of their personal engagement reinforced the lively presentation of the text. The bidirectional nature of such relationships is consistent to the theory of emotional contagion (Hatfield *et al.* 1994). Hence, there is a constant adaptation between teachers and children which enables the affective and cognitive tuning of both parts. The interactive sequences that emerged from this study illustrate how intersubjectivity is achieved during class book reading with a variety of book genres, an achievement which may account for some of the better attention and memory shown by infants with picturebooks as compared to television and touchscreens (Barr 2013).

As young children have not fully developed regulatory processes, the transmission of emotional states during interaction is facilitated not only between the teacher and the child, but also among children. During the observation of the 80 sessions, it became evident that the expression of enjoyment by a child was transmitted to the whole group, and most children reacted in a similar manner. Moreover, strategies such as voice intonation and dramatization make the text appealing and assist children's text comprehension. Finally, text features such as rhyming prompt children's language play and manage to affectively engage them.

Book reading styles and young children's developmental outcomes

Research during book-sharing interaction in preschool settings has illustrated a variety of book reading styles. Dickinson and Smith (1994) have identified three approaches: the performance-oriented style, the didactic interactional, and the co-constructive style. Teachers in the performance-oriented style presented the whole text with minimal interruption, with discussion taking place before and after text reading. The other two styles engaged children in extended discussion during the reading of text. However, the didactic interactional approach focused on labeling and story recall, whereas the co-construction style engaged children in cognitive-challenging talk. Similar book-reading styles have also emerged in the present study, yet such styles varied according to book genre. Teachers adopted either the performance-oriented style or the interactional didactic style during the reading of the two fiction books. The co-constructive style is better suited to the presentation style of the information books, since a lot of high-cognitive-demand discussion takes place during the presentation of such books (Moschovaki and Meadows 2005).

Parents also adopt different book-reading styles. Haden *et al.* (1996) have revealed three maternal styles with children aged from 3½ to 6: describers, who portray characters and illustrations; comprehenders, who engage children in more evaluations, inferences, and sharing of personal experiences and focus on print knowledge; and collaborators, who encourage children's active participation as they become older. Hammett *et al.* (2003) have identified five styles on the basis of parents' extratextual utterances. Notably, the majority of parents (60 out of 96), who formed one of the five styles, focused primarily on text reading and offered limited extratextual utterances of varied cognitive demand. Such a style matches the performance-oriented style of class book reading.

Additionally, there are numerous intervention studies related to the impact of dialogic reading on children's language and literacy development (e.g. Landry *et al.* 2012). Dialogic reading is an interactive style of reading which requires the use of open questions in order to encourage children's active participation, the use of modeling and expansion of children's utterances, the provision of positive feedback, and the ability of the adult to adapt conversation to their child's level of understanding. A meta-analysis of studies related to home book reading with the dialogic style revealed a moderate effect on the expressive vocabulary of 2- to 3-year-old children. The effect size was smaller for older children (4–5 years old) and for children who were at risk for language and literacy impairment (Mol *et al.*, 2008). Furthermore, a meta-analysis of experimental studies using the dialogic style of book reading in preschool settings revealed a moderate effect on children's expressive vocabulary and on their alphabetic knowledge. The effect of such interaction was greater for older children than for younger ones (Mol *et al.* 2009).

On the other hand, Dickinson and Smith (1994) found that children who participated in the performance-oriented group showed greater gains on tests of vocabulary and story comprehension as compared with the other two styles. In another study, 4-year-old children attended story-reading sessions for a period of six weeks with teachers who were trained in one of three styles: the describer style, the comprehender style, and the performance-oriented style of reading (Reese and Cox 1999; Reese *et al.* 2003). The children were pre- and post-tested on vocabulary, print, and story comprehension skills. In relation to vocabulary, children with higher language scores benefited more from a performance-oriented style of reading, whereas children with a lower initial vocabulary level benefited more from the describer style. Furthermore, children with high initial comprehension skills who were exposed to the describer style scored better in their print skills, while children with low initial comprehension skills benefited more from the performance-oriented style. Surprisingly, no effect was found on children's comprehension skills. Thus, different book-reading styles yield different developmental outcomes and, most importantly, these outcomes vary according to children's initial skills. Moreover, the outcomes differ according to children's age and their background, especially for those who are at risk of failing in school, whereas similar book-reading styles may have different impacts depending on the context of implementation. At home, there is a one-to-one interaction, whereas at school, shared book-reading interaction usually involves a large number of children, and children might not have immediate access to the book. Furthermore, children's individual characteristics such as their interest in books, their attentive span, and their temperament may also affect their learning outcomes (Fletcher and Reese 2005). Research has to disentangle such relationships if a clear picture is to emerge on what features of book reading have the optimal effect on children's current level of development while taking into account their individual characteristics and the context of implementation (home or school).

The current study points out that teachers' affective presentation is causally related to young children's affective reactions. Such a relationship also functions in the opposite direction since children's demonstration of their affective engagement encourages teachers' affective representation of texts. Our research (Moschovaki 2009) has also shown that children have higher concentration on fiction books, where the use of affective strategies is accentuated compared to information ones. Moreover, variation in the use of teachers' affective strategies had a significant impact on children's attentive behavior in the unfamiliar fiction book *Winnie the Witch*. In particular, high affective presentation of the particular story elicited higher concentration than low affective presentation of the same story (Moschovaki 2009), indicating that the affective strategies of the teachers simplify the cognitive demand of the activity and make a difficult or unfamiliar task interesting and appealing for young children whose attention span is limited and whose abilities in text comprehension have not fully developed. Given the fact that the affective quality of home book reading predicted children's later motivation to read (Sonnenschein and Munsterman 2002) and reading ability (Bingham 2007), it seems that, apart from the quality of discussion, affect is also an essential component of a read-aloud style. Further support is given by the outcomes of another study on home book reading that found a significant correlation between children's use of affective words such as love, like, and want and their development of their print concepts (book orientation, print direction, letter word concepts, etc.) a year later, when children were 3 years old (Watson and Shapiro 1988).

The style of reading that seems to accentuate the affective representation of text is the performance-oriented style. In such a style, teachers treated "reading as a performance to be enjoyed", and usually discussion occurred at the end (Dickinson and Smith 1994: 116). Reading becomes a strong aesthetic experience, as the affective qualities of its presentation assist children to merge to the story. Interestingly, research has not yet examined the impact of affect on children's cognitive abilities. Experimental studies suggest that affective states influence children's abilities in recall and their evaluative judgments (Clore *et al.* 1994; Bugental *et al.* 1995). Future research might fruitfully explore how children's affective engagement influences their cognitive engagement within the context of book reading while taking into account children's individual differences. Such a description could explain the benefits of the performance-oriented styles for children's receptive vocabulary, the development of print skills, and story comprehension.

The outcomes of the current study support the idea that teachers' affective representation of texts (intonation, dramatization, and personal involvement) invokes children's affective engagement. Text features (emphatic particles, rhyming, and dialogue) have considerable impact on teachers' choice of affective strategies. In this study, the coding of affect focused mainly on the verbal strategies and reactions of both teachers and children. Future research should incorporate nonverbal behavior (e.g. facial expression and body posture) in the coding system of affect through the use of video recording.

Moreover, this study did not explicitly examine the effect of illustrations on children's affective reactions. Book illustrations can become a considerable source of aesthetic delight, and visual codes may have considerable effect on children's affective engagement. Styles and Arizpe (2001) found that children's drawings after book reading depicted the emotions induced by the images of the story, and the empathy they felt for the book's characters. Future research may examine how particular features of book illustrations influence young children's affective reactions and to what extent teachers shape such affective responses.

The bidirectional relationship between teachers' personal involvement comments and children's personal engagement does not depend on book genre and text genre. On the other hand, the use of particular features of voice intonation, dramatization, and language play depend more on text features. The current study used a minimal expository text, and therefore we do not know what sort of affective strategies teachers use in more extended types of expository texts. Further research with a variety of children's books could elucidate the impact of various text features and the effect of illustrations on the use of affective strategies and children's affective behavior while taking into account children's interest on book reading, since research has shown that some children are highly engaged regardless of parental behaviors (see the review by Fletcher and Reese 2005).

The results of this study have considerable implications for practitioners. Many children, especially those who lack book-reading experiences at home, find it difficult to divide their attention between an adult and a book, in particular when such an interaction occurs at school, where there is not a one-to-one interaction and immediate access to the book's illustrations is unavailable. The use of various affective strategies such as voice reenactment of dialogue, or comments where the teacher displays her personal interest, enjoyment, or sorrow, is a particularly effective means of retaining children's attention. Teachers should become aware that their emotional state can be transmitted to children and can manage to affectively engage them even with books of increased difficulty. If children are to consider book reading as a positive emotional experience, teachers should pay attention not only to the quality of discussion but also to the affective representation of text. The present findings point out that teachers' training in the use of affective strategies can optimize the quality of book-reading experiences offered to preschool-age children.

Appendix

Examples of the coding system

TEACHER 10: *Fire*
116 T: (Shows illustration) Here children, the fire did a lot of damage (sad voice). (Teacher. Personal involvement).
117 T: What did it do? (sad voice). (Teacher. Personal involvement).
118 C1: It broke the window. (Child, 0)
119 T: All the windows (sad voice). (Teacher. Personal involvement).
120 C2: And the poor teddy bear. (Child. Personal engagement)
121 T: It burned the house (sad voice). (Teacher. Personal involvement).

TEACHER 10: *The Three Little Wolves*
119 T: (reads) And the three little pigs hitch a ride. (Teacher, 0)
120 T: How do we hitch a ride with our hand (raises her thumb)? (Teacher. Dramatization)
121 Cs: Stop (raise their thumb). (Children. Dramatization)
122 T: They stopped a rhino that was driving a lorry and they said to him. (Teacher, 0)

123 T (reads with a thin voice): Please rhino, will you give us some of your barbed wire, a few iron bars and armor plates, and some heavy metal padlocks? (Teacher. Dramatization)
124 T (reads with a heavy voice): "Sure," said the rhino, whose name was Popo Libopo. (Teacher. Dramatization).
125 Cs: Popo Libopo (laughing). (Children. Language play).
126 T: Funny name (with amusement). (Teacher. Personal involvement).

Note

1 T: Teacher; C: child; Cs: children; C1: a child; C2: a different child.

References

Primary sources

Paul, Korky and Valerie Thomas. 1990. *Μάγισσα Παλάβω* (*Winnie the Witch*). Athens: Margarita.
Rius, Maria and Joseph M. Parramon. 1992. *Τα τέσσερα στοιχεία: Φωτιά* (*The Four Elements: Fire*). Athens: Kedros.
Rius, Maria and Joseph M. Parramon. 1994. *Η ζωή κάτω από τη Γη* (*Life Underground*). Athens: Kedros.
Trivizas, Eugenios. 1993. *Τριβιζάς, Ευγένιος* (*The Three Little Wolves*). Athens: Minoas.

Secondary sources

Bakeman, Roger and Vicenç Quera. 1995. *Analyzing Interaction: Sequential Analysis with SDIS and GSEQ*. Cambridge: Cambridge University Press.
Barr, Rachel. 2013. "Memory constraints on infant learning from picture books, television, and touchscreens". *Child Development Perspectives* 7: 205–210.
Beals, Diane E., Jeanne M. DeTemple, and David K. Dickinson. 1994. "Talking and listening that support early literacy development of children from low-income families". In *Bridges to Literacy: Children, Families and Schools*, edited by David K. Dickinson. 19–40. Cambridge, MA: Blackwell.
Berghout-Austin, Ann M. and Craig J. Peery. 1983. "Analysis of adult–neonate synchrony during speech and nonspeech". *Perceptual and Motor Skills* 57: 455–459.
Bingham, Gary E. 2007. "Maternal literacy beliefs and the quality of mother–child bookreading interactions: Associations with children's early literacy development". *Early Education and Development* 18: 23–49.
Blok, Henk. 1999. "Reading to young children in educational settings: A meta-analysis of recent research". *Language Learning* 49: 343–371.
Bugental, Daphne B., Eta K. Lin, and Joshua E. Susskind. 1995. "Influences of affect on cognitive processes of different ages: Why the change?" In *Social Development*, edited by Nancy Eisenberg. 159–184. London: Sage.
Bus, Adriana G. and Marinus H. van IJzendoorn. 1988. "Mother–child interactions, attachment and emergent literacy: A cross-sectional study". *Child Development* 59: 1262–1272.
Bus, Adriana G., Marinus H. van IJzendoorn, and Anthony Pellegrini. 1995. "Joint book

reading makes for success in learning to read: A meta-analysis on intergenerational transmission of literacy". *Review of Educational Research* 65: 1–21.

Chafe, L. Wallace. 1982. "Integration and involvement in speaking, writing and oral literature". In *Spoken and Written Language: Exploring Orality and Literacy. Advances in Discourse Practices*, edited by Deborah Tannen. Vol. 9. 35–53. Norwood, NJ: Ablex.

Chukovsky, Kornei. 1971. *From Two to Five*. Berkeley: University of California Press.

Clore, Gerald L., Norbert Schwarz, and Michael Conway. 1994. "Affective causes and consequences of social information processing". In *Handbook of Social Cognition*. Vol. 1: *Basic Processes*, edited by Robert S. Wyer Jr. and Thomas K. Srull. 323–417. Hillsdale, NJ: Lawrence Erlbaum.

Cochran-Smith, Marilyn. 1984. *The Making of a Reader*. Norwood, NJ: Ablex.

Cook, Guy. 2000. *Language Play, Language Learning*. Oxford: Oxford University Press.

Crystal, David. 2001. *Language Play*. Chicago: University of Chicago Press.

Dickinson, David K. and Miriam W. Smith. 1994. "Long-term effects of pre-school teachers' book readings on low-income children's vocabulary and story comprehension". *Reading Research Quarterly* 29: 104–122.

Egan, Kieran. 1988. *Primary Understanding: Education in Early Childhood*. New York: Routledge.

Field, Tiffany M., Robert Woodson, Debra Cohen, Reena Greenberg, Robert Garcia, and Kerry Collins. 1983. "Discrimination and imitation of facial expressions by term and preterm neonates". *Infant Behavior and Development* 6: 485–489.

Fletcher, Kathryn L. and Elaine Reese. 2005. "Picture book reading with young children: A conceptual framework". *Developmental Review* 25: 64–103.

Goodsitt, Jan, Jayne G. Raitan, and Marion Perlmutter. 1988. "Interaction between mothers and preschool children when reading a novel and familiar book". *International Journal of Behavioral Development* 11: 489–505.

Grusec, Joan E. and Rona Abramovitch. 1982. "Imitation of peers and adults in a natural setting: A functional analysis". *Child Development* 53: 636–642.

Haden, Catherine A., Elaine Reese, and Robyn Fivush. 1996. "Mothers' extratextual comments during storybook reading: Stylistic differences over time and across texts". *Discourse Processes* 21: 135–169.

Hammett, Lisa A., Anne Van Kleeck, and Carl J. Huberty. 2003. "Patterns of parents' extratextual interactions during book sharing with preschool children: A cluster analysis study". *Reading Research Quarterly* 38: 442–468.

Hammett Price, Lisa, Anne Van Kleeck, and Carl J. Huberty. 2009. "Talk during book sharing between parents and preschool children: A comparison between storybook and expository book conditions". *Reading Research Quarterly* 44: 171–194.

Hammett Price, Lisa, Barbara A. Bradley, and Jana Michele Smith. 2012. "A comparison of preschool teachers' talk during storybook and information book read-alouds". *Early Childhood Research Quarterly* 27: 426–440.

Hatfield, Elaine, John T. Cacioppo, and Richard L. Rapson. 1994. *Emotional Contagion*. Cambridge: Cambridge University Press.

Hatfield, Elaine, Megan Carpenter, and Richard L. Rapson. 2014. "Emotional contagion as a precursor to collective emotions". In *Collective Emotions: Perspectives from Psychology, Philosophy and Sociology*, edited by Christian von Scheve and Mikko Salmella. 108–122. Oxford: Oxford University Press.

Kitsaras, George. 1993. *The Illustrated Book in Early Childhood: A Theoretical and Empirical Investigation*. Athens: Papazizis (in Greek).

Landry, Susan H., Karen E. Smith, Paul R. Swank, Tricia Zucker, April D. Crawford, and

Emily F. Solari. 2012. "The effects of a responsive parenting intervention on parent–child interactions during shared book reading". *Developmental Psychology* 48: 969–986.

Lepola, Janne, Julie Lynch, Eero Laakkonen, Maarit Silvén, and Pekka Niemi. 2009. "The role of inference making and other language skills in the development of narrative listening comprehension in 4–6-year-old children". *Reading Research Quarterly* 47: 259–282.

Malatesta, Carol Z. and Jeannette M. Haviland. 1982. "Learning display rules: The socialization of emotion expression in infancy". *Child Development* 53: 991–1003.

Mason, Jana M., Carol L. Peterman, and Bonnie M. Kerr. 1989. "Reading to kindergarten children". In *Emerging Literacy: Young Children Learn to Read and Write*, edited by Dorothy S. Strickland and Lesley Mandel Morrow. 52–62. Newark, DE: International Reading Association.

Meadows, Sara. 2010. *The Child as Social Person*. Hove, UK: Routledge.

Mol, Suzanne E., Adriana G. Bus, Maria T. de Jong, and Daisy J. H. Smeets. 2008. "Added value of dialogic parent–child book readings: A meta-analysis". *Early Education and Development* 19: 7–26.

Mol, Suzanne E., Adriana G. Bus, and Maria T. de Jong. 2009. "Interactive book reading in early education: A tool to stimulate print knowledge as well as oral language". *Review of Educational Research* 79: 979–1007.

Moschovaki, Eleni. 2009. "Teachers' affective presentation of children's books and young children's attention and participation during classroom book reading". In *Early Education*, edited by Janet B. Mottely and Anne R. Randall. 47–62. New York: Nova Science Publishers.

Moschovaki, Eleni and Sara Meadows. 2005. "Young children's cognitive engagement during classroom book reading: Differences according to book, text genre and story format". *Early Childhood Research and Practice* 7. Online. Available at: http://ecrp.uiuc.edu/v7n2/moschovaki.html (accessed January 12, 2010).

Moschovaki, Eleni, Sara Meadows, and Anthony Pellegrini. 2007. "Teachers' affective presentation of children's books and young children's display of affective engagement during classroom book reading". *European Journal of Psychology of Education* 22: 405–420.

Pellegrini, Anthony D., Jane C. Perlmutter, Lee Galda, and Gerie H. Brody. 1990. "Joint reading between black Head Start children and their mothers". *Child Development* 61: 443–453.

Reese, Elaine and Adell Cox. 1999. "Quality of adult book reading affects children's emergent literacy". *Developmental Psychology* 35: 20–28.

Reese, Elaine, Adell Cox, Diane Harte, and Helena McAnally. 2003. "Diversity in adults' styles of reading books to children". In *On Reading Books to Children*, edited by Anne Van Kleeck, Steven A. Stahl, and Eurydice B. Bauer. 37–57. Mahwah, NJ: Lawrence Erlbaum.

Reese, Elaine, Alison Sparks, and Diana Leyva. 2010. "A review of parent interventions for preschool children's language and emergent literacy". *Journal of Early Childhood Literacy* 10: 97–117.

Rogoff, Barbara. 1990. *Apprenticeship in Thinking*. New York: Oxford University Press.

Rosenblatt, Louise M. 1978. *The Reader, the Text, the Poem: The Transactional Theory of Literary Work*. Carbondale: Southern Illinois University.

Scarborough, Hollis S. and Wanda Dobrich. 1994. "On the efficacy of reading to preschoolers". *Developmental Review* 14: 245–302.

Sonnenschein, Susan and Kimberley Munsterman. 2002. "The influence of home-based reading interactions on 5-years-olds' reading motivations and early literacy development". *Early Childhood Research Quarterly* 17: 318–337.

Stamou, Anastasia. 2012. "Representations of linguistic variation in children's books: register stylization as a resource for (critical) language awareness". *Language Awareness* 21: 313–329.

Styles, Morag and Evelyn Arizpe. 2001. "A gorilla with 'Grandpa's eyes': How children interpret visual texts – a case study of Anthony Browne's *Zoo*"; *Children's Literature in Education* 32: 261–281.

Sulzby, Elizabeth and William H. Teale. 1987. *Young Children's Storybook Reading: Longitudinal Study of Parent–Child Interaction and Children's Independent Functioning*. Final report to the Spencer Foundation. Ann Arbor: University of Michigan (ERIC: ED 334 541).

Tannen, Deborah. 1985. "Relative focus on involvement in oral and written discourse". In *Literacy, Language and Learning: The Nature and Consequences of Reading and Writing*, edited by David R. Olson, Nancy Torrance, and Angela Hildyard. 124–147. Cambridge: Cambridge University Press.

Thompson, A. Ross. 2006. "The development of the person: Social understanding, relationships, conscience, self". In *Handbook of Child Psychology, Social, Emotional and Personality Development*, edited by William Damon, Richard M. Lerner, and Nancy Eisenberg. Vol. 6. 24–98. New York: John Wiley.

Watson, Rita and Jon Shapiro. 1988. "Discourse from home to school". *Applied Psychology: An International Review* 37: 395–409.

Part III
Learning language skills from picturebooks

9 Word learning via shared storybook reading

Jessica S. Horst

Storybooks as a method to teach words

One of the most ubiquitous activities in early childhood is shared storybook reading (Simcock and DeLoache 2006). Both receptive and expressive vocabulary are predicted by the number of times parents read to their children and the number of trips they take to the library (Arterberry *et al.* 2007), and shared storybook reading also promotes later academic achievement (Lonigan and Whitehurst 1998). Importantly, preschool children are able to learn words via shared storybook reading (Blewitt and Reese, this volume, Chapters 6 and 10 respectively). Given how common shared storybook reading is in children's everyday lives (Simcock and DeLoache 2006), it presents a naturalistic domain in which to explore empirically how children really learn words in real life.

Storybooks in experiments

Storybooks can be used as an experimental tool to better understand the processes by which children learn new words. However, it is possible to unintentionally make it difficult for children to learn new words from shared storybook reading during an experimental study. For example, lack of familiarity with the plot situation can make it more difficult for 7- to 8-year-old children to learn words from a storybook (Elley 1989), as can the number of times the story is read for 3- to 4-year-old children (Sénéchal 1997). In addition, including too many new words to learn at once, or including too few repetitions of these words, or investigating too many different types of words (e.g. nouns, verbs) can also generally make word learning from storybooks difficult in experimental settings (Horst 2013).

Depending on the current goal of the study, it may be more appropriate to use either commercially available storybooks or purpose-written storybooks. There are advantages and disadvantages to both approaches. Commercially produced books are useful because they are readily available and readers can fairly easily obtain a copy of the same storybook to replicate the study or to have a better look at the materials. However, one cannot always be certain how many of the words in the story are new to the children before the study – which is important to ensure the experiment is testing what the researchers intend to test. One solution to this problem is to pretest the children on the target words to ensure the words are really unknown at the start of the experiment (e.g. Wilkinson and Houston-Price 2013). Another concern with commercially available books is that target words may be repeated different numbers of times (Robbins and Ehri 1994), which means some words may be easier to learn than others.

Creating purpose-written storybooks enables better control over factors such as how many new words are in the story, how often the new words are repeated, and that they are really unknown to the children at the start of the experiment (so any learning must be the result of shared storybook reading during the study). One possibility is to include pseudo-words, such as novel words that sound like real words (e.g. *cheem*, *blicket*, *fode*), which children could not have encountered before the experiment. Of course, creating purpose-written storybooks takes time, which may defer data collection. For example, it took four months for Horst *et al.* (2011) to create the nine storybooks used in their experiment. Each storybook was ten pages long, including a title page, and was created by photographing models acting out a "scene" (e.g. a young girl pouring salt instead of sugar into her cookie dough) and then editing the photographs by using Photoshop to make them look more like illustrations (for more information, see Horst *et al.* 2011). Previous research demonstrates that children learn better from picturebooks with realistic photos than from black-and-white line drawings (Ganea *et al.* 2009; Simcock and DeLoache 2006).

Throughout each storybook in the Horst *et al.* (2011) study, unusual objects – unlikely to be known to preschool children – were named (e.g. an inverted slingshot called a *tannin*) because the use of synonyms for known concepts makes it difficult to pinpoint exactly how much learning occurred as a result of the study (Ard and Beverly 2004). This also ensures that the study is not testing children on words they might already know or partially know (Bornstein and Mash 2010). In addition, other research demonstrates that young children have a bias to attend to novelty in word-learning tasks (Horst *et al.* 2011; Mather and Plunkett 2012); therefore, it was important that all of the targets be equally novel (see also Axelsson and Horst 2013). In creating the text and "scenes", the authors also considered whether the target names and objects appeared together or separately, which facilitates cross-situational word learning (McMurray *et al.* 2012; Yu and Smith 2007) and the number of target name–object pairs. In this case, the authors only included two target name–object pairs in each storybook, because young children only learn approximately three to four new words each week via shared storybook reading (e.g. Brett *et al.* 1996; Elley 1989; Sénéchal and Cornell 1993), regardless of how many new words they encounter. Horst and colleagues included more than one target name–object pair per story to ensure children were learning the name–object association and not just remembering which object was the only one named (Axelsson and Horst 2013).

Testing words from storybooks

Word learning is an extended process, during which time words become increasingly familiar until they are integrated into the child's lexicon (Horst 2013). After shared storybook reading, there are a variety of ways in which to test children's word comprehension. A rigorous test of word comprehension involves presenting the child with a to-be-learned word and several possible candidate meanings to choose from. For example, one common method for testing word learning involves presenting children with multiple pictures and asking them to point to the target picture (e.g. Goodman *et al.* 1998; Horst *et al.* 2011; Wilkinson and Houston-Price 2013; Ard and Beverly 2004; Sénéchal 1997). However, if the target (correct answer) is presented only with other objects that were not pictured in the story, or other objects that are all completely unknown, then there is only one reasonable answer. This means the test is more like "choose the one thing we learned about earlier" (Axelsson *et al.* 2012; Axelsson and Horst 2013).

Importantly, that kind of test can be solved without learning the actual phonetic information of the new word (Schafer and Plunkett 1998). It is important that the test trials form a valid test – that is, it would be possible to fail to obtain the desired result (i.e. it would be possible to show no evidence of learning). For example, testing a child on *penguin* and *chimpanzee* with pictures of both a penguin and a chimpanzee creates a situation where it is possible for children to make mistakes and give incorrect (undesired) responses – for example, choosing the black-and-white animal for *chimpanzee*. Such errors can also be informative for understanding what children have learned (Horst and Samuelson 2008). When more test alternatives are plausible, children's performance does decline (Axelsson and Horst 2013), but children are still able to learn more words than expected by chance. It is important to keep in mind that introducing too many target words may also make a test *too* difficult. Note children under 6 years only learn about three words per day (Bion *et al.* 2013; see also Biemiller and Boote 2006 for a review of how the number of targets influences word learning from shared storybook reading).

Well-designed empirical tests of children's word comprehension also include a benchmark against which to compare children's performance, such as a baseline (pretest) word comprehension score or a level for chance responding. That is, if children failed to learn any words from the storybook, what would their responses look like? Such benchmarks are important to include because there may be differences between groups, but still no evidence of word learning for either group. For example, if children are asked to find a target from among four pictures (chance = 25 percent), it is possible for one group (mean = 38 percent) to perform significantly better than another group (mean = 21 percent) but for neither group to perform statistically differently from chance. In such cases, it may be informative to know that one condition performed better but that no significant *learning* occurred, calling into question whether the study was really successful.

It may be tempting to give children a production test after introducing words via shared storybook reading. After all, the ability to spontaneously produce and use a word is the pinnacle of word learning. However, word production is much more challenging than word comprehension (McMurray *et al.* 2012; Reznick and Goldfield 1992). Not surprisingly, then, children perform worse on production tests than on comprehension tests for words learned via shared storybook reading (e.g. Sénéchal 1997; Sénéchal *et al.* 1995). Two-year-old children may also fail to produce any words during an experimental session (e.g. Horst and Samuelson 2008). Finally, more repetitions of each word may be required for production than comprehension (McMurray *et al.* 2012). For example, Pinkham and colleagues (2011) recently demonstrated that 5-year-old children require 24 exposures to produce a new word.

How children use storybooks to learn words

Children do learn to comprehend new words learned via shared storybook reading, especially when they are repeatedly read the same storybooks. This is encouraging, as children often request the same storybooks over and over (Sulzby 1985). Previous research has shown that preschool (3- to 4-year-old) children learn more words when a story is read three times rather than just once (Sénéchal 1997) and schoolchildren learn more words when a story is read four times rather than twice (Biemiller and Boote 2006). Unfortunately, in these cases children who hear a story repeated have also had more exposures to the target words and therefore more opportunities to learn the new words.

McLeod and McDade (2011) controlled for the amount of word exposure. Three- and 4-year-old children either received a single reading of a story that included each target word three times or received three readings of a story that included each target word once. Importantly, both groups of children heard the target words the same number of times (three). Children who heard the words by hearing the same story repeated learned the words significantly better than children who only heard the story once. At first glance, this may seem counter-intuitive, because children who heard the story once had more varied exposures to the target words, which could lead to a deeper understanding. These findings suggest that repetition – and encountering a word in fewer contexts – facilitates word learning via shared storybook reading.

However, the amount of time engaged in shared reading was also different for the two groups in the McLeod and McDade (2011) study, just as it had been in previous research (Biemiller and Boote 2006; Sénéchal 1997). Recently, Horst and colleagues (2011) also investigated the effects of repetition and context on word learning via shared storybook reading independently of McLeod and McDade (2011), but controlled for the overall amount of time engaged in shared storybook reading.

Horst and colleagues read 3-year-old children either the same storybooks repeatedly or different storybooks, using the nine storybooks described above. Among these nine storybooks, three books included the same name–object pairs, so children could hear a target word the same number of times either by being read a set of three books or by being read one of the books three times. In the same-stories group, children were read a story three times in a row. The researchers read to children on three days and these children heard a different story on each day (i.e. nine story exposures to three stories). In the different-stories group, children were read three different stories in a row. These children heard three different stories on each day (i.e. nine story exposures to nine stories). Importantly, children in both groups were exposed to the target words the same number of times (12 exposures per target word).

Each day after reading, children were tested on their immediate recall for that day's target words. Children who heard the same stories repeatedly recalled significantly more words than children who heard three different stories (see Table 9.1, top row). On the final day of the study, children were also tested on their retention of the words they had heard on days 1 and 2. The children had not read those stories or heard those words in the intervening two to six days. Children who heard the same stories repeatedly retained significantly more words than children who heard three different stories.

Because children in both groups had the same amount of shared reading time and the same number of exposures to the target words, the only difference was whether the words occurred in the same contexts or in different contexts. Rather than there being a benefit for variable contexts, this finding provides converging evidence for the benefit of repetition during the early stages of word learning shortly after a new word is initially encountered (see also McLeod and McDade 2011). It is possible, however, that variable contexts aid later stages of word learning. Horst and colleagues have since replicated the advantage of reading the same stories repeatedly rather than different stories (Horst 2013). In one study, they found that this effect persists even when all children encounter three different stories each day, but the stories are the same or different over the course of one week. In a second study, they found that while there is a significant, persistent advantage to hearing the same stories repeatedly rather than different stories, children who hear different stories are able to learn words well if they encounter the stories in a bedtime setting (Williams and Horst 2014) – that is, if they hear stories immediately before sleeping, which is known to facilitate memory consolidation (Henderson *et al.* 2012). A word-learning advantage from reading the same stories repeatedly rather than different stories has also been observed in a classroom reading setting (Wilkinson and Houston-Price 2013).

Clearly, there are differences in the methods between the studies in this research area. However, as can be seen in Table 9.1, there is a consistent pattern of a word-learning benefit arising from reading of the same stories repeatedly. In addition, as can also be seen in the table, children's performance at test decreases as the number of target words introduced increases. Note: all of the studies in Table 9.1 tested 3- to 4-year-old children and did not include dialogical reading techniques, which enhance learning via shared storybook reading (e.g. pointing; Sénéchal and Cornell 1993; Rohlfing *et al.*, this volume,

Table 9.1 Shared storybook reading studies testing noun word learning as a function of repeated readings

Study	Ages	Nouns per test	Total exposures per noun	Test type	Test occurrence	Word learning rates (%) Repeated stories	Word learning rates (%) Different stories	Word learning rates (%) Single story
Horst et al. (2011)	3.5 yrs	2	12	Recall	Same day	81 (3)	58 (3)	–
Williams and Horst (2014)	3.5 yrs	2	12	Recall	Same day	82 (3)	57 (3)	–
Ard and Beverly (2004) (joint book reading condition only)	3–4 yrs	5[a]	3	Recall	Same day (read across 3 days)	64 (3)	–	–
Williams et al. (2011)	3.5 yrs	6	12	Recall	Same day	45 (3)	37 (3)	–
Sénéchal (1997) (nonquestioning conditions)	3–4 yrs	10[b]	3[d]	Recall	Same day (read across 2 days)	46 (3)	–	32
Sénéchal et al. 1995 (Experiment 1 only)	4 yrs	13[c]	2	Recall	Same day (read across 2 days)	15 (2)	–	–
Williams and Horst (2014) (no nap conditions only)	3.5 yrs	2	12	Retention	7 days later	75 (3)	58 (3)	–
Horst et al. (2011)	3.5 yrs	4	12	Retention	2–6 days later	66 (3)	25 (3)	–
McLeod and McDade (2011)	3–4 yrs	5[a]	3	Retention	1 day later	43 (3)	–	31
Sénéchal et al. (1995) (Experiment 1 only)	4 yrs	13[c]	2	Retention	5–7 days later	13 (2)	–	–

Notes

Number of repeated readings and number of different stories, respectively, in parentheses.

a Children were also tested on five verbs, in addition to the five nouns.
b This total includes two verbs.
c This total includes three verbs and 1 adjective.
d Children in the single reading condition received only one exposure to each target word.

Chapter 5). This table focuses on comparing learning rates for nouns, because previous research demonstrates differences in children's ability to learn different types of words from shared storybook reading (verbs and adjectives are more challenging than nouns; Robbins and Ehri 1994). For a similar review table with older children, see Biemiller and Boote (2006).

Why does contextual repetition help?

Taken together, this growing body of research demonstrates not only that repetition facilitates learning, but that contextual repetition facilitates learning. One might wonder, why should this be the case?

Each time a storybook is read again, the child has less information to encode, because at least some of the information was encoded during a previous reading. The first time a storybook is read, everything about it is completely new – although in some cases the child might know the characters from another book or movie and might be familiar with some elements of the story (e.g. going to the zoo). When a story is completely new, the child has a lot to take in and process: the general plot, the setting, the characters, the rhythm, whether the story is in the first person (e.g. "I wrote to the zoo…"; Campbell 2010: 1) or third person (e.g. "Buster loves the zoo"; Campbell 2012: 1), whether the story has tabs to open or parts to touch and feel – as well as any unknown words. The next time a book is read, however, several of these aspects will be at least somewhat familiar. For example, the child may recall that the story takes place at a zoo and there is a different animal on each page. Because some aspects are now familiar, the child does not need to devote as many cognitive resources to processing these elements and can move on to the finer details, such as new words (Horst 2013; see also Crawley *et al.* 1999; Mares 2006; Perrachione *et al.* 2011 in other research domains). You may have observed the phenomenon yourself; perhaps you have noticed finer details in children's storybooks when you have read them repeatedly or when you have watched a movie for a second time.

The benefit of repeatedly viewing the same visual information has been well researched in cognitive psychology, where it is known as *contextual cueing* (Chun 2000; Chun and Jiang 1998). Contextual cueing is a form of implicit learning. Because the visual world is predictable and highly structured, when visual contexts are repeated one's attention is guided to the to-be-learned item – and guided away from the less-relevant visual background. Contextual repetition facilities and accelerates object recognition within a scene and enables *inhibition of return* (Chao and Yeh 2006), which is avoiding going back and attending to something to which one has already attended. Overall, contextual repetition both reduces the complexity of the scene and increases predictability.

Children can use the predictability of repeated readings to guide their attention to the to-be-learned items. They are likely able to predict what will happen next and which words will come next in a story, as evidenced by their ability to correct readers who deviate from a familiar text (Robinson and Sulzby 1984) and their ability to fill in missing words when a reader leaves a word out (Beck et al. 1983). Once children are also reading themselves, repeatedly reading the same text aids reading fluency (Chafouleas et al. 2004; Hindin and Paratore 2007; Therrien et al. 2006; Weinstein and Cooke 1992), most likely because it helps readers to predict what will come next (Ardoin et al. 2008). Being able to predict what will come next decreases the attentional demands necessary to attend to new words in the story (Horst 2013).

Young children enjoy hearing the same books repeatedly (Williams and Horst 2014; Sulzby 1985). This is part of why they ask for familiar books to be read again and again. Another research area where we also observe a preference for something "old" and familiar is the infant cognition literature. For example, after being habituated to a video of a three-dimensional object being rotated, 3-month-old male infants prefer looking at a video of that same, familiar object being rotated in a different way rather than a video of a novel object being rotated (Moore and Johnson 2011). The widely accepted explanation for why infants prefer something familiar is that they are not done processing it (for additional reviews, see Perone and Spencer 2013; Roder et al. 2000; Rose et al. 2004). When infants are still processing something, they prefer to continue taking it in. Then, after they are done, they move on to something novel. It is possible that the same trajectory is at work in learning from shared storybook reading. Children may unconsciously know that they are not quite done processing something from a story, and that may drive their impulse to ask for the same story to be read again. Importantly, storybooks are very rich stimuli, involving characters, plots, detailed illustrations, new words, etc. Depending on the complexity of the book, many repetitions may be needed before children have taken in all that they can from the storybook (see also Rose et al. 2004 for a discussion of how complexity interacts with infant familiarity preferences). In addition, parents often add complexity by elaborating on information presented in stories that are repeated – for example, providing definitions of new words and asking questions linking what children are reading to their own experiences. In such cases, children may be encoding new or deeper information on subsequent readings.

Shouldn't variability help?

It may remain unintuitive that reading the same stories repeatedly is more advantageous than reading several different books (for a similar argument, see Ardoin et al. 2008). After all, we often hear that the number of books at home (e.g. Payne et al. 1994) and the number of trips to the library (e.g. Arterberry et al. 2007) are related to later academic performance. In addition, some studies do show that variation helps in other areas of language acquisition, such as learning phonetics (Apfelbaum et al. 2013; Rost and McMurray 2009, 2010) and generalizing words (Perry et al. 2010).

However, in situations where variability aids learning, children are often learning multiple things in parallel. For example, the other letters in words are also letters children need to learn in order to read (Apfelbaum *et al.* 2013). Variability appears to help children learn targets among targets. In storybook reading, the advantage is for less variability among the irrelevant information (Horst 2013). Contextual repetition appears to help children learn targets embedded in irrelevant information (a penguin is a *penguin* whether it is in a story about going to the zoo or a story about Antarctica).

Further, when the target words occur multiple times within the same storybook, there is some variability. For example, in my collection of storybooks the target name–object pairs appear on four different pages, offering some variation in how the characters hold them, where in the illustration they occur, etc. Even reading the same storybook repeatedly provides some variability because the child now has some background knowledge of the story and can pay attention to different things on subsequent readings (Horst 2013). As Heraclitus explained, you cannot step into the same river twice (Barnes 1987). We might also argue: you cannot read the same book twice.

It is also possible that reading different stories does help, but we have not yet fully tapped into when different stories are most advantageous. For example, it may be that when children are read different stories, they ultimately learn more about an object or concept, but we have thus far tested children too early in the encoding process. Variable contexts may also be more beneficial for learning grammatical and pragmatic information. Further, it may be that the greatest benefit comes from reading a variety of books while also reading each individual book repeatedly. This is likely to be the case with bedtime stories, where parents might read more than one book on any given night but read the same storybooks repeatedly over the course of several days. Recall, children are very good at learning new words when read different stories each day if these stories are read repeatedly during the study (Horst 2013).

Conclusions

Reading storybooks is a wonderful way to explore children's early word learning because children enjoy reading stories. Teaching words through shared storybook reading is unique as a method because it can be conducted in a variety of settings, including homes (Cornell *et al.* 1988), daycare centers (Williams and Horst 2014), and the lab (Evans and Saint-Aubin 2013). Not only researchers (Horst *et al.* 2011) but also parents (Whitehurst *et al.* 1988) and teachers (Wilkinson and Houston-Price 2013) can read stories to children. In addition, children can extend what they read in books to real objects (Ganea *et al.* 2009; Ganea and Canfield, this volume, Chapter 2), and the same processes involved in word learning via shared storybook reading are involved in other word-learning situations (Horst 2013). Thus, insights from word learning via shared storybook reading have great generalizability. Because reading picture and storybooks is such a common activity in many homes (Simcock and DeLoache 2006), this method also has great ecological validity: it is empirically testing how children learn words in a situation in which they do learn words in real life.

Children do learn words via shared storybook reading (Ard and Beverly 2004; Blewitt, this volume, Chapter 6; Horst *et al.* 2011; McLeod and McDade 2011; Reese, this volume, Chapter 10; Sénéchal and Cornell 1993). Word learning via shared storybook reading can be enhanced through pointing to pictures as new concepts are introduced (Cornell *et al.* 1988; Sénéchal *et al.* 1995; Rohlfing *et al.*, this volume, Chapter 5), when brief explanations of new concepts are provided (Brett *et al.* 1996), and when children are asked questions as they read (Blewitt *et al.* 2009). Importantly, simply reading the same storybook repeatedly significantly facilitates word learning (Horst 2013; Horst *et al.* 2011; McLeod and McDade 2011; Robbins and Ehri 1994; Sénéchal 1997; Wilkinson and Houston-Price 2013). The word-learning benefits of repeatedly reading the same story are useful to keep in mind as children continually request the same stories to be read again and again.

References

Primary sources

Campbell, Rod. 2010. *Dear Zoo*. 2nd edition. London: Macmillan Children's Books.
Campbell, Rod. 2012. *Buster's Zoo*. London: Macmillan Children's Books.

Secondary sources

Apfelbaum, Keith S., Eliot Hazeltine, and Bob McMurray. 2013. "Statistical learning in reading: Variability in irrelevant letters helps children learn phonics skills". *Developmental Psychology* 49: 1348–1365.
Ard, Lisa M. and Brenda L. Beverly. 2004. "Preschool word learning during joint book reading: Effect of adult questions and comments". *Communication Disorders Quarterly* 26: 17–28.
Ardoin, Scott P., Tanya L. Eckert, and Carolyn A. S. Cole. 2008. "Promoting generalization of reading: A comparison of two fluency-based interventions for improving general education student's oral reading rate". *Journal of Behavioral Education* 17: 237–252.
Arterberry, Martha E., Corina Midgett, Diane L. Putnick, and Marc H. Bornstein. 2007. "Early attention and literacy experiences predict adaptive communication". *First Language* 27: 175–189.
Axelsson, Emma L. and Jessica S. Horst. 2013. "Testing a word is not a test of word learning". *Acta Psychologica* 144: 264–268.
Axelsson, Emma L., Kirsten Churchley, and Jessica S. Horst. 2012. "The right thing at the right time: Why ostensive naming facilitates word learning". *Frontiers in Developmental Psychology* 3: 1–8.
Barnes, Jonathan. 1987. *Early Greek Philosophy*. London: Penguin Books.
Beck, Isabel L., Margaret G. McKeown, and Ellen S. McCaslin. 1983. "Vocabulary development: All contexts are not created equal". *Elementary School Journal* 83: 177–181.
Biemiller, Andrew and Catherine Boote. 2006. "An effective method for building meaning vocabulary in primary grades". *Journal of Educational Psychology* 98: 44–62.

Bion, Ricardo A. H., Arielle Borovsky, and Anne Fernald. 2013. "Referent selection and word learning in 18- and 24-month-old infants". *Cognition* 126: 39–53.

Blewitt, Pamela, Keiran M. Rump, Stephanie E. Shealy, and Samantha A. Cook. 2009. "Shared book reading: When and how questions affect young children's word learning". *Journal of Educational Psychology* 101: 294–304.

Bornstein, Marc H. and Clay Mash. 2010. "Experience-based and on-line categorization of objects in early infancy". *Child Development* 81: 881–897.

Brett, Arlene, Liz Rothlein, and Michael Hurley. 1996. "Vocabulary acquisition from listening to stories and explanations of target words". *Elementary School Journal* 415–422.

Chafouleas, Sandra M., Brian K. Martens, Robin L. Dobson, Kristen S. Weinstein, and Kate B. Gardner. 2004. "Fluent reading as the improvement of stimulus control: Additive effects of performance-based interventions to repeated reading on students' reading and error rates". *Journal of Behavioral Education* 13: 67–81.

Chao, Hsuan-Fu and Yeh, Yei-Yu. 2006. "Inhibition of return lasts longer at repeatedly stimulated locations than at novel locations". *Psychonomic Bulletin and Review* 13(5): 896–901.

Chun, Marvin M. 2000. "Contextual cueing of visual attention". *Trends in Cognitive Science* 4: 170–177.

Chun, Marvin M. and Yuhong Jiang. 1998. "Contextual cueing: Implicit learning and memory of visual context guides spatial attention". *Cognitive Psychology* 36: 28–71.

Cornell, Edward H., Monique Sénéchal, and Lorri S. Broda. 1988. "Recall of picture books by 3-year-old children: Testing and repetition effects in joint reading activities". *Journal of Educational Psychology* 80: 537–542.

Crawley, Alisha M., Daniel R. Anderson, Alice Wilder, Marsha Williams, and Angela Santomero. 1999. "Effects of repeated exposures to a single episode of the television program *Blue's Clues* on the viewing behaviors and comprehension of preschool children". *Journal of Educational Psychology* 91: 630–637.

Elley, Warwick B. 1989. "Vocabulary acquisition from listening to stories". *Reading Research Quarterly* 24: 174–187.

Evans, Mary Ann and Jean Saint-Aubin. 2013. "Vocabulary acquisition without adult explanations in repeated shared book reading: An eye movement study". *Journal of Educational Psychology* 105: 596–608.

Ganea, Patricia A., Melissa L. Allen, Lucas Butler, Susan Carey, and Judy S. DeLoache. 2009. "Toddlers' referential understanding of pictures". *Journal of Experimental Child Psychology* 104: 283–295.

Goodman, Judith C., Laraine McDonough, and Natasha B. Brown. 1998. "The role of semantic context and memory in the acquisition of novel nouns". *Child Development* 69: 1330–1344.

Henderson, Lisa M., Anna R. Weighall, Helen Brown, and M. Gareth Gaskell. 2012. "Consolidation of vocabulary is associated with sleep in children". *Developmental Science* 15: 674–687.

Hindin, Alisa and Jeanne R. Paratore. 2007. "Supporting young children's literacy learning through home–school partnerships: The effectiveness of a home repeated-reading intervention". *Journal of Literacy Research* 39: 307–333.

Horst, Jessica S. 2013. "Context and repetition in word learning". *Frontiers in Psychology* 4: 1–11.

Horst, Jessica S. and Larissa K. Samuelson. 2008. "Fast mapping but poor retention by 24-month-old infants". *Infancy* 13: 128–157.

Horst, Jessica S., Kelly L. Parsons, and Natasha M. Bryan. 2011. "Get the story straight: Contextual repetition promotes word learning from storybooks". *Frontiers in Developmental Psychology* 2: 1–11.

Lonigan, Christopher J. and Grover J. Whitehurst. 1998. "Relative efficacy of parent and teacher involvement in a shared-reading intervention for preschool children from low-income backgrounds". *Early Childhood Research Quarterly* 13: 263–290.

Mares, Marie-Louise. 2006. "Repetition increases children's comprehension of television content – up to a point". *Communication Monographs* 73: 216–241.

Mather, Emily and Kim Plunkett. 2012. "The role of novelty in early word learning". *Cognitive Science* 36: 1157–1177.

McLeod, Angela N. and Hiram L. McDade. 2011. "Preschoolers' incidental learning of novel words during storybook reading". *Communication Disorders Quarterly* 32: 256–266.

McMurray, Bob, Jessica S. Horst, and Larissa K. Samuelson. 2012. "Word learning as the interaction of online referent selection and slow associative learning". *Psychological Review* 119: 831–877.

Moore, David S. and Scott P. Johnson. 2011. "Mental rotation of dynamic, three-dimensional stimuli by 3-month-old infants". *Infancy* 16: 435–445.

Payne, Adam C., Grover J. Whitehurst, and Andrea L. Angell. 1994. "The role of home literacy environment in the development of language ability in preschool children from low-income families". *Early Childhood Research Quarterly* 9: 427–440.

Perone, Sammy and John P. Spencer. 2013. "Autonomy in action: Linking the act of looking to memory formation in infancy via dynamic neural fields". *Cognitive Science* 37: 1–60.

Perrachione, Tyler K., Jiyeon Lee, Louisa Y. Ha, and Patrick C. M. Wong. 2011. "Learning a novel phonological contrast depends on interactions between individual differences and training paradigm design". *Journal of the Accoustical Society of America* 130: 461–472.

Perry, Lynn K., Larissa K. Samuelson, Lisa M. Malloy, and Ryan N. Schiffer. 2010. "Learn locally, think globally: Exemplar variability supports higher-order generalization and word learning". *Psychological Science* 21: 1894–1902.

Pinkham, Ashley M., Susan B. Neuman, and Angeline S. Lillard. 2011. "Have we underestimated repetition? Repeated exposures to promote vocabulary development". Paper presented at the annual conference of the Literacy Research Association, Jacksonville, Florida, November 30 – December 3.

Reznick, J. Steven and Beverly A. Goldfield. 1992. "Rapid change in lexical development in comprehension and production". *Developmental Psychology* 28: 406–413.

Robbins, Claudia and Linnea C. Ehri. 1994. "Reading storybooks to kindergartners helps them learn new vocabulary words". *Journal of Educational Psychology* 86: 54–64.

Robinson, Fay and Elizabeth Sulzby. 1984. "Parents, children, and 'favorite' books: An interview study". *Thirty-Third Yearbook of the National Reading Conferences* 33: 54–59.

Roder, Beverly J., Emily W. Bushnell, and Anne Marie Sasseville. 2000. "Infants' preferences for familiarity and novelty during the course of visual processing". *Infancy* 1: 491–507.

Rose, Susan A., Judith F. Feldman, and Jeffrey J. Jankowski. 2004. "Infant visual recognition memory". *Developmental Review* 24: 74–100.

Rost, Gwyneth C. and Bob McMurray. 2009. "Speaker variability augments phonological processing in early word learning". *Developmental Science* 12: 339–349.

Rost, Gwyneth C. and Bob McMurray. 2010. "Finding the signal by adding noise: The role of noncontrastive phonetic variability in early word learning". *Infancy* 15: 608–635.

Schafer, Graham and Kim Plunkett. 1998. "Rapid word learning by fifteen-month-olds under tightly controlled conditions". *Child Development* 69: 309–20.

Sénéchal, Monique. 1997. "The differential effect of storybook reading on preschoolers' acquisition of expressive and receptive vocabulary". *Journal of Child Language* 24: 123–138.

Sénéchal, Monique and Edward H. Cornell. 1993. "Vocabulary acquisition through shared reading experiences". *Reading Research Quarterly* 28: 360–374.

Sénéchal, Monique, Eleanor Thomas, and Jo-Ann Monker. 1995. "Individual differences in 4-year-old children's acquisition of vocabulary during storybook reading". *Journal of Educational Psychology* 87: 218–229.

Simcock, Gabrielle and Judy DeLoache. 2006. "Get the picture? The effects of iconicity on toddlers' reenactment from picture books". *Developmental Psychology* 42: 1352–1357.

Sulzby, Elizabeth. 1985. "Children's emergent reading of favorite storybooks: A developmental study". *Reading Research Quarterly* 20: 458–481.

Therrien, William J., Katherine Wickstrom, and Kevin Jones. 2006. "Effect of a combined repeated reading and question generation intervention on reading achievement". *Learning Disabilities Research and Practice* 21: 89–97.

Weinstein, Gloria and Nancy L. Cooke. 1992. "The effects of two repeated reading interventions on generalization of fluency". *Learning Disability Quarterly* 15: 21–28.

Whitehurst, Grover J., Francine L. Falco, Christopher J. Lonigan, Janet E. Fischel, Barbara D. DeBaryshe, Marta C. Valdez-Menchaca, and Marie Caulfield. 1988. "Accelerating language development through picture book reading". *Developmental Psychology* 24: 552–559.

Wilkinson, Kathryn S. and Carmel Houston-Price. 2013. "Once upon a time, there was a pulchritudinous princess…: The role of word definitions and multiple story contexts in chldren's learning of difficult vocabulary". *Applied Psycholinguistics* 34: 591–613.

Williams, Sophie E. and Jessica S. Horst. 2014. "Goodnight book: The benefit of sleep consolidation on word learning via storybooks". *Frontiers in Developmental Psychology* 5: 1–12.

Williams, Sophie E., Jessica S. Horst, and Jane Oakhill. 2011. "The same old story: Contextual cueing facilitates word learning in shared storybook reading". Poster presented at the biannual meeting of the Cognitive Development Society, Philadephia, October 13–15).

Yu, Chen and Linda B. Smith. 2007. "Rapid word learning under uncertainty via cross-situational statistics". *Psychological Science* 18: 414–420.

10 What good is a picturebook?
Developing children's oral language and literacy through shared picturebook reading

Elaine Reese

Benjamin Franklin purportedly countered, "What good is a newborn baby?" when queried about the point of the new technology of hot air ballooning (Chapin 1985). Like a baby (or a hot air balloon), does a picturebook justify its existence simply from being a delight to behold, complete in and of itself?

In this chapter, I will present evidence that picturebook reading has a function beyond the aesthetic and hedonic: shared picturebook reading enhances children's oral language development. Yet I will also present evidence that shared picturebook reading, as it is normally practiced between adults and young children, does not necessarily advance children's early reading skills. For shared picturebook reading to accelerate early reading skills, particular kinds of interactions need to take place.

Yet that does not mean that picturebook reading is unimportant for children's reading. Children who have better oral language skills at school entry experience greater success in reading by the middle of primary school (Dickinson and Porche 2011; Sénéchal and LeFevre 2002), when good reading involves comprehension as well as decoding. The components of oral language that appear to be most important for later reading are vocabulary knowledge, comprehension of stories heard aloud, as well as production of stories (narrative skills) and an awareness of the sounds of words (phonological awareness). Vocabulary knowledge and narrative skills both support children's later reading skill (Reese *et al.* 2010b), and phonological awareness supports early decoding efforts (Bradley and Bryant 1983; Chow *et al.* 2008). All of these oral language skills have been developing throughout early childhood via interactions with adults.

In this chapter, I will review my own work and that of others on the various ways children's oral language skills and literacy develop through shared picturebook-reading interactions. I will focus on each of these components of oral language – vocabulary, narrative, phonological awareness – to review the existing evidence for how picturebook interactions can support each skill. Most of the studies I will review are longitudinal, meaning that researchers have followed the same children over time to observe the way that parents and children naturally read picturebooks together, and to track the changes in children's oral language skills that can be attributed to shared picturebook reading. Some studies are shorter-term and experimental, in which researchers or parents are trained to use a particular style of book reading with children, and then the differences in children's skills are measured relative to children who have experienced reading as it naturally occurs. I will evaluate the evidence from these studies for shared picturebook reading as a privileged context for children's developing oral language and literacy skills. I will close the chapter with some recommendations on how parents and teachers can read picturebooks with young children in ways that matter the most for their development as communicators and as readers.

How does shared picturebook reading support young children's vocabulary development?

Perhaps the largest body of research exists on children's learning of new words from picturebooks. This research has explored children's receptive vocabulary (their understanding of words) and expressive vocabulary (their ability to produce these words). Early research in this area was correlational, and focused primarily on the frequency with which parents shared picturebooks with their children. In these studies, parents estimated how often they engaged in picturebook reading with their young children per day or per week, and then children's vocabulary knowledge was measured either at that same time or later in time using standardized measures. These studies reveal a moderate association between the quantity of shared picturebook reading and children's oral language growth, including vocabulary skills (see Bus *et al.* 1995 for a meta-analysis; Scarborough and Dobrich 1994 for a review). However, these studies often failed to control for other confounding factors in explaining the association, such as other types of interactions or teaching practices that parents might be engaging in with their children besides picturebook reading. Thus, a parent who reads picturebooks often with their children may also talk more often with their children, and it could be the total frequency of talk – not simply talk during book reading – that matters for children's language development. Therefore, it is difficult to ascertain the unique role that picturebook reading might be playing in children's language and literacy development from these studies alone.

In 2002, Sénéchal and LeFevre conducted an influential longitudinal study that addressed some of these confounds. Their study began when children were in kindergarten and followed those children into third grade. The children were all Canadian and English-speaking. First, Sénéchal and LeFevre developed a new way to measure the frequency of parents' book reading that circumvented parents' tendency to overreport how often they shared books with their children. (When parents know the socially desirable response, there is a strong tendency for them to report that they engage in more of that behavior with their children than they actually do.) Their book exposure checklists entailed parents noting the real book titles and authors they recognized, but, unbeknownst to the parents, the checklists also contained "foil" items that were not real books or authors. Parents' frequency of book reading was calculated as the number of real books and authors they checked minus the number of foils they checked. This final measure may be a more accurate count of how often parents are actually reading picturebooks with their children. Second, they controlled for parents' education levels, which could be acting as a proxy influence on their book-reading habits and many other activities. In other words, highly educated parents may be doing more of all sorts of things, in addition to reading picturebooks, that help their children's development. Third, they contrasted the frequency of book reading with the frequency of another important interaction for children's reading: parents' reports of teaching their children to recognize and print letters and words. Finally, they also controlled for children's analytic IQ scores in the analyses, another strong contributor to children's skills and achievement. The results were clear: even after controlling for these other potential influences on children's language and literacy, the frequency of parents' book reading was uniquely linked to children's receptive vocabulary development one year later, but not to their phonological awareness or early reading skills. Note that this study did not measure other aspects of children's oral language, such as their expressive vocabulary, listening comprehension, or narrative skills.

These findings provided compelling evidence of the role of picturebook reading in children's vocabulary development, but they still only addressed a part of the picture. Is it merely quantity of book reading that matters for children's vocabulary, or does the quality of the picturebook reading interactions matter too? Conceivably, a parent who reads the text straight through and does not ask the child questions about the pictures or about words would not advance their children's vocabulary as much as a parent who reads the same number of books but in a more interactive fashion.

Fortunately, a large body of experimental evidence has been amassed on this very question. Note that my focus in this review is on verbal interactions during picturebook reading. Rohlfing, Grimminger, and Nachtigäller (this volume, Chapter 5) have demonstrated that young toddlers' productive vocabulary increases rapidly when parents simultaneously gesture to an object on the page as they are labeling it during picturebook reading. In contrast, most book-reading studies with older children do not assess parents' gestures. In these studies, parents or teachers are taught a more interactive style of reading which they practice with children over several weeks or months. Other parents or teachers are instructed to read picturebooks with their children in their natural style. Parents or teachers are randomly assigned to the experimental and control conditions so that preexisting differences in quantity or quality of book reading are spread equally across the two groups. Many of these studies use a technique called *dialogic reading*, in which parents or teachers are trained to ask open-ended prompts on each page spread, and to follow up those prompts by extending and praising their child's reply, which can then lead to a new cycle of prompting (see Whitehurst *et al.* 1988). Dialogic reading involves repeated readings of the same book at least three times over a week, with the parent's or teacher's prompts requesting more verbal contributions from children with each reading (Whitehurst *et al.* 1994b). In a preschool setting, dialogic reading is conducted with small groups of three to five children. Children's vocabulary knowledge is tested before and after the intervention phase to determine whether dialogic reading increases vocabulary more than would parents' or teachers' natural reading techniques. These studies reveal that dialogic reading does enhance children's vocabulary, especially their expressive vocabulary development (Whitehurst *et al.* 1988; Zevenbergen and Whitehurst 2003). The main outcome measure in dialogic reading studies is typically single-word expressive vocabulary tests, in which the researcher asks children to provide a label for a picture; however, some dialogic reading studies have also included measures of children's verbal expression, syntactic complexity, and narrative skills (e.g. Lonigan and Whitehurst 1998; Zevenbergen *et al.* 2003).

The dialogic reading technique was originally devised as a therapy for children with language delays; it is notable that the technique in its original form appears to work best for younger children and for those with lower initial language levels (Cutspec 2004). It does not seem to work as well for older children or for at-risk children from low-income or less educated families (Mol *et al.* 2008), perhaps because low-income parents are not as comfortable or confident with the new reading techniques. Although 98 percent of contemporary parents in the United States report reading to their children at least once or twice a week (Hindman *et al.* 2014), parents may be overestimating their book-reading habits in line with what they think they should be doing. And if parents are reading books to their young children mainly because they think they *should* be, it does not mean they feel comfortable or confident doing so. It makes sense that it will be easier for a parent to adopt a new style of reading if they are already comfortable reading books with their children. In one study we conducted with low-income US parents and their children attending Head Start enrichment programs, dialogic reading by parents alone was not effective for enhancing children's oral language development (Reese *et al.* 2010a). Instead, a conversational technique called *elaborative reminiscing*, in which parents discussed shared past events with their children, was more effective than dialogic reading for enhancing children's oral language in the form of narrative production skills. Thus, it is vital before conducting picturebook-reading interventions with low-income parents that researchers ensure parents are comfortable sharing picturebooks with their children and with the new techniques (see Reese 2012 for an extended discussion of this point).

In one experimental study that we conducted with a researcher reading in one of three different ways for six weeks with a group of 4-year-old children, a dialogic-style reading technique was most effective at advancing vocabulary (receptive vocabulary in this instance) for the younger and less advanced 4-year-olds (Reese and Cox 1999). In this *describer* style, adults provided statements and asked simple questions about the pictures (e.g. *What are Mum and Dad having for breakfast?*). In contrast, a *performance-oriented* style of book reading, in which the researcher previewed the book with the child and then asked more difficult inferential questions at the end of the book (e.g. *Why did Hemi take Rata to school as his pet?*), but did not interrupt the actual reading, resulted in greater vocabulary advances for older 4-year-olds and those with larger vocabularies at the outset of the study.

This experimental work is consistent with an earlier correlational study (Haden *et al.* 1996) in which the children with the most advanced receptive vocabularies at school entry had mothers who read to them in a high-level style in which they increased their use of prediction and inference statements and questions over the preschool period (e.g. *What do you think is going to happen next in the story? Why did Peter run away? I think Hemi is sad because he doesn't have a pet.*). These findings are also consistent with findings from the Early Childhood Longitudinal Study of nearly 700 US families that older preschoolers' vocabulary skill was linked to mothers' use of a greater variety of meaning-related talk (including word definitions and story summaries) during picturebook reading (Hindman *et al.* 2014). Moreover, these findings are consistent with other experimental work reiterating that children with larger vocabularies learn new words from picturebooks more readily than children with smaller vocabularies, and that teachers' high-level "analytic" talk during book reading with older preschoolers predicts children's later vocabulary (Dickinson and Porche 2011). Thus, the quality of book reading does matter for children's vocabulary development, but the optimal style depends on the child's current vocabulary level. Younger children and those with smaller vocabularies appear to benefit more from a highly interactive style of book reading in which the adult requests labels or asks simple open-ended questions about the pictures on nearly every page. This highly interactive style may also be necessary to keep younger children engaged in the book-reading session for longer. Older children and those with larger vocabularies, in contrast, benefit from a higher-level style of book reading in which the comments and questions do not necessarily interrupt the flow of the text. However, it is not possible to draw firm conclusions about which techniques are helpful for specific oral language skills from applied interventions such as dialogic reading, which incorporate multiple potentially beneficial strategies. For firmer answers to those questions, I turn now to basic experimental research that isolates these techniques to ascertain their specific benefits.

For instance, basic experimental research underscores the benefit of repeated readings of the same book for children to acquire new vocabulary (Horst *et al.* 2011; Horst, this volume, Chapter 9). Vocabulary in these studies was measured in terms of children's comprehension of single words, for example their ability to choose a target word from an array of four pictures, only one of which correctly depicted that word. Children's word comprehension was tested immediately after hearing a story, as well as about one week later, in order to measure acquisition and retention of new words. Thus, the repeated readings in dialogic reading techniques could be one key ingredient for its benefits. In order to learn new words from a picturebook, it is best for children to hear those new words over several readings of the same book rather than via a single reading with multiple exposures to the same new words (McLeod and McDade 2011). Preschoolers also learn nouns more readily than verbs from picturebook reading, most likely because nouns are easier to depict in the pictures than are verbs (ibid.). Finally, Ganea and colleagues' work specifies the types of books from which children of different ages learn best. Toddlers are distracted from word learning when the books are in pop-out form or if they feature abstract pictures; they learn new words best from picturebooks that use realistic images, such as photos or realistic drawings (Ganea and Canfield, this volume, Chapter 2; Ganea *et al.* 2008; Tare *et al.* 2010). Although these experimental studies use specially constructed storybooks, not commercially available picturebooks, they are critical for delineating the precise conditions under which word learning is optimized during picturebook reading.

Other basic experimental research has explored the effects of different types of adults' questions and comments during book reading on children's word learning. These studies vary the types of questions and comments adults make about target words during shared picturebook reading, with the outcome measure being children's understanding and production of these new target words both immediately and after a delay, typically of about one week. These studies clearly show that adults' questions during picturebook reading are particularly important for children's language learning. When adults ask a *wh-*question about a target word (*What's that?* or *Where's the pagoda?*), requesting the child to repeat the new word or point to a picture of it, children learn those new words more effectively than when they simply hear the word from the book's text alone (e.g. Sénéchal 1997; Sénéchal *et al.* 1995). Finally, Walsh and Blewitt (2006) found that questions containing the target word that did not even require the child to say the word (*What color is the pagoda?*) were just as effective as vocabulary-eliciting questions for word learning. Thus, adults' questions containing new words during picturebook reading help children acquire and use new vocabulary.

Yet another body of basic research has instead focused on the demand level of adults' questions – lower-level or higher-level – in children's word learning from picturebooks. This research shows that preschoolers learn to use new words most effectively when adults move from low-demand to high-demand questions over multiple readings of a picturebook (see Blewitt, this volume, Chapter 6; Blewitt *et al.* 2009). In this research, children were asked to define the new words as a test of deeper understanding that extends beyond labeling, and which requires considerable expressive language skill. Combined with the findings discussed above on the benefits of repeated readings and questions, this research shows that all children are likely to learn new words most effectively from a style of picturebook reading in which the demand level of adults' comments increases with each exposure to a new word, and when adults insert questions about the words amid their reading of the text.

Thus, shared picturebook reading is clearly an important vehicle for children's acquisition of new vocabulary, especially their ability to comprehend and use those new words in their speech, and to understand those new words at a deep level. Children learn new words from picturebooks most effectively when adults engage with them in an interactive reading style that is sensitive to the child's current vocabulary level, when they experience the same book more than once, and, if they are toddlers, when the pictures are more realistic and not in a pop-out form.

How does shared picturebook reading support young children's narrative skills?

What about higher-order oral language skills? Are young children also learning narrative skills from picturebook reading? Narrative skills include both children's understanding of story events (*narrative comprehension*) and their ability to tell stories, whether those stories are retold or new (*narrative production*).

Somewhat surprisingly, given that children's picturebooks are mainly in narrative form, and that most interventions use narrative picturebooks almost exclusively (e.g. Whitehurst et al. 1994a), there is not a great deal of research on children's acquisition of narrative skills from picturebooks. The existing research, however, echoes a finding similar to that with children's vocabulary development: children do acquire narrative skills from picturebooks, but their ability to gain narrative skills from book reading depends upon the quality of the adult–child interaction. Sheer frequency of book reading is not linked to children's storytelling skill, either for creating a story from pictures or for telling personal narratives (Sénéchal et al. 2008). At school entry, children have higher story comprehension skills, as measured by their ability to answer questions about the characters and plot during the reading of a picturebook, when their parents used higher-level questions and comments (e.g. predictions and inferences) during picturebook reading in the preschool years (Reese 1995). In contrast, dialogic reading as it is typically practiced does not appear to help children's storytelling skills, as measured by the total information from the story included in their narrative retells (Zevenbergen et al. 2003). Instead, other conversational techniques, such as elaborative reminiscing, are more effective for enhancing children's narrative production skills than dialogic reading, at least as dialogic reading is practiced by low-income parents (Reese et al. 2010a). However, dialogic reading does appear to improve children's inclusion of internal state terms (characters' thoughts and feelings) in their retold stories (Zevenbergen et al. 2003). Internal state terms are an important element for creating strong and engaging narratives.

Moreover, an enhanced version of dialogic reading, in which researchers highlighted four aspects of narrative (plot structure, descriptions, connectives, and context) with 4-year-old children during an eight-week intervention, was effective at improving children's fictional and retold stories compared to an alternative treatment that did not involve picturebook reading (Lever and Sénéchal 2011). Children in the experimental reading group improved in many aspects of narrative production for both fictional and retold stories, but especially in their provision of critical plot developments, their mention of

Table 10.1 Effects of an enhanced dialogic reading training on children's narrative production skills

Child's narrative after receiving enhanced dialogic reading	Child's narrative after receiving alternative treatment
He saw someone holding balloons from the stash. He wanted one. Then he asked to the man if he could have one of the red balloons. And he looked on the ground. The man told him five dollars. He looked in his pocket. He did not see any. He just got one. And the man said, "Only one red balloon. Only if you have five dollars." The lady got five dollars in her little purse and gave it to the man. Then both of the little girl and the little boy has two balloons that were the same color.	*He had a lot of balloons. Then he said, "Can I have one balloon?" Then he said, "No." Then he said, "No no." Then he said, "Okay." And then the bunny's walking. And then the other bunny was there. And the other bunny's walking. Then he said, "He didn't let me get a balloon." Then he said, "Oh first give the money to him." Then they got two balloons.*

Source: Lever and Sénéchal (2011: 13–14).

characters, and their inclusion of internal states in their stories, after the eight-week intervention. Table 10.1 contains illustrative excerpts of children's posttest fictional narratives in response to a wordless picturebook after receiving the enhanced dialogic reading training or the alternative treatment.

Thus, similarly to what was found in the research on the importance of picturebook reading for children's vocabulary, sharing books with preschoolers can also enhance their narrative skills. The caveats are that a style of book reading that focuses explicitly on narrative elements is most effective; moreover, this style appears to enhance children's narrative production skills, though not necessarily their narrative comprehension skills (see Zevenbergen and Whitehurst 2003). However, research has not adequately tested the hypothesis that shared book reading also helps children's narrative comprehension, because the experimental studies often include measures only of narrative production and not comprehension.

How does shared picturebook reading support young children's phonological awareness?

Children's understanding of the individual sounds, or phonemes, that make up words is a critical skill for their early reading efforts in alphabetic languages. Children with impaired phonological awareness skills have great difficulty learning to read (Pullen and Justice 2003). At first glance, picturebook reading seems like an ideal setting for children to learn more about the sounds of words. During picturebook reading, children are learning new words and hearing familiar words in supportive interactions with an adult.

The evidence tells a different story. Simply put, there is little empirical evidence to support the notion that picturebook reading, as it occurs naturally between parents and children, helps develop children's awareness of the sounds of their language. For instance, Stadler and McEvoy (2003) noted that parents do not naturally talk about the sounds of words during shared picturebook reading, although there was a genre difference in that parents talked more about letter sounds in the context of an alphabet book than they did for a narrative picturebook. When reading narrative texts, their natural tendency is to discuss the content of the story. Hindman *et al.* (2014) confirmed this pattern for a large, representative sample in the United States. In their study, parents rarely made code-related comments during book reading, which included references to the sounds of words and to print, and neither these code-related comments nor their meaning-related comments were linked to a composite score of children's phonological awareness and print skill. Neither did Foy and Mann (2003), in their correlational study, find any links specifically between frequency of shared picturebook reading and children's phonological awareness (see also Sénéchal and LeFevre 2002). Instead, children's phonological awareness was linked to other environmental sources besides parent–child picturebook reading, such as time spent playing reading-related computer games. Other research underscores the effectiveness of computer games that engage young children in explicit teaching of letters and letter–sound associations for children's phonological awareness (What Works Clearinghouse 2006).

However, experimental research does reveal a link between interactive book-reading in early childhood settings and preschool children's phonological awareness (Mol *et al.* 2009). Specially designed interactions with picturebooks can enhance children's phonological awareness even more. In these studies, parents or teachers are taught to talk explicitly about the sounds of words in the course of reading picturebooks (e.g. *What sound does "duck" start with? That's right, "d"*). Children who experience picturebook reading in this fashion advance faster in their phonological awareness than do children who experience typically occurring book reading (e.g. Carroll *et al.* 2013; Chow *et al.* 2008). In one study with kindergarteners, children's phonological awareness developed faster when their teacher read alphabet books that included example words (*The Cat in the Hat Comes Back!*) compared to children whose teacher read alphabet books containing only the letters of the alphabet (*Dr. Seuss's ABC*) or narrative picturebooks that did not refer to letters (*The Cat in the Hat*). All of the existing evidence points to the same conclusion: when adults specifically refer to the sounds of letters or words while reading picturebooks, either through their extratextual utterances or because the comments are embedded in the text itself, children's phonological awareness is increased relative to children who receive typical book-reading interactions focused on the content of the story.

How does shared picturebook reading support young children's reading skills?

It seems common sense to assume that reading picturebooks to children would help their reading skills. After all, children are getting experience with books.

They are watching how one holds a book, turns pages, and reads from one side of the page to the other. They are seeing words on the page. They are observing adults draw meaning from text.

However, careful experimental research shows that young children are looking pretty much everywhere but at the text when they are experiencing a picturebook. In fact, eye-tracking studies reveal that 4-year-old children are looking at the print a mere 4 percent of the time during picturebook reading (Justice *et al.* 2008). Instead, they are primarily looking at the pictures while they are listening (or not) to the story. In that sense, picturebook reading is akin to watching a film of static pictures with a story voice-over, although of course in the case of high-quality picturebook reading, the child is also engaging in a dialogue about the story with an adult.

The eye-tracking studies help us understand the at first puzzling lack of a direct association between the frequency or quality of shared book reading in the preschool years and children's early reading skills when they are figuring out letter-sound correspondences and first learning to read words. Neither correlational nor experimental work shows a firm direct link between shared book reading with preschoolers and children's early reading skills in English (e.g. Hindman *et al.* 2014; Mol *et al.* 2009; Sénéchal and LeFevre 2002; although see Davidse *et al.* 2011, for a link between parents' shared book reading and children's letter recognition in Dutch). However, interactive book reading in early childhood settings with older children (5-year-olds) is moderately effective at increasing their letter knowledge, probably because older children are becoming more interested in print (Mol *et al.* 2009). In experimental work with younger children in early childhood settings, picturebook reading promotes print skills *only* when add-on interventions specifically focusing on print are part of the intervention (e.g. Whitehurst *et al.* 1994b). In fact, in one large-scale study in which preschool teachers were trained in interactive picturebook reading, the intervention even had a negative effect on children's letter knowledge by the end of the school year (see Wasik *et al.* 2006), presumably because of the time the picturebook reading intervention took away from other letter-based activities in the classroom.

Once again, however, picturebook reading *can* be used as a way for children to learn print skills if the interaction is tailored accordingly. When adults talk explicitly about print or point to the words in the book, children look more often at the text during picturebook reading (e.g. *What letter is this?*; Justice *et al.* 2008). In one intervention with preschool teachers, children from classrooms whose teachers were trained to reference print explicitly during picturebook reading over the school year advanced faster in their print skills than children from classrooms in which teachers engaged in their typical reading styles (Justice *et al.* 2010). Fortunately, these advances in print skills did not occur at the cost of children's language development; the two reading styles were indistinguishable in their effects on children's language growth across the school year.

Typically occurring picturebook reading is thus more important for children's oral language growth, especially vocabulary growth, than for their early reading skill. And oral language growth in turn is strongly linked to children's ability to understand what they read later in the reading acquisition process, at around Year 3 or 4 in school. At this age, they should now be reading to learn, rather than learning to read. And it is at this point that the hours of shared picturebook reading pay off: children with large vocabularies and strong narrative skills have much better reading comprehension skills than children who may be good decoders but who lack strong oral language skills (Dickinson and Porche 2011; Reese 2013; Sénéchal and LeFevre 2002).

The message for parents and teachers

The first message for parents and teachers is that shared picturebook reading is a positive activity in which to engage with young children. It is also a flexible activity that can be tailored to the individual child's needs and interests. Children are always going to learn more from books that they enjoy, and with a conversational partner to whom they are securely attached and with whom they can hold high-quality interactions (Bus and van IJzendoorn 1995). Young children are also going to benefit more from interactive book-reading sessions than from a straight reading of the text, but the style of that interaction can be adapted to the age and language level of the child. As far as we know, all of these techniques also work for bilingual children in both languages (e.g. Chow et al. 2010; McBride-Chang 2012), although a great deal more research needs to be dedicated to this topic. Finally, although typical book reading is more beneficial for children's oral language development than for their phonological awareness and early reading skills, teachers and parents can learn to read in styles that support these skills as well (see Mol et al. 2009). Because it is difficult for teachers to read in ways that support oral language development with large groups of children, my recommendation is that teachers can be using group book-reading sessions to advance children's phonological awareness and print skills. Extrapolating from the experimental work, parents who include alphabet books in their picturebook reading diet, especially books containing explicit information about letter sounds (e.g. *The Cat in the Hat Comes Back!*; *Chicka Chicka Boom Boom*), will likely help their children's phonological awareness.

Focusing on print during picturebook reading appears to work equally well for young children of all levels and ages, even in a large-group setting (Justice et al. 2010). One interesting direction for future research would be to teach low-income parents these techniques as a way of supporting young children's early reading skills. Dialogic reading does not appear to work as well as other conversational strategies with low-income parents for enhancing children's oral language development (Mol et al. 2008; Reese et al. 2010a). Perhaps other book-reading styles that focus specifically on phonology or print would be more palatable and easier to teach to low-income and less educated parents than dialogic-type book-reading styles. Hindman et al. (2014) found that parental education, not parental ethnicity or home language use, was the main correlate of parents' natural use of higher-level comments during narrative picturebook reading (although see Doan and Wang 2010 for cultural differences in parents' use of internal state terms during book reading).

In conclusion, like newborn babies, picturebooks *are* important simply because they are a delight and a wonder to children and adults alike. However, like babies who grow into useful and productive adults, picturebooks also serve an important purpose in growing young children's oral language skills and – eventually – their reading.

References

Primary sources

Martin, Bill Jr., John Archambault, and Lois Ehlert. 2000. *Chicka Chicka Boom Boom*. New York: Beach Lane Books.
Dr. Seuss. 2013. *Dr. Seuss's ABC*. New York: Random House.
Dr. Seuss. 1957. *The Cat in the Hat*. New York: Random House.
Dr. Seuss. 1958. *The Cat in the Hat Comes Back*. New York: Random House.

Secondary sources

Blewitt, Pamela, Keiran M. Rump, Stephanie E. Shealy, and Samantha A. Cook. 2009. "Shared book reading: When and how questions affect young children's word learning". *Journal of Educational Psychology* 101: 294–304.
Bradley, Lynette and Peter E. Bryant. 1983. "Categorizing sounds and learning to read: A causal connection". *Nature* 301: 419–421.
Bus, Adriana G. and Marinus H. van IJzendoorn. 1995. "Mothers reading to their 3-year-olds: The role of mother–child attachment security in becoming literate". *Reading Research Quarterly* 30: 998–1015.
Bus, Adriana G., Marinus H. van IJzendoorn, and Anthony D. Pellegrini. 1995. "Joint book-reading makes for success in learning to read: A meta-analysis on intergenerational transmission of literacy". *Review of Educational Research* 65: 1–21.
Carroll, Jane, Gail Gillon, Bridget B. McNeill, and Elizabeth Schaughency. 2013. "The effects of a professional development model to enhance early childhood teachers' storybook reading". Poster presentation at IWORDD: International Workshop On Reading and Developmental Dyslexia, San Sebastian, Spain.
Chapin, Seymour L. 1985. "A legendary bon mot? Franklin's 'What is the good of a newborn baby?'" *Proceedings of the American Philosophical Society* 129: 278–290.
Chow, Bonnie Wing-Yin, Catherine McBride-Chang, Him Cheung, and Celia Sze-Lok Chow. 2008. "Dialogic reading and morphology training in Chinese children: Effects on language and literacy". *Developmental Psychology* 44: 233–244.
Chow, Bonnie Wing-Yin, Catherine McBride-Chang, and Him Cheung. 2010. "Parent–child reading in English as a second language: Effects on language and literacy development of Chinese kindergarteners". *Journal of Research in Reading* 33: 284–301.
Cutspec, Patricia A. 2004. "Influences of dialogic reading on the language development of toddlers". *Bridges: Practice-Based Research Syntheses* 2: 1–12.
Davidse, Neeltje J., Maria T. de Jong, Adriana G. Bus, Stephan C. J. Huijbregts, and Hanna Swaab. 2011. "Cognitive and environmental predictors of early literacy skills". *Reading and Writing* 24: 395–412.

Dickinson, David K. and Michelle V. Porche. 2011. "Relation between language experiences in preschool classrooms and children's kindergarten and fourth-grade language and reading abilities". *Child Development* 82: 870–886.

Doan, Stacy N. and Qi Wang. 2010. "Maternal discussions of mental states and behaviors: Relations to emotion situation knowledge in European American and immigrant Chinese children". *Child Development* 81: 1490–1503.

Foy, Judith G. and Virginia Mann. 2003. "Home literacy environment and phonological awareness in preschool children: Differential effects for rhyme and phoneme awareness". *Applied Psycholinguistics* 24: 59–88.

Ganea, Patricia A., Megan Bloom Pickard, and Judy S. DeLoache. 2008. "Transfer between picture books and the real world by very young children". *Journal of Cognition and Development* 9: 46–66.

Haden, Catherine A., Elaine Reese, and Robyn Fivush. 1996. "Mothers' extratextual comments during storybook reading: Stylistic differences over time and across texts". *Discourse Processes* 21: 135–169.

Hindman, Annemarie H., Lori E. Skibbe, and Tricia D. Foster. 2014. "Exploring the variety of parental talk during book reading and its contributions to preschool children's language and literacy: Evidence from the Early Childhood Longitudinal Study – Birth Cohort". *Reading and Writing* 27: 287–313.

Horst, Jessica S., Kelly L. Parsons, and Natasha M. Bryan. 2011. "Get the story straight: Contextual repetition promotes word learning from storybooks". *Frontiers in Developmental Psychology* 2: 1–11.

Justice, Laura M., Paige C. Pullen, and Khara Pence. 2008. "Influence of verbal and nonverbal references to print on preschoolers' visual attention to print during storybook reading". *Developmental Psychology* 44: 855–866.

Justice, Laura M., Anita S. McGinty, Shayne B. Piasta, Joan N. Kaderavek, and Xitao Fan. 2010. "Print-focused read-alouds in preschool classrooms: Intervention effectiveness and moderators of child outcomes". *Language, Speech, and Hearing Services in Schools* 41: 504–520.

Lever, Rosemary and Monique Sénéchal. 2011. "Discussing stories: On how a dialogic reading intervention improves kindergartners' oral narrative construction". *Journal of Experimental Child Psychology* 108: 1–24.

Lonigan, Christopher J. and Grover J. Whitehurst. 1998. "Relative efficacy of parent and teacher involvement in a shared-reading intervention for preschool children from low-income backgrounds". *Early Childhood Research Quarterly* 13: 263–290.

McBride-Chang, Catherine. 2012. "Shared book-reading: There is no downside for parents". In *Contemporary Debates in Childhood Education and Development*, edited by Sebastian Suggate and Elaine Reese. 51–58. London: Routledge.

McLeod, Angela N. and Hiram L. McDade. 2011. "Preschoolers' incidental learning of novel words during storybook reading". *Communication Disorders Quarterly* 32: 256–266.

Mol, Suzanne E., Adriana G. Bus, Maria T. de Jong, and Daisy J. H. Smeets. 2008. "Added value of dialogic parent–child book readings: A meta-analysis". *Early Education and Development* 19: 7–26.

Mol, Suzanne E., Adriana G. Bus, and Maria T. de Jong. 2009. "Interactive book-reading in early education: A tool to stimulate print knowledge as well as oral language". *Review of Educational Research* 79: 979–1007.

Pullen, Paige C. and Justice, Laura M. 2003. "Phonological awareness, print awareness, and oral language skills in preschool children". *Intervention in School and Clinic* 39: 87–98.

Reese, Elaine. 1995. "Predicting children's literacy from mother–child conversations". *Cognitive Development* 10: 381–405.

Reese, Elaine. 2012. "The tyranny of shared book-reading". In *Contemporary Debates in Childhood Education and Development*, edited by Sebastian Suggate and Elaine Reese. 59–68. London: Routledge.

Reese, Elaine. 2013. *Tell Me a Story: Sharing Stories to Enrich Your Child's World*. New York: Oxford University Press.

Reese, Elaine and Adell Cox. 1999. "Quality of adult book reading affects children's emergent literacy". *Developmental Psychology* 35: 20–28.

Reese, Elaine, Diana Leyva, Alison Sparks, and Wendy Grolnick. 2010a. "Maternal elaborative reminiscing increases low-income children's narrative skills relative to dialogic reading". *Early Education and Development* 21: 318–342.

Reese, Elaine, Sebastian Suggate, Jennifer Long, and Elizabeth Schaughency. 2010b. "Children's oral narrative and reading skills in the first three years of reading instruction". *Reading and Writing: An Interdisciplinary Journal* 23: 627–644.

Scarborough, Hollis S. and Wanda Dobrich. 1994. "On the efficacy of reading to preschoolers". *Developmental Review* 14: 245–302.

Sénéchal, Monique. 1997. "The differential effect of storybook reading on preschoolers' acquisition of expressive and receptive vocabulary". *Journal of Child Language* 24: 123–138.

Sénéchal, Monique and JoAnn LeFevre. 2002. "Parental involvement in the development of children's reading skill: A five-year longitudinal study". *Child Development* 73: 445–460.

Sénéchal, Monique, Eleanor Thomas, and Jo-Ann Monker. 1995. "Individual differences in 4-year-old children's acquisition of vocabulary during storybook reading". *Journal of Educational Psychology* 87: 218–229.

Sénéchal, Monique, Stephanie Pagan, Rosemary Lever, and Gene P. Ouellette. 2008. "Relations among the frequency of shared reading and 4-year-old children's vocabulary, morphological and syntax comprehension, and narrative skills". *Early Education and Development* 19: 27–44.

Stadler, Marie A. and Mary A. McEvoy. 2003. "The effect of text genre on parent use of joint book reading strategies to promote phonological awareness". *Early Childhood Research Quarterly* 18: 502–512.

Tare, Medha, Cynthia Chiong, Patricia Ganea, and Judy DeLoache. 2010. "Less is more: How manipulative features affect children's learning from picture books". *Journal of Applied Developmental Psychology* 31: 395–400.

Walsh, Bridget A. and Pamela Blewitt. 2006. "The effect of questioning style during storybook reading on novel vocabulary acquisition of preschoolers". *Early Childhood Education Journal* 33: 273–278.

Wasik, Barbara A., Mary Alice Bond, and Annemarie Hindman. 2006. "The effects of a language and literacy intervention on Head Start children and teachers". *Journal of Educational Psychology* 98: 63–74.

What Works Clearinghouse. 2006. *WWC Intervention Report: Beginning Reading (Daisyquest)*. US Department of Education: Institute of Education Sciences, September 28.

Whitehurst, Grover J., Francine L. Falco, Christopher J. Lonigan, Janet E. Fischel, Barbara D. DeBaryshe, Marta C. Valdez-Menchaca, and M. Caulfield. 1988. "Accelerating language development through picture-book reading". *Developmental Psychology* 24: 552–558.

Whitehurst, Grover J., David S. Arnold, Jeffery N. Epstein, Andrea N. Angell, Meagan

Smith, and Janet E. Fischel. 1994a. "A picture book reading intervention in day care and home for children from low-income families". *Developmental Psychology* 30: 679–689.

Whitehurst, Grover J., Jeffrey N. Epstein, Andrea L. Angell, Adam C. Payne, Deanne A. Crone, and Janet E. Fischel. 1994b. "Outcomes of an emergent literacy intervention in Head Start". *Journal of Educational Psychology* 86: 542–555.

Zevenbergen, Andrea A. and Grover J. Whitehurst. 2003. "Dialogic reading: A shared picture book reading intervention for preschoolers". In *On Reading Books to Children: Parents and Teachers*, edited by Anne van Kleeck, Steven A. Stahl, and Eurydice B. Bauer. 177–200. Mahwah, NJ: Lawrence Erlbaum.

Zevenbergen, Andrea A., Grover J. Whitehurst, and Jason A. Zevenbergen. 2003. "Effects of a shared-reading intervention on the inclusion of evaluative devices in narratives of children from low-income families". *Applied Developmental Psychology* 24: 1–15.

11 Tense acquisition with picturebooks[1]

Linda Stark

Introduction

In many varieties of spoken German, the *Präteritum* (simple past) – with the exception of some verbs – is almost extinct (Dannerer 2012: 196). However, it is a standard tense in written German with a narrative function. In contrast, the *Perfekt* (present perfect) is the main tense with past time reference in spoken language. This way of using the tenses raises the question of how children acquire the *Präteritum* before they learn how to code and decode writing from a medial point of view. Against this background, it seems likely that the shared reading of picturebooks promotes children's tense acquisition process by providing them with written and narrative contexts – that is, with the *Präteritum* in its prototypical use domain (Quasthoff 2002: 184).

Before one can estimate the role of picturebooks as a specific input in the process of past tense acquisition, it is necessary to investigate to what extent picturebooks are adequate for providing such a specific input. Thus, the corpus analysis presented in this chapter aims at demonstrating the characteristics of picturebooks that could be useful to children in helping them to acquire the German past tense. Basically, these characteristics consist in the accommodation of picturebooks to children's tense acquisition process.

This accommodation of picturebooks can only be described as a function of the tense acquisition task and the way children manage it. This gives rise to the following outline of the present contribution. In the first section, the acquisition object *Präteritum* is presented in contrast to the *Perfekt*. A short overview of existing research will show what is known about how children accomplish the three *Präteritum* acquisition tasks of form, meaning, and use. Against this background, it will be possible in the second section to analyze the linguistic accommodation of picturebooks to the children's tasks in this process. Nineteen picturebooks for children of different ages have been analyzed with regard to the use and the function of the German tense paradigm. In addition to the linguistic analysis, the images of the picturebooks will be discussed where relevant. These analyses reveal that picturebooks not only take into consideration children's tense acquisition development but even respond to their acquisition tasks in a didactic way. What form this didactic response takes will be demonstrated with more detailed analyses of some picturebooks from the corpus.

Perfekt and *Präteritum* in German: three acquisition tasks and their accomplishment by children

In this section, the acquisition of the *Präteritum* is described by outlining the three acquisition tasks form, meaning, and use. As the *Präteritum* is closely linked to the *Perfekt* regarding all three acquisition tasks, it is included in the following description where necessary.

Form

The German paradigm of verbal inflection distinguishes strong and weak verbs. Whereas the formation of weak verbs follows one uniform rule, the inflectional forms of strong verbs present a certain degree of variance. Weak verbs form their *Präteritum* synthetically: the suffix *-te* is attached to the verb stem. The *Präteritum* form of strong verbs has no affixes. Instead, German strong verbs involve different stem vowel changes. There are a total of three types of vowel change patterns (Szagun 2011: 734): ABA (the vowel of the present tense and the past participle stem is the same; the vowel of the *Präteritum* stem differs: e.g. *sehen sah gesehen*), ABB (the vowel of the past participle and the *Präteritum* stem is the same; the vowel of the present tense stem differs: e.g. *biegen bog gebogen*), and ABC (all stems have different vowels: e.g. *gehen ging gegangen*).

Because of this irregularity in the inflection of strong verbs, the acquisition task form is the one that children are slowest to learn in the acquisition of the *Präteritum*: up to the end of primary school, they produce incorrect *Präteritum* forms (Kieferle 2006: 76f.). At the age of 1;6, children start to use the past participle of weak verbs (Szagun 2011: 743). A high frequency of *-t* suffixation and present-tense stem vowels with past participles of strong verbs, as in **genehmt* (**taked) (cf. Rau 1979: 363) or **gehte* (**goed) (Behrens 1993: 98), shows that children tend to overregularize the morphological rules of the inflection of weak verbs (Szagun 2011: 756). But this is not the only way of marking past tense inflection erroneously. In addition to *-t* suffixation on strong verbs, and vowel errors, children omit prefixes and suffixes, and even use the suffix *-en* on weak verbs (ibid.: 755f.).

Thus, there are at least two main difficulties in the morphological acquisition task: the differentiation between strong and weak verbs, and the correct stem vowel change. Both depend to a high degree on the frequency that is present in the children's input (Szagun 2011: 759).

Meaning

The meanings of the *Perfekt* and *Präteritum* overlap in the relation of event time and speech time: the event time is located before the speech time. This relation holds for both tenses. Therefore, they can substitute for each other in many cases, which leads to the question of their use in such cases.

According to Reichenbach (1947), all (English) tenses can be analyzed on the basis of the relationships between three points in time: the event time, the speech time, and the reference time. The event time (E) is defined as the moment when an event takes place. The speech time (S) is the moment when the statement is made, and the reference time (R) can be interpreted as "a point in time relative to which the event time is located" (Rothstein 2008: 8). In the Reichenbachian tradition, the German tenses *Perfekt* and *Präteritum*, both of which express the temporal relation anteriority, are analyzed as follows:

The meaning of the German *Präteritum*: (E) and (R) are located before (S). Similarly for the meaning of the German *Perfekt*: (E) is located before (S) and (R).

As these analyses show, both tenses have one relationship in common: (E) is located before (S) (Musan 2002: 88). Even if the reference time in this definition is located differently, in many cases the *Präteritum* can be replaced by the *Perfekt* and vice versa (ibid.: 88):

1   Lola **ist gerannt**. (*Perfekt*)
    Lola is run
    "Lola has run."
2   Lola **rannte**. (*Präteritum*)
    Lola ran
    "Lola ran."

The agreement in the relationship of E and S between *Perfekt* and *Präteritum* leads to the assumption that children have to develop a mental concept of past to process the meaning of both tenses. The essential step in this development is the child's ability to decentralize from the here-and-now of the communicative situation. Since for both the anteriority meaning is due to the relation between event time and speech time – which is (E) before (S) for both the *Perfekt* and the *Präteritum* – the mental concept of the past is assumed to be similar for both tenses.

Behrens (1993: 127) found that children are able to express past events "by using verbs, verbal particles, and adverbs" before they have acquired the inflectional forms of the German past tenses. These findings have led to the assumption that children develop a mental concept of the past before mastering the adequate tense.

As the grammatical category aspect describes a smaller distance from the here-and-now of the speaker than tense does (Kruse 2007: 41), it has often been suspected to be acquired before the past tense. When one transfers this idea to tense acquisition in German, the following problem emerges: in German, the semantic category aspect is not marked morphologically. Nevertheless, a similar tendency has been observed in German studies: German children tend to produce their first inflectional past tense forms by using telic verbs that refer to events of the immediate past, such as *buddemacht* (broke) or *ausgekippt* (spilled) at the age of 2;0 (Behrens 1993: 165). Children seem to prefer these verbs because they describe changes in situation whose results are appreciable from the child's here-and-now – that is, they have a visible end state for the child (Wagner 2001: 663; Shirai 2009: 179). These completed changes in situation can be interpreted aspectually.

Use

The interchangeability of the *Perfekt* and *Präteritum* in cases such as the one shown above is due to the fact that linguistically and/or contextually the reference time can be underspecified (Musan 2002: 90). When the previous discourse does not provide a temporal specification or the statement itself does not contain an appropriate adverbial (e.g. "[a]m Freitagabend" *on Friday evening*; ibid.: 76), the reference time is not specified. Without a temporal specification, one cannot attribute to the reference time a more or less determined time interval or time value. Hence, "as long as in an utterance, it only matters where the situation time [event time, L.S.] of the verb is located, both constructions [*Perfekt* and *Präteritum*, L.S.] can be used. This leads to a considerable overlap in applicability of the two constructions" (ibid.: 90).

If, because of the temporal underspecification, this interchangeability of the *Perfekt* and the *Präteritum* (as with the examples (1) and (2) shown above) is possible "without a significant change in meaning" (Rothstein 2008: 112), there have to be factors other than semantic ones that govern a speaker's choice of the *Perfekt* or *Präteritum* (Musan 2002: 90). These factors determine the distribution of the *Präteritum* and *Perfekt* in cases of possible interchangeability. In a usage-oriented grammar, Fabricius-Hansen (2009: 513ff.) describes the different uses of the *Präteritum* and *Perfekt* as a function of spoken and written language: the *Präteritum* serves as the main tense in chronological narratives of the written standard language. In these linguistic contexts, one avoids the *Perfekt*. In contrast, in everyday spoken language the *Präteritum* is widely replaced by the *Perfekt*. Only *sein* (to be), the modals, and some frequent verbs are used in the *Präteritum* in such contexts. According to a corpus analysis by Sieberg (2003: 295), these verbs are *kommen* (to come), *sagen* (to say), *gehen* (to go), *stehen* (to stand), *fahren* (to drive), *kriegen* (to get), *wissen* (to know), *geben* (to give), *tun* (to do), *machen* (to make), *liegen* (to lie), *denken* (to think), *laufen* (to walk), *fallen* (to fall), *nehmen* (to take), *bleiben* (to stay), *heißen* (to be called), and *finden* (to find).

The overall tendency – *Präteritum* in written, *Perfekt* in spoken language contexts – has been confirmed by an exemplary statistic based on the corpora of the Institute of German Language Mannheim (Strecker 2008: 33f.). It indicates that in written language contexts, the *Präteritum* of the investigated verbs is used more often than the corresponding past participle as one part of the analytic *Perfekt*, e.g. *treten* (to tread) 122,090 (*Präteritum*) vs. 27,532 (past participle) and *sprechen* (to speak) 213,165 vs. 87,398. As examples of prototypical written language contexts where the *Präteritum* is most frequently used, Strecker (ibid.: 33) gives the text types *narrative* and *report*.

In the following, it will be shown that narratives and reports – although they are prototypical written language contexts – can be realized in spoken language. For example, when a grandmother tells an old fairy tale to her grandchild, this can be seen as a written language context that becomes manifest in spoken language. As this example shows, written language contexts are not restricted to writing in a medial sense. This is also the case with the *Präteritum*. Thus, it is necessary to distinguish between written language contexts, such as a told (not written) fairy tale, and writing in a medial sense. The model of immediacy and distance from Koch and Oesterreicher (1985: 23) helps to make the differences clear and to establish the relation between written language and writing and their impact on the distribution of the *Präteritum* and *Perfekt*.

In their model, Koch and Oesterreicher (see Koch 1997 for its publication in English) distinguish two dimensions of utterances, which they call the conceptual and the medial. This is relevant for the present argumentation, as one dimension is independent of the other, which allows cross-classifications such as the following: a fairy tale told by a grandmother to her grandchild is fixed in the medial dimension of orality, whereas its conception is written. In contrast, an online chat takes place in the medium of writing, whereas its conception is oral.

The conceptual dimension, which becomes manifest in the mode of expression, i.e. the register, depends on the "situational characteristics or communicative parameters" (Koch 1997: 151) listed in Table 11.1 that belong either to the pole of distance (= written conception) or to the pole of immediacy (= oral conception) (ibid.: 151).

In cases of possible interchangeability, the *Präteritum* is basically used in conceptual written language contexts, thus in situations demonstrating the communicative parameters on the right-hand side of Table 11.1. In contrast, the communicative parameters on the left side account for the use of the *Perfekt* as a tense of conceptual orality.

However, the communicative parameters in this table do not merely explain the differences in linguistic conception, for example in the distribution of the past tenses in German. They are also used to describe and distinguish different text types (Helbig 1975: 73). Depending on these communicative parameters, the choice of the appropriate past tense in cases of possible interchangeability is linked not only to the dimension of conception but also to special text types. Subsequently, the past tenses in German can be related to different text types, i.e. text linguistic purposes. As the text type of narratives, e.g. fairy tales, is a prototypical written context, it is an important field of application of the *Präteritum*. In contrast, the text type of informal conversations with familiar speakers, as it is linked to the communicative parameters of the left-hand side of Table 11.1, provokes the use of the *Perfekt*. This tense distribution shows the extent to which the use of either the *Präteritum* or the *Perfekt* is not entirely self-evident. This is an important task on its own in the acquisition of the past tenses

214   L. Stark

Table 11.1 Communicative parameters of conceptual oral (pole of immediacy) and written (pole of distance) language (see Koch 1997: 151)

Immediacy	Distance
I Physical immediacy vs. distance Face-to-face interaction with partners	Distance in space and time
II Social immediacy vs. distance Private setting of the communicative event Familiarity of the partners Emotional involvement Context embeddedness	Public setting of the communicative event Unfamiliarity of the partners Detachment Contextual dissociation of a discourse
III Referential immediacy vs. distance Reference to the EGO-HIC-NUNC and to elements of the immediate situational context	Reference to elements that are far from the EGO-HIC-NUNC and from the situational context
IV Elocutional immediacy vs. distance Dialogue Maximum cooperation of partners Free topic Spontaneity	Monologue Minimum cooperation of partners Fixed topic Reflection

that has to be taken into consideration, in addition to the form and the meaning.

To my knowledge, the acquisition of this use component has never been studied from a pure tense acquisition perspective. All the clues that we find on this issue come from other research fields such as emergent literacy and the acquisition of narrative skills. Emergent literacy as the "knowledge of the forms of written language" (Purcell-Gates 2001: 14) and early narrative skills are necessary preconditions for an appropriate use of the *Präteritum* (Müller 2012: 99).

All we know about the acquisition of this use component is that children not only use *Präteritum* forms in an appropriate way from an early age on but use these forms to distinguish different narrative genres and even written and oral language. Thus, Rau's diary study shows the child using the *Präteritum* from 3;1 years of age on in narrative situations such as pretended reading from books or newspapers (1979: 368, 370) or telling stories (ibid.: 363). The results of Quasthoff's study (2002: 184ff.) indicate that children adapt their language use to different narrative genres: with personal, oral, and informal narrations that are embedded in conversations, 6-year-old children tend to use the *Perfekt*. Some of these children already use predominantly the *Präteritum* to tell a fantasy story, thus differentiating stylistically between the narrative genres. In contrast to these oral texts, when writing their narratives the majority of the children participating in the study use predominantly the *Präteritum* in both narrative genres.

Hence, the results of Rau (1979) and Quasthoff (2002) indicate that children master the acquisition task use before learning to code and decode writing. They seem to have a concept allowing them to distinguish between oral and written language on both levels: the medial and the conceptual one. As children are probably rarely exposed to the *Präteritum* because of its tendency to occur mainly in conceptually written language, the reason for children's early narrative use of the *Präteritum* seems to connect to previous literacy experience (Quasthoff 2002: 184): through the shared reading of picturebooks, children can gain access to conceptually written language, i.e. the *Präteritum*, via the medium of orality.

Children's tasks in the tense acquisition process

When acquiring the German *Präteritum*, children do not merely have to map a meaning onto a form. Because of the similarity of meaning of the *Präteritum* and *Perfekt*, they also have to process the distribution of these two past tenses, which depends (in cases of possible interchangeability) on the communicative parameters shown in Table 11.1. As these parameters become manifest in text types that differ in terms of conception (oral vs. written language), the use of the *Präteritum* requires text linguistic knowledge. The acquisition of the three tasks form, meaning, and use can be summarized in the following "course of acquisition of the verb tense system in German" (Behrens 1993: 185).[2]

In the first, nonfinite phase, children use primarily infinitives, stems, verbal particles, and first finite (inflected for person and number) verbs that are "not yet [used] productively but in formulas" (Behrens 1993: 185). This small number of linguistic patterns enables children to "express a variety of temporal notions" (ibid.: 185f.) such as the reference to remote past events (ibid.: 186). This first phase is reached at about 1;5 years of age (ibid.: 114).

In the second phase, children acquire their first verb tenses and finiteness: they start to distinguish temporally between the emerging present tense paradigm and first past participles. In addition, "[f]inite modal and copulaic constructions appear" (Behrens 1993: 186). This phase is reached in Behrens' data in the age range of 1;10 up to 2;5. "The transition from Phase 2 to Phase 3 is determined by the acquisition of the auxiliary system" (ibid.: 115). This is a necessary precondition for the acquisition of complex tenses, which happens in the third phase of the tense acquisition process (ibid.: 186), which children reach at the age of approximately 2;5. The *Perfekt* is the first complex tense acquired by children. The pluperfect and future tenses follow. Although the *Präteritum* is not a complex but a synthetic tense, it is, for main verbs, acquired later than the *Perfekt*. Only in the case of modal verbs and copulas is it used earlier (ibid.: 116). "For main verbs, however, children show a preference for complex *Perfekt* over preterite [*Präteritum*]" (ibid.: 116).

Thus, there is reason to assume two more phases: a fourth phase, in which the *Präteritum* of modals and copulas as well as of very frequent verbs is acquired, which then transitions into a fifth phase, in which main-verb *Präteritum* is used, including that of less frequent strong verbs.

As children refer to past events before they use past tense forms, we can assume that the acquisition of the temporal meaning precedes the acquisition of the complex tense morphology. Not much can be said about how children acquire the use of the *Präteritum*: studies in emergent literacy and narration have shown that children start to use the *Präteritum* in conceptual written and narrative contexts at quite an early stage – that is, before learning to code and decode writing. They even use this conceptual written past tense to distinguish different genres, such as fantasy stories and personal narratives (Becker 2005: 38).

When describing the course of acquisition of the *Präteritum*, one has to bear in mind that all acquisition tasks are complicated by the fact that the use of the *Präteritum* is infrequent in the input children get in their everyday language, as their daily language use is usually fixed to orality (Maas 2008: 38). *Präteritum* forms, in contrast, tend to be used in written contexts, to which preschool children have access only in rare situations. This could be a reason for the fact that in secondary school a few pupils still use the *Perfekt* when producing both spoken and written narratives (Dannerer 2012: 208).

Tense acquisition and picturebooks

Theoretical background: children's literature and language acquisition

In his conceptual framework, Meibauer (2011) puts forward two hypotheses on the relation between children's literature and language acquisition: first, that children's literature is a specific input in the process of language acquisition; and second, that an essential characteristic of children's literature is that it takes into consideration children's linguistic and cognitive development (ibid.: 9).

In my opinion, these two ideas are inseparable insofar as children's literature can play the role of a specific input in language acquisition only if it takes into consideration children's linguistic and cognitive development. In other words, in order to be a specific input in the process of language acquisition, picturebooks have to be accommodated somehow to children's development. Thus, this section aims to demonstrate this accommodation of picturebooks with regard to the process of past tense acquisition in German.

Corpus analysis: tense use in 19 picturebooks: reflection of the course of tense acquisition

If picturebooks are accommodated to the process of tense acquisition, they have to somehow reflect the order of this process (Kümmerling-Meibauer and Meibauer 2011: 104). Thus, the first step in testing Meibauer's second hypothesis on the basis of my corpus,[3] which was randomly compiled on the basis of the inventory of picturebooks from a public library in a city in southwest Germany, consisted in the following: I classified the 19 picturebooks according to their tense use. This classification revealed a correspondence to the five phases of tense acquisition described in the section on children's tasks in the tense acquisition process. Additionally, the tense use in the picturebooks and the corresponding acquisition phases match with the age recommendation for the picturebooks given by the publishers. Thus, the correlation between the presented picturebook groups and the age recommendation can be seen as a result of the grouping, but it was not a criterion for classification.[4] In the following, I will give a description of the five groups, including a short analysis of the tense use in the picturebooks.

The picturebooks of the first group contain only present-tense forms or even infinitives. The picturebooks in this group are:

- *Mein erster Grüffelo* (My First Gruffalo[5]) by Scheffler;
- *Wenn die Sonne scheint* (When the Sun Shines) by Heyduck;
- *Drei Vögel* (Three Birds) by Heyduck-Huth.

Most of the inflected present-tense forms in these books belong to the third person singular. Thus, the acquisition task under focus in this first phase is the finiteness of verbs with regard to the inflectional categories number and person. The picturebooks representing this phase address children between 1 and 2 years of age.

The second group of picturebooks is also characterized by the predominant use of present-tense forms. In addition to these forms, the books of this group contain single *Perfekt* forms, past participles, or verbal particles with past time reference. The books showing this tense distribution are:

- *Papa ist glücklich* (Daddy Is Happy) by Le Saux;
- *Kleiner weißer Fisch* (Little White Fish) by Genechten;
- *Wo ist Lola* (Where Is Lola?) by Godon;
- *1, 2, 3, – bringt Trost herbei!* (1, 2, 3 – Give Comfort!) by Moost.

The *Perfekt* forms, particles, and participles in these books are *verliebt* (in love), *gefangen* (caught), *weg* (gone) in *Daddy*, *hat verloren* (has lost) in *Fish*, *ist gefallen* (has fallen) in *Comfort*, and *hast gesucht* (has looked for) in *Lola*. By focusing basically on visible end states, these past constructions indicate the aspectual interpretation of completeness (see also p. 211). Thus, they can be seen as an introduction to the meaning of the past.

The predominant use of *Perfekt* forms differentiates the third group of picturebooks:

- *Eine Wolke in meinem Bett* (A Cloud in My Bed) by Janisch;
- *Das ganz, ganz kleine Schwein mit dem ganz, ganz großen Hunger* (The Very, Very Little Pig with the Very, Very Big Hunger) by Auer;
- *Tagebuch eines Wombats* (A Wombat's Diary) by French.

Whereas most of the text of the first two examples consists of direct speech, the final book is in the form of a diary that tells about the Wombat's week in short, even one-word, sentences such as *Morgens: Geschlafen.* (Morning: slept.). Thus, all these examples contain language that tends towards the pole of immediacy (see Table 11.1), i.e. the *Perfekt*. These picturebooks of phase III are suggested for children aged 3–5 years and illustrate the *Perfekt* as belonging to conceptual oral language.

The fourth group consists of picturebooks containing *Präteritum* forms in addition to *Perfekt* or present-tense forms:

- *Hallo, roter Fuchs* (Hello, Red Fox) by Carle;
- *Der Mondhund* (The Moondog) by Moost;
- *Geschichte ohne Ende und Anfang* (Story without End and without Beginning) by Usatschow;
- *Warum der Schnee weiß ist* (Why the Snow Is White) by Janisch;
- *Es war einmal eine Ente* (Once upon a Time There Was a Duck) by Straaten.

The alternating tense distribution is realized by embedded direct speech in the narrative text in the first three examples and by two interlaced narrative levels in *Snow* and *Duck*. The narrative texts of the first three examples and the second narrative level of the fourth and fifth examples contain *Präteritum* forms of either weak or highly frequent strong verbs. Examples of these weak verbs include *schaute* (looked) and *sagte* (said) in *Fox* and *without End*. The *Präteritum* form *kam* (came) appears in both *Fox* and *Duck*. It is an example of a strong verb whose *Präteritum* form is frequently used even in conceptual spoken language (see p. 212). Thus, within this phase the *Präteritum* is introduced basically for frequent and weak verbs. The books of this phase, which are intended for children aged 4–5, do not contain the *Präteritum* as the main tense, but it alternates with other tenses such as the *Perfekt* or the present tense. The alternating tense distribution in these books emphasizes the narrative function of the *Präteritum* and thereby demonstrates its different use as compared with the *Perfekt*.

In the fifth group, the *Präteritum* is the predominant narrative tense in the picturebook texts. In contrast to the preceding group, the following picturebooks contain not only weak or frequent verbs but also less frequent strong *Präteritum* verbs:

- *Ente, Tod und Tulpe* (Duck, Death, and Tulip) by Erlbruch;
- *Pozor* (Pozor) by Maar;
- *Otto. Autobiographie eines Teddybären* (Otto: Autobiography of a Teddy Bear) by Ungerer;
- *Reiner der Weiner* (Reiner the Cryer) by Seefeldt.

The percentage of weak, frequent, and strong verbs of all *Präteritum* forms in the text for all four picturebooks does not vary much. The amount of weak *Präteritum* verbs ranges from 45 percent to 47 percent, the percentage of frequent verbs is between 30 percent and 37 percent, and the strong verbs amount to

18–24 percent. Compared to the picturebooks of the preceding phases, which contained mainly *Präteritum* forms of weak and frequent verbs, a continuous increase in the amount of strong verbs characterizes this last phase, which starts with picturebooks for children at about 5 years of age. This goes hand in hand with an increase in the amount of narrative text and a decrease in the amount of quoted speech. Thus, the acquisition task best reflected in this last phase focuses on the complex inflectional paradigm with the objective of providing children with a greater number of *Präteritum* forms of strong verbs and their characteristic stem vowel changes.

The different ways of using the tenses in these phases reflected by the picturebooks are accompanied by the following formal properties of the picturebooks, which reflect a continuous increase in children's linguistic and cognitive abilities:

- length of sentences: this ranges from short main clauses with verb-only predicates up to hypotactic constructions;
- amount of text: this ranges from one sentence per double spread as in *Sun* up to 12 sentences per double spread as in *Otto*;
- complexity of the narrative structure: this ranges from isolated up to narratively structured narratives (Boueke *et al.* 1995);
- number of objects and details depicted in the illustrations: this ranges from one object per double spread in the first group up to an uncountable number of details in the fifth;
- number of pages: this ranges from 9 up to 29 pages.

These formal properties and the age recommendations given by the publishers, ranging from 1 year for the first phase up to 7 years for the fifth phase, confirm both the classification of the picturebooks and the proposed order. Table 11.2 shows that this order is in line with the tense acquisition stages described on p. 215 and summarizes the current findings.

Procedures of past tense comprehensibility enhancement in the picturebooks

Further analyses of the tense use in the picturebooks revealed that they not only reflect the order of tense acquisition but also contain *procedures of tense comprehensibility enhancement*[6] which respond in a didactic way to the identified tense acquisition tasks, as they make explicit either the meaning of past or the prototypical use domains of the *Perfekt* or the *Präteritum*. The following gives examples of the selection of these procedures in the picturebooks:

- **An example of Phase II: illustrations of grammatical aspect in the pictures**
  Children at the age of about 3 years seem to mark "a grammatical aspect and not a tense distinction" (Wagner 2001: 678) when using past tenses. Although the linguistic category of aspect is not morphologically marked in

Table 11.2 Overview of the findings of the picturebook analysis

	Phase I	Phase II	Phase III	Phase IV	Phase V
Tense use	Infinitives or present tense	Present tense forms, verbal particles referring to past events, first *Perfekt* forms	*Perfekt*	*Präteritum* of weak and frequent strong verbs	*Präteritum* of both weak and strong words
Acquisition task under focus	Finiteness (person and number) → form	Meaning of past/anteriority → meaning	Medial differences between orality and literacy → use	Conceptual differences between orality and literacy → use	Inflectional paradigm of strong verbs → form
Picture-books	*Sun* *Gruffalo* *Birds*	*Comfort* *Fish* *Lola* *Daddy*	*Cloud* *Pig* *Wombat*	*Fox* *Moondog* *without End* *Duck* *Snow*	*Tulip* *Pozor* *Otto* *Reiner*
Age recommendation	1–2 years	Approx. 3 years	3–5 years	4–5 years	From 5 years on

German, the expression of completeness which connects to grammatical aspect can be seen as a cognitive milestone in the process of tense acquisition. Perfective grammatical aspect indicates the point of beginning and the point of end of an eventuality. Thus, a completed eventuality can be seen as a whole that is accomplished by the moment of speech.

This relationship between completeness and the *Perfekt*, whose aspectual interpretation is still under discussion in current research (Rothstein 2008: 30), is used to illustrate the past meaning of this tense in the following example.

In *Comfort*, the illustration of a bear lying on the ground is accompanied by a resultative *Perfekt* form: *Der Bär ist auf die Nase gefallen.* (The bear has fallen on his nose.) Thus, the illustration showing the completed action denoted by the verb promotes an aspectual interpretation of the *Perfekt* form *ist gefallen*.

- **An example of Phase III: imitation of special genres**
  Typically, diaries are a very personal text type; they are not written for a wide audience but rather are very intimate or even secret, and usually they include descriptions of emotions and feelings. Thus, in the continuum of linguistic conception they tend towards the pole of immediacy (Table 11.1). As we have seen, the German *Perfekt* is the tense of this immediacy pole. Accordingly, the tense of anteriority used in the diary genre, as imitated by *Wombat*, is the *Perfekt*.

- **An example of Phase III: alternating tense use from a medial point of view**
  The implementation of a story within a background story allows the use of different tenses in one picturebook and illustrates the characteristics of a given communicative situation. The picturebook *Pig* makes use of this procedure, as the protagonist of the background story, a little boy, tells a story to his mother during lunch. The background story is anchored in the present tense but the conversationally embedded story told by the little boy contains the *Perfekt*. First, it is realized in the medium of orality as the boy tells the story to his mother. Second, its conception tends towards the pole of immediacy, as it displays the following characteristics of conceptual oral language: it is a face-to-face interaction between mother and son, it is a private setting with a high degree of familiarity between the partners, and it is embedded in the context provided by the family lunch.

- **Two examples of Phase IV: alternating tense use from a conceptual point of view**
  Janisch's picturebook *Snow* has two different narrative levels that are connected in the following way: the background story introduces the story within the story on the first double spread: Mira, the protagonist of the background story, wants her father to tell her a fairy tale. This explanation of the narrative context in the background story leads to the story within the story, which begins on the next double spread with the fairy tale told by Mira's father. After this fairy tale, the reader returns to the background

story, i.e. to Mira and her father, who talk about the fairy tale. The transition between the introduction, which creates a narrative context, and the narrative itself in terms of the fairy tale is made explicit by a number of changes on both the text and visual levels: whereas the background story is told in the present tense, the fairy tale contains the *Präteritum* as the narrative tense. The background story frames the fairy tale with two almost identical pictures on the first and on the last double spread. Even in terms of typography, the two levels can be distinguished: the background story is written in white letters on a dark red backdrop whereas the letters of the fairy tale are black. All these markers that set apart the two story levels from each other spell out the narrative context in which the fairy tale is embedded. Thus, they first create a contrast with the change in tense use and second they illustrate the *Präteritum*'s prototypical use domain.

Duck – again a Phase IV picturebook – also contains this double structure obtained by having a story within the story. The background story introduces the story within the story in the following way: Duck, the protagonist, writes a story with a pen that he has found. His friend Frog is able to read the story with the help of his reading glasses. So, Duck asks Frog to read the story he wrote out loud to Duck and to two other friends. The story written by Duck and read out loud by Frog is the story within the story. When Frog finishes reading Duck's story, the reader returns to the background story.

These two different narrative levels of this interlaced story structure are distinguished by linguistic and visual markers. In terms of linguistic markers, the contrastive use of the present tense in the background story and the *Präteritum* in the story within the story can be seen as a procedure of tense comprehensibility enhancement that illustrates the *Präteritum*'s prototypical use domain. In this picturebook, it is linked to a narrative context that is constructed in a very explicit way by the background story. On the double spread of Figure 11.1, one can see the transition from the background story to the beginning of the story written by Duck. It is introduced by the following text: *Frosch nimmt seine Lesebrille und bläht sich auf, so weit er kann. [...] Dann fängt er an vorzulesen.* (Frog takes his reading glasses and draws a deep breath. [...] Then he starts to read.) (Straaten 2004: 17).

This transition from the narrative context created by the background story to the story within the story is accompanied by the following textual and visual features that motivate the use of the *Präteritum* and can in part be seen on the depicted double spread:

- a change in the mode of illustration in terms of a sepia brown tint that covers all the pictures of the story within the story;
- a change in the mode of text type, as the letters of the story within the story are italic while the letters of the background story are roman.

Figure 11.1 Illustration from Harmen van Straaten and Arnica Esterl: *Es war einmal eine Ente*.

(These two features establish a visual border between the two narrative levels in such a way that children can recognize it.)

- the reference to the reading process from a medial point of view by the reading glasses in the text and pictures;
- the reference to the writing process from a medial point of view by the depiction of the writing materials used by the duck when producing its story, such as the pen and the paper, in the text and illustrations;
- meta-narrative cues on the text level, such as *Geschichte* (story), *vorlesen* (read out loud) and the title "Die Geschichte von Ente" (*The Story of Duck*) on the depicted title page of the story within the story.

With these features which concentrate on the writing of Duck's story with a medial focus, a connection is created between the written conception based on the use of the *Präteritum* and the medium of writing which is attached to this conception in the present example.

This section has shown that some of the picturebooks of the presented corpus not only reflect the order of tense acquisition phases in terms of an accommodated tense use but, additionally, they contain procedures of past tense comprehensibility enhancement – for example, implicit explanations of the use or the meaning of the *Perfekt* or *Präteritum*. As I have shown, these explanations are provided on different levels of the picturebooks: the illustrations, the vocabulary, the story structure, the genre, and the typography. The described procedures of past tense comprehensibility enhancement are only examples from the corpus I have considered; this list does not claim to be exhaustive. These examples only indicate that picturebooks are accommodated to the children's tense acquisition tasks not only in terms of tense use but also in terms of providing – on different levels – an accommodated stage to this tense use, which can be seen as an additional source for the tense acquisition process.

Conclusions

The analysis of the small sample of 19 German picturebooks has shown that these picturebooks are accommodated to the children's process of tense acquisition in two ways. First, a classification of the picturebooks on the basis of their tense use revealed five homogeneous groups which correspond not only to the five phases of children's tense acquisition but also to the picturebooks' age recommendations by the publishers. These groups reflect the children's order of tense acquisition and the corresponding acquisition tasks. Second, these acquisition tasks are supported by manifold procedures of tense comprehensibility enhancement, which operate on the text level, the narrative structure, the picture level, and even the typographic level.

Thus, the present corpus analysis confirms Meibauer's second hypothesis regarding the process of tense acquisition. It indicates that picturebooks do indeed take children's tense development into consideration on different levels. As picturebooks are accommodated to the process of tense acquisition, it seems likely that they can play an important role in this process. Against the background of the past tense distribution in German, it seems even more probable that the accommodated picturebooks provide a specific input in the acquisition of the *Präteritum*, as they furnish children with conceptually written contexts. Additionally, this assumption aligns with findings of Müller (2012: 169–184), who showed that children with less literacy experience use fewer *Präteritum* forms in their narratives than children with varied experience in picturebook reading do. Accordingly, the results of the present corpus analysis also substantiate Meibauer's first hypothesis (2011: 9) concerning the impact of picturebooks on language acquisition for the *Präteritum* as an acquisition object. This hypothesis needs to be tested in further empirical investigations in order to finally define the role of the described accommodations of picturebooks in the process of tense acquisition.

Notes

1 I would like to thank Bettina Kümmerling-Meibauer, Jörg Meibauer, Katharina J. Rohlfing, and Björn Rothstein for their very helpful comments and remarks during the development of this chapter. Without their friendly support, the chapter would not have its present form. However, any remaining errors are not their responsibility but solely my own.
2 In terms of language acquisition, the age specification of the described developmental stages can only be seen as a rough orientation. Children smoothly change from one stage to another. These consecutive transitions from stage to stage are individual processes that can differ in length from child to child.
3 The corpus contains both books originally written in German and translations. I did not differentiate between them because I assumed adult readers would confront children with both types of books in the same way without being aware of the fact of translation. I would like to thank Jörg Meibauer for remarks concerning this question.
4 An analysis that aims at determining any accommodation to the age and the language development of children should not be based on the publishers' age recommendations for picturebooks because it is unclear what criteria these are based on. An analysis

could, however, explore whether the age recommendations match with the accommodation investigated here (see Gressnich 2013). But on the basis of the present findings, it can only be speculated whether tense use is one of the criteria that publishing houses rely on.
5 In what follows, only the short titles of the picturebooks will be given, which are the words underlined in the full title.
6 This term is based on Finkbeiner's description of "procedures of 'phraseme comprehensibility enhancement'" (2011: 70) by analogy.

References

Primary sources

Auer, Martin and Manuela Olten. 2008. *Das ganz, ganz kleine Schwein mit dem ganz, ganz großen Hunger*. Weinheim: Beltz & Gelberg.
Carle, Eric. 1998. *Hallo, roter Fuchs*, translated by Edmund Jacoby. Hildesheim: Germany: Gerstenberg.
Erlbruch, Wolf. 2007. *Ente, Tod und Tulpe*. Munich: Kunstmann.
French, Jackie and Bruce Wheatley. 2005. *Tagebuch eines Wombat*, translated by Leena Fleger. Hildesheim, Germany: Gerstenberg.
Genechten, Guido van. 2007. *Kleiner weißer Fisch*. Berlin: Bloomsbury.
Godon, Ingrid. 2001. *Wo ist Lola?* Hamburg: Oetinger.
Heyduck, Hilde. 1961. *Wenn die Sonne scheint*. Ravensburg, Germany: Ravensburger.
Heyduck-Huth, Hilde. 1963. *Drei Vögel*. Ravensburg, Germany: Ravensburger.
Janisch, Heinz and Silke Leffler. 2007. *Eine Wolke in meinem Bett*. Berlin: Aufbau.
Janisch, Heinz and Isabel Pin. 2011. *Warum der Schnee weiß ist*. Vienna: Betz.
Le Saux, Alain. 2000. *Papa ist glücklich*, translated by Markus Weber. Frankfurt am Main: Moritz.
Maar, Anne and Bernd Mölck-Tassel. 2000. *Pozor*. Zürich: Bajazzo.
Moost, Nele and Anett Rudolph. 1997. *1, 2, 3, – bringt Trost herbei!* 2nd edition. Esslingen, Germany: Esslinger.
Moost, Nele and Jutta Bücker. 2000. *Der Mondhund*. Stuttgart: Thienemann.
Scheffler, Axel and Julia Donaldson. 2012. *Mein erster Grüffelo – Geräusche und Bewegungen*. Weinheim: Beltz & Gelberg.
Seefeldt, Philipp. 2007. *Reiner der Weiner*. Berlin: Tulipan.
Straaten, Harmen van and Arnica Esterl. 2004. *Es war einmal eine Ente*. Stuttgart: Freies Geistesleben.
Ungerer, Tomi. 1999. *Otto. Autobiographie eines Teddybären*, translated by Anna von Kramer-Klett. Zürich: Diogenes.
Usatschow, Andrej and Alexandra Junge. 2008. *Geschichte ohne Ende und Anfang*. Zürich: NordSüd.

Secondary sources

Becker, Tabea. 2005. "Mündliche Vorstufen literaler Textentwicklung. Vier Erzählformen im Vergleich". In *Literale Textentwicklung. Untersuchungen zum Erwerb von Textkompetenz*, edited by Helmuth Feilke. 19–42. Frankfurt am Main: Lang.
Behrens, Heike. 1993. *Temporal Reference in German Child Language: Form and Function of Early Verb Use*. Zutphen, Netherlands: Wöhrmann.

Boucke, Dieter et al. 1995. *Wie Kinder erzählen. Untersuchungen zur Erzähltheorie und zur Entwicklung narrativer Fähigkeiten*. Munich: Fink.

Dannerer, Monika. 2012. *Narrative Fähigkeiten und Individualität: Mündlicher und schriftlicher Erzählerwerb im Längsschnitt von der 5. bis zur 12. Schulstufe*. Tübingen: Stauffenburg.

Fabricius-Hansen, Catherine. 2009. "Das Verb". In *Duden. Die Grammatik*, edited by Matthias Wermke et al. 389–566. Mannheim: Dudenverlag.

Finkbeiner, Rita. 2011. "Phrasenerwerb und Kinderliteratur. Verfahren der 'Verständlichmachung' von Phraseologismen im Kinder- und Jugendbuch am Beispiel von Otfried Preußlers 'Die kleine Hexe' und 'Krabat' ". *Zeitschrift für Literaturwissenschaft und Linguistik* 162: 47–73.

Gressnich, Eva. 2013. "Feinabstimmung im Bilderbuch. Die Darstellung von Raum in Text und Bild". Unpublished lecture given at Ruhr-University Bochum, January.

Helbig, Gerhard. 1975. "Zu Problemen der linguistischen Beschreibung des Dialogs im Deutschen". *Deutsch als Fremdsprache* 12: 65–80.

Kieferle, Christa. 2006. "Was wissen Dritt- und Viertklässler über die Bildung von Vergangenheitsformen? Eine Analyse". In *Gesteuerter und ungesteuerter Grammatikerwerb*, edited by Tabea Becker. 75–86. Baltmannsweiler, Germany: Schneider Verlag Hohengehren.

Koch, Peter. 1997. "Orality in literate cultures". In *Writing Development: An Interdisciplinary View*, edited by Clotilde Pontecorvo. 149–172. Amsterdam: John Benjamins.

Koch, Peter and Wulf Oesterreicher. 1985. "Sprache der Nähe – Sprache der Distanz. Mündlichkeit und Schriftlichkeit im Spannungsfeld von Sprachtheorie und Sprachgeschichte". *Romanistisches Jahrbuch* 36: 15–43.

Kruse, Silke. 2007. *Kindlicher Grammatikerwerb und Dysgrammatismus. Verstehen – erkennen – behandeln*. 2nd edition. Bern: Haupt.

Kümmerling-Meibauer, Bettina and Jörg Meibauer. 2011. 'Early concept-books: Acquiring nominal and verbal concepts'. In *Emergent Literacy: Children's Books from 0 to 3*, edited by Bettina Kümmerling-Meibauer. 91–114. Amsterdam: John Benjamins.

Maas, Utz. 2008. *Sprache und Sprachen in der Migrationsgesellschaft. Die schriftkulturelle Dimension*. Göttingen: V&R-Unipress.

Meibauer, Jörg. 2011. "Spracherwerb und Kinderliteratur". *Zeitschrift für Literaturwissenschaft und Linguistik* 162: 9–26.

Müller, Claudia. 2012. *Kindliche Erzählfähigkeiten und (schrift-)sprachsozialisatorische Einflüsse in der Familie. Eine longitudinale Einzelfallstudie mit ein- und mehrsprachigen (Vor-)Schulkindern*. Baltmannsweiler, Germany: Schneider Verlag Hohengehren.

Musan, Renate. 2002. *The German Perfect: Its Semantic Composition and Its Interactions with Temporal Adverbials*. Dordrecht: Kluwer.

Purcell-Gates, Victoria. 2001. "Emergent literacy is emerging knowledge of written, not oral language". *New Directions for Child and Adolescent Development* 92: 7–22.

Quasthoff, Uta. 2002. "Tempusgebrauch von Kindern zwischen Mündlichkeit und Schriftlichkeit". In *Grammatik und Grammatikvermittlung*, edited by Corinna Peschel. 179–197. Frankfurt am Main: Lang.

Rau, Marie Luise. 1979. "Die Entwicklung von Vergangenheitsstrukturen in der Sprache eines Dreijährigen". *Folia Linguistica* 13: 356–412.

Reichenbach, Hans. 1947. *Elements of Symbolic Logic*. London: Routledge & Kegan Paul.

Rothstein, Björn. 2008. *The Perfect Time Span: On the Present Perfect in German, Swedish and English*. Amsterdam: John Benjamins.

Shirai, Yasuhiro. 2009. "Temporality in first and second language acquisition". In *The Expression of Time*, edited by Wolfgang Klein and Ping Li. 167–193. Berlin: De Gruyter.

Sieberg, Bernd. 2003. "Regelhafte und normale Anwendung von Perfekt und Präteritum: Mit Anregungen für den DaF-Bereich". In *Jahrbuch der ungarischen Germanistik*, edited by Magdolna Orosz and Andreas Herzog. 291–315. Budapest: GuG.

Strecker, Bruno. 2008. "'Die Vorstellung hat bereits begonnen' oder 'Die Vorstellung begann bereits'? Unterschiede beim Gebrauch von Präteritum und Präsensperfekt". *Sprachreport* 3: 31–35.

Szagun, Gisela. 2011. "Regular/irregular is not the whole story: The role of frequency and generalization in the acquisition of German past participle inflection". *Journal of Child Language* 38: 731–762.

Wagner, Laura. 2001. "Aspectual influences on early tense comprehension". *Journal of Child Language* 28: 661–681.

Index

1, 2, 3 – bringt Trost herbei! (Moost and Rudolph) 217

aesthetics 3, 4, 14, 21, 66, 73, 172
affective engagement 7, 156, 163, 165–6, 171–2
affective strategies 7, 157, 161–3, 166, 171–3
Allison, Alida 23
Amant, Kathleen 82
ambience 56, 72–3, 88
Anna Brushes Her Teeth (Amant) 82
anthropomorphic story 39–40
Antons ganze Welt (Drews) 15
attunement 25, 156
Auer, Manfred 217
Awdry, Wilbert 56

B Is for Bear (Bruna) 16
Baby Sees Farm Animals (Picthall) 16
Baby's My First ABC 72
Baby's Very First Black and White Library (Baggot) 72
Baggot, Stella 72
Berner, Rotraut Susanne 28
bidirectional relationship 7, 166–7, 172
Bravi, Soledad 15
bricolage 142–3
Brooks, Ron 25
Browne, Anthony 52
Bruna, Dick 14, 16, 52, 56, 66, 82
Buster's Zoo (Campbell) 187

Campbell, Rod 187
Carle, Eric 218
categoriziation 16–17, 28, 53
Cat in the Hat, The (Dr. Seuss) 202
Cat in the Hat Comes Back, The (Dr. Seuss) 202, 204

Chicka Chicka Boom Boom (Martin, Archambault and Ehlert) 204
Chii dekita yo! (Mori) 22
child engagement 127–32
children's literature 51, 54, 66, 117–18, 124, 131, 216
Child's Book of Things, A (Stickland) 16
Cho, Shinta 23
"Cleanliness" starring Johnny Toothbrush (Parkinson) 24
co-constructive reading 170
cognitive development 4, 8, 13, 18, 27, 101, 139, 216
cognitive theory 51, 66
coherence 16–19, 28, 53, 59, 64
cohesion 17–18, 28, 53, 64
color discrimination 76–7, 81
color naming 73, 77, 88
color vision 6, 72–9, 81–2, 84–5, 87–9
Comenius, Johann Amos 51
concept book 5, 15–19, 29
conceptual domain 15–19, 28
contextual cueing 187
contextual repetition 187, 189
contrast sensitivity 78–9
Cornille, Didier 15
corpus analysis 8, 209, 212, 216, 224

Dear Zoo (Campbell) 187
deixis 16, 18–19
descriptive frame 16
descriptive picturebook 1, 5–6, 13, 18, 51–67
descriptive–narrative continuum 21, 23–4, 52
developmental scenario 27, 62, 65
developmental stage 8, 14, 27–8, 71, 224n2
dialogic reading 170, 196–8, 200–1, 204
Discovery Farm 82

distributed cognition 67n7, 139, 148
Dr. Seuss's ABC (Dr. Seuss) 202
dramatization 7, 161–5, 167–70, 172–3
Drei Vögel (Heyduck) 217
Drews, Judith 15

early-concept book 1, 5, 14–17, 19, 27, 29, 51, 62, 66, 67n1, 71, 103, 105
early lexicon 15–16, 27
early literacy 4, 13–28, 51, 67n6, 156
early mark making 5, 7, 153
early narrative 14, 18–19, 214–15
early vocabulary growth 117
education 29, 43, 51, 128, 148, 156, 161, 196, 204
Egner, Thorbjørn 23–4
Eine Wolke in meinem Bett (Janisch) 217
elaborative reminiscing 197, 200
emotion 2–4, 8, 14, 18–21, 24–6, 29, 38, 56, 66, 72, 111, 137–40, 142, 147, 152, 156–7, 163, 166–7, 169, 172–3, 214, 221
empathy 18–19, 26, 29, 56, 163, 165–6, 172
Ente, Tod und Tulpe (Erlbruch) 218
Eriksson, Eva 19, 52
Erlbruch, Wolf 23, 218
Erste Bilder (Bruna) 52
Es war einmal eine Ente (van Straaten and Esterl) 218, 223
Esterl, Arnica 223
Everyone Poops (Gomi) 23
extratextual talk 124, 126–7, 131–2

fast mapping 6, 118–20, 126–31
film 148, 203
First concepts ABC (Graham and Pinnington) 41
Flotsam (David Wiesner) 52
forced preferential looking (FPL) 74, 81
Fire (Rius and Parammon) 158–66, 173
Fox (Wild and Brooks) 25
frame 16–18, 28, 61
French, Jackie 217
Fun with Peter Rabbit (Potter) 82

ganz ganz kleine Schwein mit dem ganz ganz großen Hunger, Das (Auer) 217
Gas We Pass, The (Cho) 23
Genechten, Guido van 217
generalization 35–8, 46
genre 5, 7, 14, 27–8, 67, 157–8, 160, 166–7, 169–70, 202, 214, 216, 220–1, 223

Geschichte ohne Ende und Anfang (Usatschow) 218
gestures 4, 6, 17, 20, 99–114, 149, 156, 162, 196
Godon, Ingrid 217
Gomi, Taro 23
Grammar Can Be Fun (Leaf) 25
graphic marking 149
grayscale 6, 72–3, 81–9

Hallo, roter Fuchs (Carle) 218
Haring, Keith 16
Heute spiele ich (Wiesner) 19
Heyduck, Hilde 217
Hoban, Tana 14–16
Holzwarth, Werner 23

iconic picture 37
illustrated book 1
In the Night Kitchen (Sendak) 147
interaction routine 6, 101
intersubjectivity 156–7, 169
intonation 7, 156, 161–3, 168–70, 172–3
Izawa, Tadasu 41

Janisch, Heinz 217–18, 221
joint attention 1–2, 101, 106
joint focus 99–102, 127

Karius and Bactus (Egner) 23
Kleiner weißer Fisch (van Genechten) 217

labeling 6, 25, 99, 102–3, 106–7, 111, 113, 170, 196, 199
Lange, Annette 15
language acquisition 18, 53, 67n4, 67n5, 99, 101–2, 111–14, 131, 188, 216, 224n2
language play 7, 163–5, 168, 170, 173
Leaf, Munro 25
learning situation 2–3
Le Saux, Alain 217
letters 16, 33–5, 41–3, 46, 139, 188–9, 196, 202
lexical acquisition 14
Life Underground (Rius and Parammon) 158–60, 162–9
Lindgren, Babro 19, 52
linguistics 4–5, 29, 54
literary character 3, 5, 14, 23–9, 29n4, 56
literature acquisition 13, 66
livre des bruits, Le (Bravi) 15
longitudinal study 6, 102–3, 117, 195
low-income parents 197, 200, 204

Maar, Anne 218
manipulative book 41–3
Max blöja (Lindgren and Eriksson) 19, 52
Mein erster Grüffelo (Scheffler) 217
Mein Spielzeug (Spanner) 16
Mickey Mouse 146–8, 156n2
Miffy (Bruna) 56, 82
Mini maxi – le livre des contraires (Cornille) 15
Mitgutsch, Ali 52
Mondhund, Der (Moost) 218
Moost, Nele 218
Mori, Mari 22
morphology 56, 58–9, 216
multimedia 139
multimodality 111–14, 139–40, 143, 145, 153n3
My ABC Book (Izawa) 41

narrative script 17
narrative skill 5, 65, 194, 196–7, 200–1, 204, 214
narratology 20
Noch mal! Meine ersten Lieblingswörter (Lange) 15
nonfiction literature 51–2
nonverbal behavior 6, 99–100, 102–6, 112–14, 172

optokinetic nystagmus (OKN) 74–6
oral language development 194, 197, 204
Orbis Sensualium Pictus (Comenius) 51
Otto. Autobiographie eines Teddybären (Ungerer) 218
Oxenbury, Helen 15, 159

Papa ist glücklich (Le Saux) 217
paralinguistic cues 163, 165–6
Parammon, Joseph 158
parental input 44
Parkinson, Virginia 24
Patricelli, Leslie 23
phonological awareness 8, 29, 194, 196, 201–4
phonology 56, 58–9, 204
photography 36–9, 45–6, 66, 67n3, 80–1, 104, 141–2, 182
Picthall, Chez 16
pictorial realism 36–7
picturebook spurt 14, 16, 29
picture–text relation 4, 71
Pinnington, Andrea 41
Pip and Posy: The Little Puddle (Scheffler) 82

Playing (Oxenbury) 15
pointing 16–17, 27, 64, 81, 83, 99–103, 105–12
pointing saccades 108–9, 111, 113
Pom-Pom Tidilly-Pom (Worth) 82
pop-up book 41
Pororo the Little Penguin 82
Potter, Beatrix 82
Potty (Patricelli) 23
Pozor (Maar) 218
pragmatic strategies 102, 107–8
pragmatics 3, 58, 60, 102
pretend play 29
proto–narrative 103
psychology 4–5, 7, 18, 29, 187
Push/Pull – Empty/Full (Hoban) 15

question, eliciting/non-eliciting 99, 101–2, 108, 123, 126, 199

reading comprehension 117, 204
reading skill 194, 196, 202–4
Recycling (Stokham) 82
Red, Blue, Yellow Shoes (Hoban) 16
Reiner der Weiner (Seefeldt) 218
rhyme 16, 27, 29, 159, 161, 163–4, 168
Rius, Maria 158
Ross, Diana 56
Rundherum in meiner Stadt (Mitgutsch) 52

Scheffler, Axel 82, 217
script 17
Seefeldt, Philipp 218
semantics 4, 6, 53, 56, 58–60, 107–8, 111, 113–14, 119–20, 152, 161, 211–12
shared picturebook reading 8, 37, 194–65, 199–204
shared storybook reading 7–8, 181–90
simple descriptive picturebook 6, 18, 51–4, 62, 66–7
slow mapping 6, 119–21, 128–31
social interaction 2, 4, 156–7, 169
social referencing 157
Sougez, Emmanuel 14
Spanner, Helmut 16
speech act 16, 60
Steichen, Edward 14
Stickland, Paul 16, 18–19, 51–2, 54, 57
Stokham, Jess 82
Story of the Little Red Engine, The (Ross and Wood) 23
Straaten, Harmen van 218

symbolic learning 7, 137, 140
symbol–referent relation 33, 47
syntax 56, 59–60

Tagebuch eines Wombats (French and Wheatley) 217
Ten (Haring) 16
tense acquisition 8, 209–24
testimony 14, 21, 23, 29, 54, 61
textless picturebook 1, 71; *see also* wordless picturebook
theory of mind 17
Thomas the Tank Engine (Awdry) 56
Thomas, Valerie 159
Three Little Wolves, The (Trivizas) 159–60, 162–8, 173
Toddler's Potty Book (Allison) 23
transactional theory 156
Trivizas, Eugenios 159
Trucks (Stickland) 6, 18, 51–68

Ungerer, Tomi 218
Usatschow, Andrej 218

verbal responsiveness 127–8, 130–1
visual acuity 75, 78–80, 82, 87
visual code 14, 172
visual development 6, 73
visual literacy 2, 14
visual schema 14, 20
visual system 2, 72–3, 75, 78, 89
visually evoked cortical potential (VEP) 73–6

visually evoked response (VER) 73–6
vocabulary breadth 119–21, 123–4, 132
vocabulary depth 121, 124
vocabulary growth 6–7, 117, 119, 124, 128, 131–2, 203
vocabulary spurt 14, 16, 29
Voices in the Park (Browne) 52
Vom kleinen Maulwurf, der wissen wollte, wer ihm auf den Kopf gemacht hat (Holzwarth and Erlbruch) 23

Warhol, Andy 14
Warum der Schnee weiß ist (Janisch) 218
Wenn die Sonne scheint (Heyduck) 217
Wiesner, Angela 19
Wiesner, David 52
Wild, Margaret 25
wimmelbook 28, 52–3
Winnie the Witch (Paul and Thomas) 159–64, 167–9, 171
Wir besuchen den Zahnarzt (Wittenburg) 24
Wittenburg, Christiane 24
Wood, Leslie 56
Wo ist Lola? (Godon) 217
word learning 5, 7–8, 45, 118–20, 124–32, 181–90, 199
wordless picturebook 28, 201; *see also* textless picturebook
Worth, Bonnie 82

eBooks
from Taylor & Francis

Helping you to choose the right eBooks for your Library

Add to your library's digital collection today with Taylor & Francis eBooks. We have over 50,000 eBooks in the Humanities, Social Sciences, Behavioural Sciences, Built Environment and Law, from leading imprints, including Routledge, Focal Press and Psychology Press.

Choose from a range of subject packages or create your own!

Benefits for you
- Free MARC records
- COUNTER-compliant usage statistics
- Flexible purchase and pricing options
- 70% approx of our eBooks are now DRM-free.

Benefits for your user
- Off-site, anytime access via Athens or referring URL
- Print or copy pages or chapters
- Full content search
- Bookmark, highlight and annotate text
- Access to thousands of pages of quality research at the click of a button.

Free Trials Available

We offer free trials to qualifying academic, corporate and government customers.

eCollections

Choose from 20 different subject eCollections, including:

- Asian Studies
- Economics
- Health Studies
- Law
- Middle East Studies

eFocus

We have 16 cutting-edge interdisciplinary collections, including:

- Development Studies
- The Environment
- Islam
- Korea
- Urban Studies

For more information, pricing enquiries or to order a free trial, please contact your local sales team:

UK/Rest of World: **online.sales@tandf.co.uk**
USA/Canada/Latin America: **e-reference@taylorandfrancis.com**
East/Southeast Asia: **martin.jack@tandf.com.sg**
India: **journalsales@tandfindia.com**

www.tandfebooks.com